PIPE FITTINGS

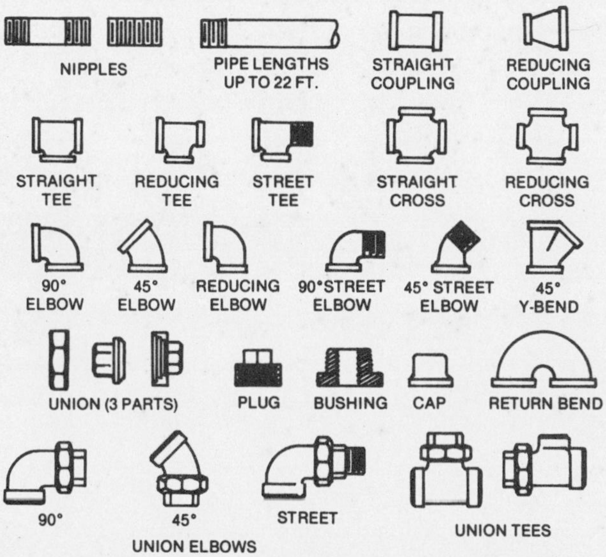

Here are the common steel pipe fittings. Nipples are simply short lengths of pipe threaded on both ends. Reducing fittings join two different sizes of pipe.

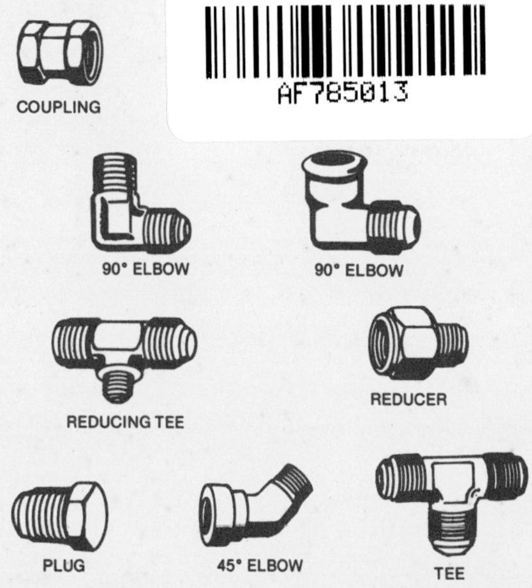

Compression fittings of the flared-tube type are the easiest for the novice to handle when working with copper tubing.

STANDARD STEEL PIPE (All Dimensions in Inches)					
Nominal Size	Outside Diameter	Inside Diameter	Nominal Size	Outside Diameter	Inside Diameter
1/8	0.405	0.269	1	1.315	1.049
1/4	0.540	0.364	1 1/4	1.660	1.380
3/8	0.675	0.493	1 1/2	1.900	1.610
1/2	0.840	0.622	2	2.375	2.067
3/4	1.050	0.824	2 1/2	2.875	2.469

SQUARE MEASURE

144 sq in = 1 sq ft
9 sq ft = 1 sq yd
272.25 sq ft = 1 sq rod
160 sq rods = 1 acre

VOLUME MEASURE

1728 cu in = 1 cu ft
27 cu ft = 1 cu yd

MEASURES OF CAPACITY

1 cup = 8 fl oz
2 cups = 1 pint
2 pints = 1 quart
4 quarts = 1 gallon
2 gallons = 1 peck
4 pecks = 1 bushel

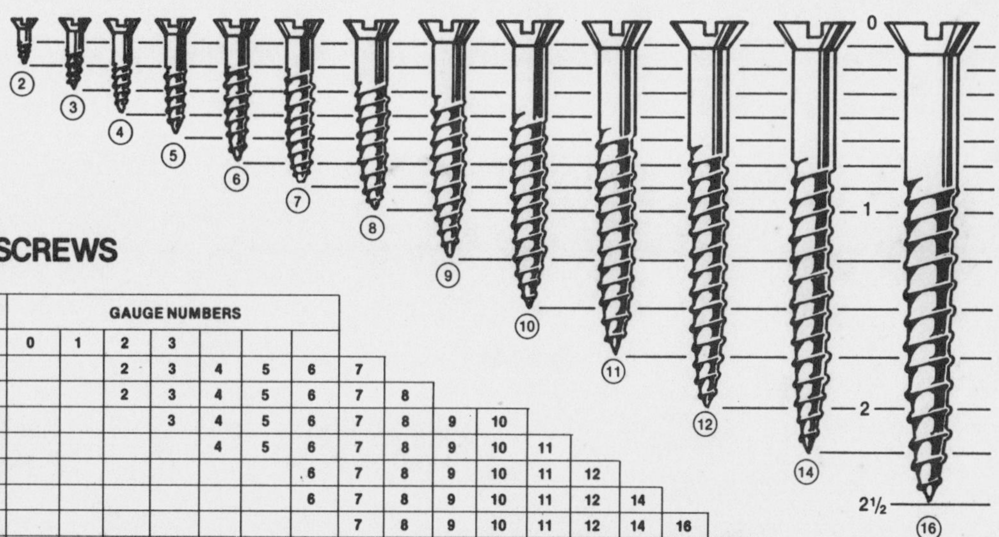

WOOD SCREWS

LENGTH	GAUGE NUMBERS																
1/4 INCH	0	1	2	3													
3/8 INCH			2	3	4	5	6	7									
1/2 INCH			2	3	4	5	6	7	8								
5/8 INCH				3	4	5	6	7	8	9	10						
3/4 INCH					4	5	6	7	8	9	10	11					
7/8 INCH							6	7	8	9	10	11	12				
1 INCH							6	7	8	9	10	11	12	14			
1 1/4 INCH								7	8	9	10	11	12	14	16		
1 1/2 INCH							6	7	8	9	10	11	12	14	16	18	
1 3/4 INCH									8	9	10	11	12	14	16	18	20	
2 INCH									8	9	10	11	12	14	16	18	20	
2 1/4 INCH										9	10	11	12	14	16	18	20	
2 1/2 INCH													12	14	16	18	20	
2 3/4 INCH														14	16	18	20	
3 INCH															16	18	20	
3 1/2 INCH																18	20	24
4 INCH																18	20	24

WHEN YOU BUY SCREWS, SPECIFY (1) LENGTH, (2) GAUGE NUMBER, (3) TYPE OF HEAD—FLAT, ROUND, OR OVAL, (4) MATERIAL—STEEL, BRASS, BRONZE, ETC., (5) FINISH—BRIGHT, STEEL BLUED, CADMIUM, NICKEL, OR CHROMIUM PLATED.

BUILD THIS FINE pool table and save hundreds of dollars. See the detailed plans on page 2256.

In this volume . . .

CHOOSE THE PROP that's right in diameter and pitch, and you'll add knots. See page 2345.

KEEP THAT BEAUTIFUL electric range in topnotch condition. Actually, it's one of the simplest appliances in your home to service. See the troubleshooting charts on page 2391.

HERE ARE SOME IDEAS for attractive privacy screens that will add pleasure and value to your home. You'll find others—and construction details—on page 2334.

PLYWOOD IS THE MOST VERSATILE of building materials. You can even use it as a ceiling material, indoors or out. Learn to buy the grade that will save money on page 2244.

THIS COLORFUL LITTLE circus train, built from your shop scraps, will be the pride and joy of any young ringmaster. Five cars carry 10 animals. For plans see page 2348.

THERE ARE SCORES of kinds of plywood, and countless uses. See details on page 2244.

EXTERIOR PLYWOOD, in many textures, can improve the appearance of almost any building.

THIS BEAUTIFUL retaining wall is faced with attractive redwood. On page 2446, Vol. 16, you'll find plans for all kinds of retaining walls.

BEAUTIFUL VACATION HOME is faced with warm, textured plywood. See page 2244.

Popular Mechanics

do-it-yourself encyclopedia

in 20 volumes

a complete how-to guide for the homeowner, the hobbyist—
and anyone who enjoys working with mind and hands!

All about:

home maintenance
home-improvement projects
wall paneling
burglary and fire protection
furniture projects
finishing and refinishing furniture
outdoor living
home remodeling
solutions to home problems
challenging woodworking projects
hobbies and handicrafts
model making
weekend projects
workshop shortcuts and techniques
hand-tool skills
power-tool know-how
shop-made tools
car repairs
car maintenance
appliance repair
boating
hunting
fishing
camping
photography projects
radio, TV and electronics know-how
clever hints and tips
projects just for fun

volume 15

ISBN 0-87851-080-X
Library of Congress Catalog Number 77 84920

MANUFACTURED IN THE UNITED STATES OF AMERICA

contents

VOLUME 15

HIGHLY DECORATIVE plywood paneling for study or office is called "brushed reverse board and batten."

All about plywood

By RICHARD NUNN

■ IF YOU'RE NEW to doing-it-yourself you should think of plywood as a single board measuring up to 4 feet wide and 8 feet long with a thickness from ¼ to ¾ in. Some building material retailers furnish it in smaller sizes and lesser thicknesses, in panels from 1 foot in width up, and in thicknesses down to ⅛ in. These panels are usually called "pre-cuts" and have A-C faces and backs (more later).

SEE ALSO
Finishes, wood . . . Lumber . . . Nails . . . Paneling, plywood . . . Sanding . . . Siding . . . Table saws . . . Wood finishes . . . Woods

Actually, plywood is a series of thinly-cut wood veneers that have been crosslaminated with alternating grain patterns under extreme pressure to provide a dimensionally-stable and water-resistant panel board. Panel fabrication is almost always the same regardless of the top veneers used.

Plywood is available faced with some of the finest cabinet woods, both domestic and exotic, from ash to zebrawood. Some of the finer hardwood facings (top veneers) are very expensive. Plywoods with softwood facings are relatively inexpensive. With such a broad range plywood may be used to build houses, boats, cabinets, furniture, fences, toys.

In the marketplace, plywood is plentiful in two basic types, the one with *hardwood* facings of a wide variety, the other in a variety of *softwood* facings. The latter are most widely used in common applications, largely because of versatility and lower cost per square foot. Both types have back veneers of lesser, but quality, facings, since the backs of the panels seldom show. If both sides will show, panels may be purchased with similar veneers on both facings.

Plywood is sold almost anywhere lumber and other building materials are sold. If you can't find the panels you want, check cabinet and millwork specialty shops and local plywood distributors. These outlets may be found in the advertising pages of the telephone directory.

hardwood-faced plywoods

Hardwood-faced plywoods are graded somewhat differently than softwood-faced panels. The best grade is *custom* grade (No. 1), free of the patches, knots and plugs that are permissible in the lower grades. It's suitable for the finest work where the wood must be exposed.

Next comes *good* grade (No. 2) with clean, smoothly cut facing and the joints precisely matched so the grain runs true.

The *sound* grade, commonly No. 3, has no open, visible defects but the grain may not be as closely matched and minor mineral streaks and stains are permissible.

In the *utility* grade (No. 4) somewhat greater defects and discolorations are more or less general and in the final, or *reject* grade (No. 5) knot holes and splits are permissible in manufacture. The latter two or three grades are suitable only for rough work where sectional strength and not appearance is the desirable feature.

Hardwood-faced plywoods also come to you in three types of bonds (adhesives) classified as faced with a series of laminated veneers. This plywood is widely used in furniture construction and built-ins. *Particle-board* core is actually a board made up of resin-coated wood particles to a given width and then faced on both sides with laminated veneers in the same manner as lumber core.

All these panels are lightweight, easily workable with hand or power tools and are exceptionally stable.

softwood plywoods

Many plywoods used for medium and light construction and do-it-yourself projects, are commonly termed "softwood plywoods." These panels are generally classified as to strength and type of glue bond. The face veneers are available in a variety of wood species such as Douglas fir, western larch, and the southern loblolly and longleaf pines. The top facing or veneer may be smooth or finished with any number of different textures and grooves. Strength of the panels is ranked into groups from 1 through 5. Group 1, for example, is the strongest panel; Group 5 is the weakest panel. Group 1 has 10 wood species including beech, birch, fir, and pine—all strong woods. Group 5 has 3 species—basswood, poplar, and balsam—considered "weak" woods. In all, there are some 83 species of woods classified in the five groups. Therefore, when you select a plywood panel, look to the group number for the strength you want. If you are paneling a room, Group 2 is plenty strong enough. If you are installing underlayment Group 1 is required. Panels in Group 1 sometimes are priced higher than those in Groups 2 through 5 for obvious reasons: strength, durability.

Two types of adhesives are used to laminate the wood veneers: exterior and interior, or only exterior. (Interior/intermediate glue sometimes is used, but this type of bond is not commonly available.) Panels designated as "exterior" or EXT are recommended for use where permanent exposure to weather or moisture will be involved. These panels have an exterior glue bond.

Panels designated as "INT" or "interior" or "Exposure 1" are recommended for use where the panels will be subjected to temporary exposure to weather or moisture. Typical would be roof and wall sheathing, interior paneling, cabinets, furniture, shelving. Panels marked with "Exposure 2" usually have an interior/exterior glue bond and may be used in the same applications as those marked "Exposure 1."

cores for softwood plywoods

Panels are available with a variety of cores or base material to which the facings (top and back) are bonded. *Veneer* cores probably are the most common. They consist of a series of laminated veneers, the laminations alternating at right angles. *Composite* cores are manufactured by gluing reconstituted wood cores—instead of veneers—between the top and back facings of the panels. Composites for all practical purposes look and act similar to all-veneer plywood. Composites are specified for many building projects and are interchangeable with all-veneer plywood panels.

Nonveneered panels are made from structural

wood generically classified as waferboard, oriented strand board (OSB), and some classes of structural particleboard. Oversimplified, waferboard is large wafer-like wood flakes that are bonded together with a resin adhesive. OSB is fabricated from cross-laminated and compressed layers of resin-bonded wood strands. Particleboard is made up of wood particles that are bonded at random with a resin adhesive.

All panels are lightweight, with the exception of particleboard. They all may be worked with hand or power tools and are exceptionally stable, free of the tendency of solid-stock construction to warp or "wind." For special projects, plywood is available on special order with fiberglass-reinforced plastic (FRP) and metal overlays bonded to the panel faces. Plywood also can be purchased fire-retardant-treated (FRT) and pressure-preservative-treated.

APA rated trademarks

Plywood, composite, and nonveneered panels manufactured by mills subscribing to the American Plywood Association (APA) are produced in strict accordance with government standards. These standards are so noted on the edge and back stamps on APA panels as PS 1-74, the government standard that applies to this product. All APA performance-rated panels are recognized by the member model building code organizations of the National Research Board (NRB), the International Building Officials and Code Administrators (BOCA) and the Uniform Building Code (UBC), and the Southern Building Code Congress International (SBCCI), promulgators of the Standard Building Code (SBC). You may find some of the panels stamped with these letters, which indicates various code approvals. Another marking may be FHA, UM-66. This stands for Federal Housing Administration Use of Materials Bulletin Number 66. As a rule of thumb, all APA performance-rated panels, regardless of composition or configuration, may be used for structural projects if they are rated with the PS 1-74 stamp. Most building codes will accept this rating.

The trademarks contain a wealth of information. The large, square trademarks are stamped on the back facings of the panels. The long, narrow trademarks are stamped on the edges of the panels. This is done so the veneer is not damaged by the ink used in the stamping process. Here's how to read a typical stamp:

The APA stands for American Plywood Association and means that the mill that manufactured that specific panel is a member of APA. The A-C letters denote the grade of veneer. The A or "good face" is smooth and paintable. The C or "back face" has tight knots and a solid surface. Group 1 means that the panel is fabricated from the strongest wood species. Exterior means that the panel has an exterior glue bond and may be used where permanent exposure to weather or moisture will be involved. The 000 numbers will be real numbers indicating the mill location where the panel was made. The PS 1-74 mark indicates that the panel meets the government requirement for this plywood specification.

Sheathing stamps are somewhat different. For example: the APA stands for American Plywood Association. Rated Sheathing means the panel has been rated by APA for sheathing according to the specification set down by the National Research Board (NRB-108). The numbers 42/20 (they may be different) mean that the sheathing may be used over rafters that are spaced no more than 42 in. on center, or over joists that are no more than 20 in. on center. The first number always applies to rafters; the second to joists or studs. The ⅝ figure means the sheathing is ⅝-in. thick. Sized for spacing indicates that the panel is slightly undersized so the joints between adjoining panels may be spaced ⅛ in. to allow for expansion/contraction of the panel. Exterior indicates an exterior glue bond; 000 is the mill number. Illustrations of these various trade marks may be found on Page 2367 and 2368.

Still another stamp is the APA Rated Sturdi-I-Floor. This is a touch-sanded panel designed for residential, light-frame single-floor installations. It serves as both structural subflooring and an underlayment for finish flooring. The panels have span ratings of 16, 20, 24, and 48 in. on center, and this is so marked on the grade stamp. The panels are sized for spacing (⅛-in.), and tongue-and-grooved, noted by the inscription "T&G Net Width 47½ (in.)" with a 1 Exposure (glue bond as noted above).

softwood grades

The top and back facings or veneers of the panels are graded for appearance as well as strength. The inner plies of exterior plywood do not permit "D" graded veneers for strength reasons. Interior plywood permits A, B, C, and D graded veneers in its manufacture since strength is not as important.

The top and back facings are graded as N, A, B, C, C-plugged, and D. The facings can be any combination of these letters (grades).

SOME COMMON GRADES OF PLYWOOD											
Grade Designation	Description & Common Uses	Typical Trademarks	Veneer Grade			Most Common Thicknesses (in).					
			Face	Inner Plies	Back	¼	5/16	⅜	½	⅝	¾
APA N-N, N-A, N-B INT	Cabinet quality. For natural finish furniture, cabinet doors, built-ins, etc. Special order items. (2)	N-N • G-1 • INT-APA • PS1-74 • 000	N	C	N,A or B						●
APA N-D INT	For natural finish paneling. Special order item. (2)	N-D • G-2 • INT-APA • PS1-74 • 000	N	D	D	●					
APA A-A INT	For applications with both sides on view: built-ins, cabinets, furniture, partitions. Smooth face, suitable for painting. (2)	A-A • G-1 • INT-APA • PS1-74 • 000	A	D	A	●		●	●	●	●
APA A-B INT	Use where appearance of one side is less important but where two solid surfaces are necessary. (2)	A-B • G-1 • INT-APA • PS1-74 • 000	A	D	B	●		●	●	●	●
APA A-D INT	Use where appearance of only one side is important: paneling, built-ins, shelving, partitions, flow racks. (2)	APA A-D GROUP 1 INTERIOR 000 PS 1-74 EXTERIOR GLUE	A	D	D	●		●	●	●	●
APA B-B INT	Utility panel with two solid sides. Permits circular plugs. (2)	B-B • G-2 • INT-APA • PS1-74 • 000	B	D	B	●		●	●	●	●
APA B-D INT	Utility panel with one solid side. Good for backing, sides of built-ins, industry shelving, slip sheets, separator boards, bins. (2)	APA B-D GROUP 2 INTERIOR 000 PS 1-74 EXTERIOR GLUE	B	D	D	●		●	●	●	●
APA UNDER-LAYMENT INT	For application over structural subfloor. Provides smooth surface for application of resilient floor coverings. Touch-sanded. Also available with exterior glue. (3)	APA UNDERLAYMENT GROUP 1 INTERIOR 000 PS 1-74 EXTERIOR GLUE	C Plgd.	C & D	D			●	●	● 19/32	● 23/32
APA C-D PLUGGED INT	For built-ins, wall and ceiling tile backing, cable reels, walkways, separator boards. Not a substitute for UNDERLAYMENT or STURD-I-FLOOR as it lacks their indentation resistance. Touch-sanded. Also made with exterior glue. (3)	APA C-D PLUGGED GROUP 1 INTERIOR 000 PS 1-74 EXTERIOR GLUE	C Plgd.	D	D			●	●	● 19/32	● 23/32
APA DECORA-TIVE INT	Rough-sawn, brushed, grooved, or striated faces. For paneling, interior accent walls, built-ins, counter facing, display exhibits. (5)	APA DECORATIVE GROUP 2 INTERIOR 000 PS 1-74	C or btr.	D	D		●	●	●	●	
APA PLYRON INT	Hardboard face on both sides. For countertops shelving, cabinet doors, flooring. Faces tempered, untempered, smooth or screened.	PLYRON-INT-APA • 000	C & D						●	●	●

SOME CONSTRUCTION PLYWOODS

	Grade Designation	Description & Common Uses	Typical Trademarks	Common Thicknesses (in.) 5/16	3/8	1/2	5/8	3/4
PROTECTED OR INTERIOR USE	**APA RATED SHEATHING EXP 1 or 2**	Specially designed for subflooring and wall and roof sheathing, but can also be used for a broad range of other construction and industrial applications. Can be manufactured as conventional veneered plywood, as composite, or as a nonveneered panel. For special engineered applications, including high load requirements and certain industrial uses, veneered panels conforming to PS 1 may be required. Specify Exposure 1 when long construction delays are anticipated.	APA RATED SHEATHING 32/16 1/2 INCH SIZED FOR SPACING EXPOSURE 2 000 NRB-108	●	●	● 7/16	●	●
	APA STRUCTURAL I & II RATED SHEATHING EXP 1	Unsanded all-veneer PS 1 plywood grades for use where strength properties are of maximum importance: structural diaphragms, box beams, gusset plates, stressed-skin panels, containers, pallet bins. Made only with exterior glue (Exposure 1). STRUCTURAL I more commonly available. (3)	APA RATED SHEATHING 24 oc 3/8 INCH SIZED FOR SPACING EXPOSURE 1 000 PS 1-74 C-C INT/EXT GLUE NRB-108	●	●	●	●	●
	APA RATED STURD-I-FLOOR EXP 1 or 2	For combination subfloor-underlayment. Provides smooth surface for application of resilient floor coverings and possesses high concentrated and impact load resistance. Can be manufactured as conventional veneered plywood, as a composite, or as a nonveneered panel. Available square edge or tongue-and-groove. Specify Exposure 1 when long construction delays are anticipated.	APA RATED STURD-I-FLOOR 24 oc 23/32 INCH SIZED FOR SPACING T&G NET WIDTH 47-1/2 EXPOSURE 1 000 NRB-108				● 19/32	● 23/32
	APA RATED STURD-I-FLOOR 48 oc (2-4-1) EXP 1	For combination subfloor-underlayment on 32- and 48-inch spans and for heavy timber roof construction. Provides smooth surface for application of resilient floor coverings and possesses high concentrated and impact load resistance. Manufactured only as conventional veneered plywood and only with exterior glue (Exposure 1). Available square edge or tongue-and-groove.	APA RATED STURD-I-FLOOR 48oc 1-1/8 INCH (2-4-1) SIZED FOR SPACING EXPOSURE 1 T&G 000 INT/EXT GLUE NRB-108 FHA-UM-66			1-1/8		
EXTERIOR USE	**APA RATED SHEATHING EXT**	Exterior sheathing panel for subflooring and wall and roof sheathing, siding on service and farm buildings, crating, pallets, pallet bins, cable reels, etc. Manufactured as conventional veneered plywood.	APA RATED SHEATHING 48/24 3/4 INCH SIZED FOR SPACING EXTERIOR 000 NRB-108	●	●	●	●	●
	APA STRUCTURAL I & II RATED SHEATHING EXT	For engineered applications in construction and industry where resistance to permanent exposure to weather or moisture is required. Manufactured only as conventional veneered PS 1 plywood. Unsanded. STRUCTURAL I more commonly available. (3)	APA RATED SHEATHING STRUCTURAL I 24/0 3/8 INCH SIZED FOR SPACING EXTERIOR 000 PS 1-74 C-C NRB-108	●	●	●	●	●
	APA RATED STURD-I-FLOOR EXT	For combination subfloor-underlayment under resilient floor coverings where severe moisture conditions may be present, as in balcony decks. Possesses high concentrated and impact load resistance. Manufactured as conventional veneered plywood. Available square edge or tongue-and-groove.	APA RATED STURD-I-FLOOR 20 oc 19/32 INCH SIZED FOR SPACING T&G NET WIDTH 47-1/2 EXTERIOR 000 NRB-108				● 19/32	● 23/32

N-grade is a special order "natural finish" veneer. It is select all heartwood or all sapwood. It is free of open defects, but allows some repairs. N-grade usually isn't stocked by building material retailers mainly because of its high cost. If your project calls for N-grade panels, expect to wait from four to six weeks for special-order delivery.

A-grade is smooth and paintable. Neatly made repairs in the veneer are permissible. The panels may be used for a natural finish in less demanding applications.

B-grade has a solid surface veneer. Circular repair plugs and tight knots are permitted.

C-grade has knotholes up to 1 in. Occasional knotholes ½ in. larger are permitted providing the total width of all knots and knotholes within a specified section doesn't exceed certain limits. Limited splits are permitted; minimum veneer.

C-plugged has improved C-veneer with splits

limited to ⅛ in. in width and knotholes and borer holes limited to ¼x½ in.

D-grade permits knots and knotholes to 2½ in. in width and ½ in. larger under certain specified limits. Limited splits are permitted.

"Repaired" plywood panels are just as strong as those without repairs. However, the patches are sometimes made with a synthetic material that does not absorb stain finish as evenly as the wood surrounding the patch. Therefore, if you finish with stain, use a heavy-bodied stain (not transparent) so the patches will be hidden.

interior grade use-guide

What grade and type of plywood you buy depends, of course, on the project at hand. Below is a guide to interior appearance grades:

A-A INT-APA: Both faces are the highest standard veneer grade for use where both sides will show: built-ins, cabinets, furniture, partitions, etc. The most common thicknesses are: ¼ in., ⅜ in., ½ in., ⅝ in., ¾ in. and 1 in. The veneer grade is A face, A back and D-grade inner.

A-B INT-APA: This panel is similar to A-A, but it is used where the appearance of one side is less important, and two smooth solid surfaces are desirable. Thicknesses are the same.

A-D INT-APA: Used for built-ins, paneling, shelving, partitions, etc., where only one side will show. Thicknesses are standard, with D inner plys.

B-B INT-APA: An interior utility panel for use as partitions, utility built-ins, mounting boards, etc. Both sides are smooth and may be painted. Thicknesses are standard, with D inner plys.

B-D INT-APA: For use where one smooth side is needed. Shelving, sides and backs for built-ins, economy cabinet work, slip sheets, separator boards and bins. Standard thickness; inner plys, D.

DECORATIVE PANELS: This material is rough sawn, brushed, grooved, striated or embossed on one side. Use it for accent walls, paneling, counter fronts and where wood with various surface textures is desired. The most common thicknesses are 5/16 in., ⅜ in., and ½ in. Veneer grade is C or better face, plys, D back and D inner.

PLYRON: These panels have a hardboard face and back and are used for built-ins, cabinet doors, countertops, worktables and furniture. The faces may be tempered, untempered, smooth or screened hardboard. The most common thicknesses are ½ in., ⅝ in. and ¾ in., with C and D inner plys.

N-N INT-APA: A natural finish cabinet-quality panel, designed to be used where both sides will show. Both sides are select all heartwood or all sapwood veneer. Typical uses are for cabinet doors, built-ins and furniture having a natural finish. The panels are usually a special order item. In thicknesses of ¾ in. only with C inner plys.

N-A and N-B INT-APA: This is similar to the grade listed above, but it permits an A or B-grade veneer on the backside. The panel is designed for economy when building cabinet doors, built-ins, furniture. It is a special-order item in ¾-in. thickness only with C inner plys.

N-D INT-APA: One side is select all heartwood or all sapwood veneer. Use it for interior paneling that will have a natural finish. Usually a special order item in ¼-in. thickness only with D inner plys.

UNDERLAYMENT INT-APA: For underlayment or combination subfloor-underlayment under resilient floor coverings. Ply beneath the face is C or D veneer; it is sanded or touch sanded as specified. Most common thicknesses: ¼, ⅜, ½, ⅝ and ¾ in.

A-A EXT-APA: Designed for exposed applications where both sides will show: fences, windscreens, exterior cabinets and built-ins, boats, etc. The most common thicknesses are: ¼, ⅜, ½, ⅝, ¾ and 1 in. Panels have an A face and back with C inner plys.

A-B EXT-APA: Similar uses to A-A EXT, but where the appearance of one side is less important. The thicknesses are the same with C inner plys.

MDO EXT-APA: A medium-density overlaid plywood panel with opaque resin-impregnated fiber overlay, heat-fused to one or both panel faces. It provides an ideal base for paint. Uses including siding, soffits, windscreens, exterior painted cabinet work, etc. Thicknesses: 5/16, ⅜, ½, ⅝, ¾ and 1 in. Veneer grade is B face, B or C back, C or C-plugged inner plys.

TEXTURE 1-11: The unsanded panels have parallel grooves ¼ in. deep, ⅜ in. wide on 2-in. or 4-in. centers. The edges are shiplapped for a continuous visual pattern. Uses include siding, accent paneling, fences, etc. It is available in 8 and 10-ft. lengths and sanded or with MD overlay. Thicknesses: ⅝ in. only; C or better face, C back and inner plys.

303 SPECIALTY SIDING EXT-APA: The grade covers proprietary plywood products for siding, fencing, soffits, windscreens and other exterior applications or interior panels. The panels have special surface treatments which include

IN PANELING A WALL, furring strips are applied to fit panels, then adhesive is applied to strips.

PANELING IS APPLIED over the furring strips. Be sure the edge of the first panel is vertical.

rough-sawn, striated and brushed, and may be V-grooved, channel-grooved, etc. It is available in redwood, cedar, hemlock, Douglas fir, lauan and other woods. The most common thicknesses are ⅜, ½ and ⅝ in. The veneer grade is B or better face, C back and plys.

PLYRPN EXT-APA: The panels are surfaced on both sides with tempered hardboard with smooth or screened surfaces. Thicknesses are ½, ⅝ and ¾ in. The panels have C inner plys.

MARINE EXT-APA: Marine-grade panels are made only with Douglas fir or western larch, and a special solid joined core construction. The panels are subject to special limitations on core gaps and the number of face repairs. Use them for boat hulls.

C-C PLUGGED EXT-APA: For exterior underlayment, these panels are also ideal for tile backing where a permanently waterproof material is needed. The panels are sanded or touch sanded as specified. The most common thicknesses are ¼, ⅜, ½, ⅝, ¾ and ⅞ in. The veneer grade is C (plugged) face, D back and inner plys.

The types and grades mentioned above are generally available in 4x8-ft. panels. However, other lengths and widths are manufactured. The larger sizes can be ordered by a building material retailer. You can expect a 4 to 6 week delivery delay, and, if small quantities are ordered, you may be expected to pay for freight costs.

shopping tips

Many building material retailers have "plywood bins" in which random-size pieces and trimmings are available. Some dealers also will cut panels for you in different sizes. You have to buy the entire panel, however, before your specific cuts are made. Many retailers also stock "pre-cuts" or "ready-cuts." These are priced a bit higher than panels that you would cut yourself. The face veneers of pre-cuts usually are A and C; edge voids are filled.

Before buying plywood, it is often to your advantage to preplan the project at hand so the amount of material required may be purchased at one time. Costs sometimes can be cut with quantity if you ask the retailer for this discount. Any irregular sizes may be picked out of the plywood bins and pre-cuts—another cost savings.

Most important, in structural projects such as roof sheathing, underlayment, and siding, be sure that the panels conform to local building codes. Group 1 and span-rated panels usually are accepted by all code groups. On some grade stamps on siding you may note these numbers and letters: "18-S/W." This means that there are 18 synthetic and/or wooden patches permitted in the panel. The number can go as low as 6-S/W. This is important when buying the siding if the siding will be stained. The fewer the patches, the less

HERE'S A TEXTURED exterior paneling, that is easy to apply. Seal the edges of exterior panels.

MANY PLYWOOD PANELS designed for covering walls are available prefinished.

"show-through" of patches through the stain, which should be heavy-bodied instead of clear or semi-transparent.

working with plywood

Plywood panels are easy to work with, although there are several tips that will make the job even easier:

1. To prevent waste, lay out the panel for cutting. If there will be many pieces cut from a single panel, sketch the arrangement on a piece of paper before you transfer it to the panel as a cutting pattern. Allow for the saw kerf between the pieces. Have the grain of the panel running the long way of the piece, if possible.

2. If you use a handsaw, cut the panel with the best face up. Use a saw with 10 to 15 points to the inch and support the panel on sawhorses so it won't sag. Always use a sharp saw.

3. For power sawing on a table saw, cut with the good face of the panel up. Use a sharp combination blade or fine-tooth blade without too much set. The blade should be set so it protrudes above the panel about the height of the teeth.

4. With a portable power saw, place the good face of the panel down.

5. When planing edges, work from both ends of the edge toward the center of the panel. This will prevent splitting out the plys at the end of the cut. Always use a plane with a sharp blade and set it to take a fine shaving. Work slowly.

6. Since plywood is sanded smooth at the time it is made, sanding it before a sealer or prime coat of finish should be confined to the edges. After the surface is sealed, however, you may sand in the direction of the grain only.

7. It is difficult to nail or screw into the edges of veneer-core plywood. Plan your work so you can avoid these problems.

Plywood panels can be bent to certain minimum radii depending, of course, on the thickness of the panel. In some applications you may have to bend two thin panels to build up a particular thickness. For example, ¾-in. panels can be bent only in a circle with a 10-ft. radius, while ⅜-in. panels can be bent to a radius of 36 in. Two layers of the ⅜-in. material will produce a much sharper bend and yet will give you the same effect as a ¾-in. panel.

Plywood panels are ideal for concrete forming. If the panels will be used for more than one project, the face that will be next to the concrete should be coated with form oil, which is brushed on. If you will be doing lots of concrete work where plywood forms are necessary, it is recommended that you buy APA B-B Plyform Class I or Class II panels that have a very high reuse factor. These panels are sanded both sides and are mill-oiled unless otherwise specified. The Class I panels are the strongest.

A pontoon boat for summer fun

You'll have nothing but a summer of fun on your own floating platform. It is supported by billets of buoyant plastic foam that are almost unsinkable and very lightweight

By HARRY WICKS

SEE ALSO
Boating, safety . . . Canoes . . . Kayaks . . . Outboard motors . . . Repairs, boat . . . Sailboats

FOR ALL-OUT water fun, safety and economical operation, a pontoon boat is a hard craft to beat. The version shown on these pages is intended for protected waters, and although substantially built, the lightweight materials it is constructed of provide great load-carrying ability without excessive weight.

The design is based on an 8 x 20-ft. deck plan. However, smaller versions are not only possible but may be desirable according to intended use. Named the *Sea Surrey* it can be used for powered fishing platform, small river operation, overnight camping or just plain swimming and diving-raft fun.

Constructed of Styrofoam BB plastic foam, the party barge takes about 100 man-hours to

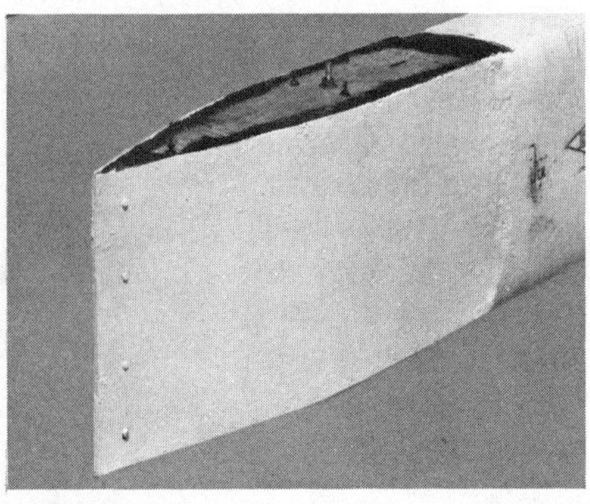

FOUR BUOYANCY billets are used for the two flotation pontoons. Bow ends (left) are notched to receive the wood framing members. Plastic foam doesn't lose buoyancy even if it's punctured. One cubic foot of the foam will hold up 55 lbs. The frames are joined using bolts, Anchorfast nails and waterproof resorcinol glue. The wood is preservative-treated to reduce the chance of decay from moisture. This also helps reduce attack by insects. All nonglued surfaces are covered with Cuprinol. The bow is skinned with ¼-in. exterior plywood (above). The edges should be carefully sealed to keep the water out. To protect the pontoons from gas and oil, which will dissolve them, apply two coats of water-mix exterior paint to the foam plastic. The styrofoam may also have to be covered with hardboard or wire netting to keep muskrats from burrowing in it.

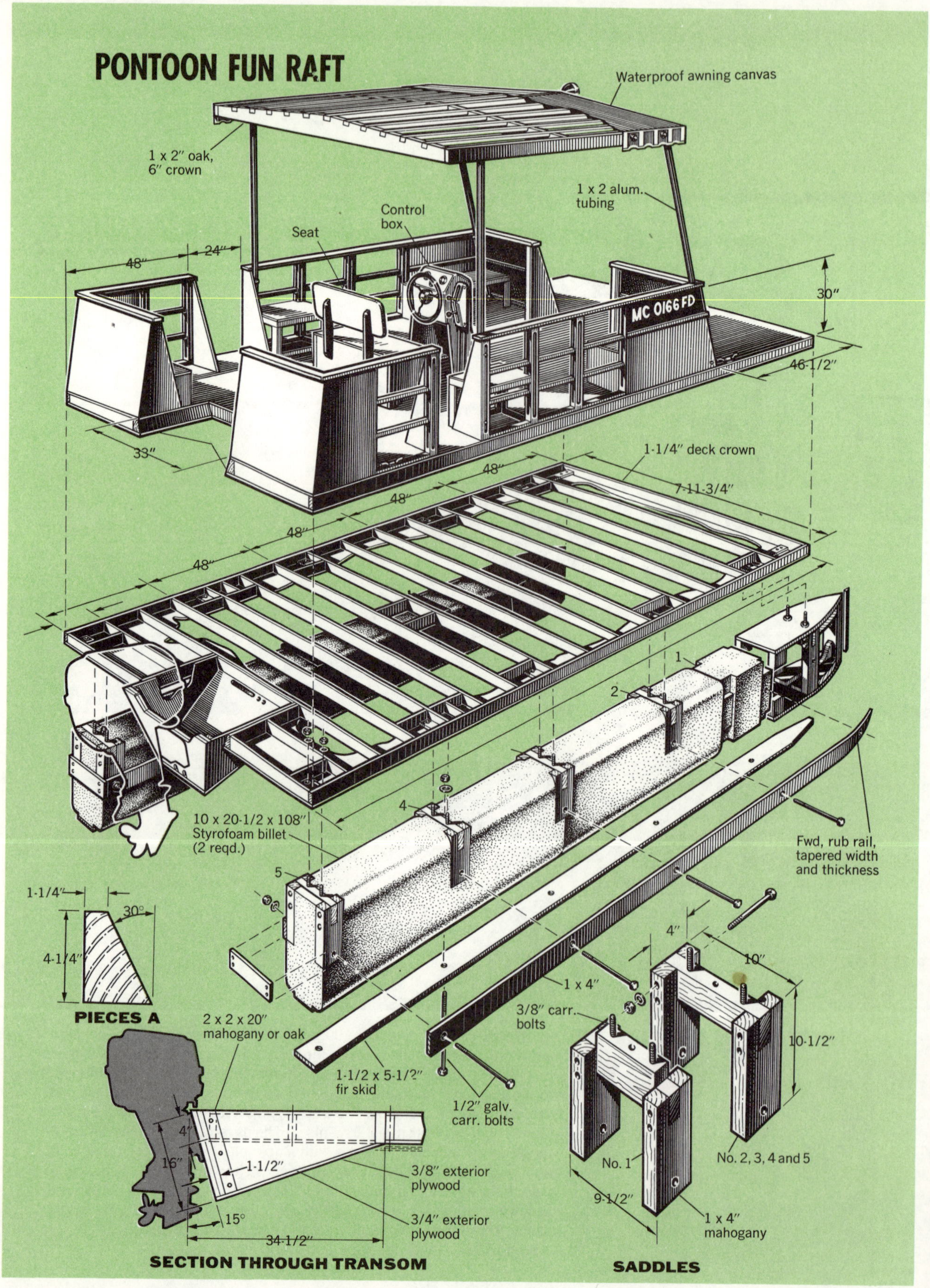
PONTOON FUN RAFT
Waterproof awning canvas
1 x 2" oak,
6" crown
1 x 2 alum.
tubing
Control
box
Seat
48"
24"
30"
MC 0166 FD
46-1/2"
33"
1-1/4" deck crown
48"
7-11-3/4"
1
2
4
5
10 x 20-1/2 x 108"
Styrofoam billet
(2 reqd.)
Fwd, rub rail,
tapered width
and thickness
1-1/4"
30°
4-1/4"
PIECES A
1 x 4"
3/8" carr.
bolts
4"
10"
10-1/2"
2 x 2 x 20"
mahogany or oak
1-1/2 x 5-1/2"
fir skid
1/2" galv.
carr. bolts
4"
16"
1-1/2"
3/8" exterior
plywood
3/4" exterior
plywood
15°
34-1/2"
No. 1
No. 2, 3, 4 and 5
9-1/2"
1 x 4"
mahogany
SECTION THROUGH TRANSOM
SADDLES

PROFILE AND END VIEWS

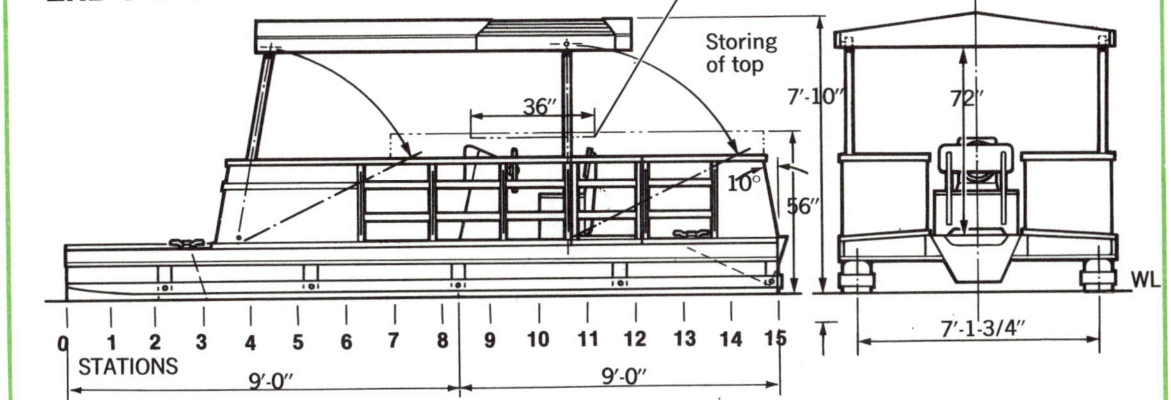

build. Though we've shown construction drawings on these pages, a brochure on the craft, which includes complete construction details, is available free at your Styrofoam dealer or directly from Styrofoam Buoyancy Plans, Functional Products & Systems, The Dow Chemical Co., Midland, MI 48640.

The plans call for a railing, a control box for steering and controlling the craft, a captain's seat and a "surrey" top. In constructing any of the topside area, you can turn your imagination loose, and vary or customize to suit your needs and imagination. If you plan to add power, the *Sea Surrey* is designed to accommodate outboard motors from 5½ to 40 hp.

treat the wood

You would be wise to use only treated wood, or wood naturally resistant to decay or insect attack, for the wooden parts of the boat to make them last longer. If you choose the first, make certain it is clean, dry and free of oily residue. (Clean wood treated with pentachlorophenol is suitable for fresh-water structures.) If you treat the wood yourself, avoid spilling the liquid preservatives on the Styrofoam BB (buoyancy billet) plastic since they will dissolve the foam. If the craft is to be used in saltwater, protect all submerged parts the way you would a wooden hull boat. In some locations muskrats like to burrow in styrofoam. To solve the problem, cover it with hardboard or wire netting.

For surfaces above the waterline, a spokesman for Dow recommends an undercoat and finishing coat of a good quality marine topside paint. If desired, the deck can be fiberglassed. But if you plan to, don't apply preservatives to any surface to be fiberglassed.

EXPLODED VIEW OF PONTOON BOW

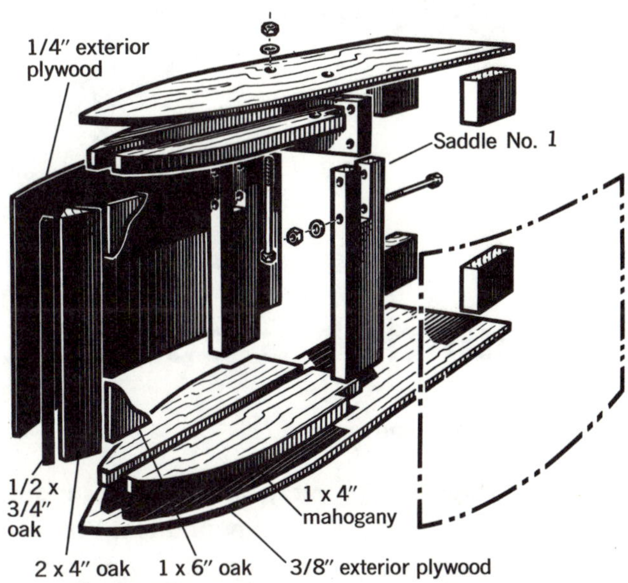

FOR OVERLAND portage, it is easy to haul your fun raft from lake to lake using an ordinary boat trailer.

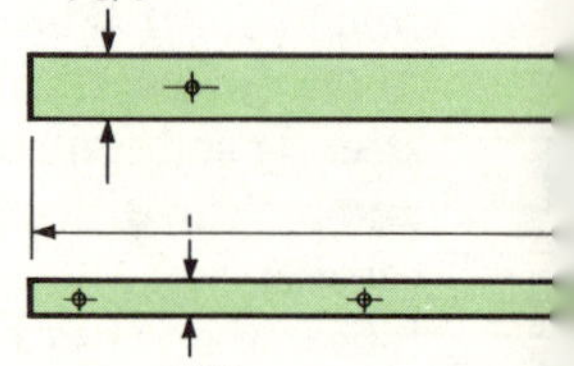

Build this beautiful pool table

By JOHN CAPOTOSTO

With billiards growing rapidly as a favorite indoor sport, everyone wants a pool table. You can build this sturdy, full-size model yourself and save nearly $200

IF YOU HAVE DONE any shopping lately you know that a pool table is an expensive item to buy. However, if you are good at working with tools you can save almost $200 by building this beauty. Believe it or not, I only spent about $107 to build it, and that includes everything—even the balls and cues. Such hard-to-get items as billiard cloth, cushion rubber and foam padding come in a kit (a source of these necessities for any pool table is given at the end of the article).

This table is well-designed and if constructed

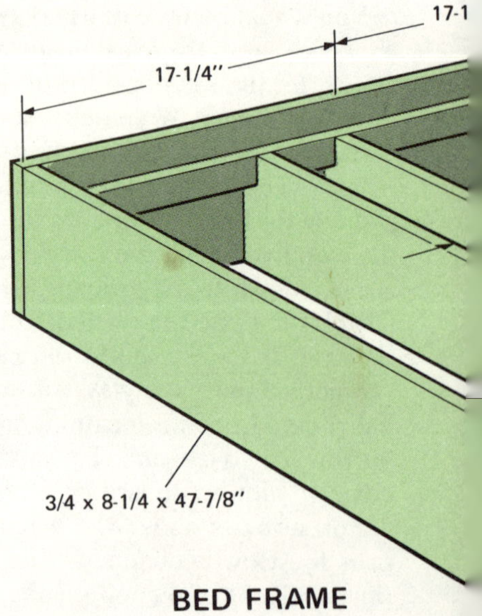

BED FRAME

SEE ALSO

Air games . . . Chess sets . . . Cribbage boards . . . Family rooms . . . Game tables . . . Games . . . Party tables . . . Shuffleboard tables

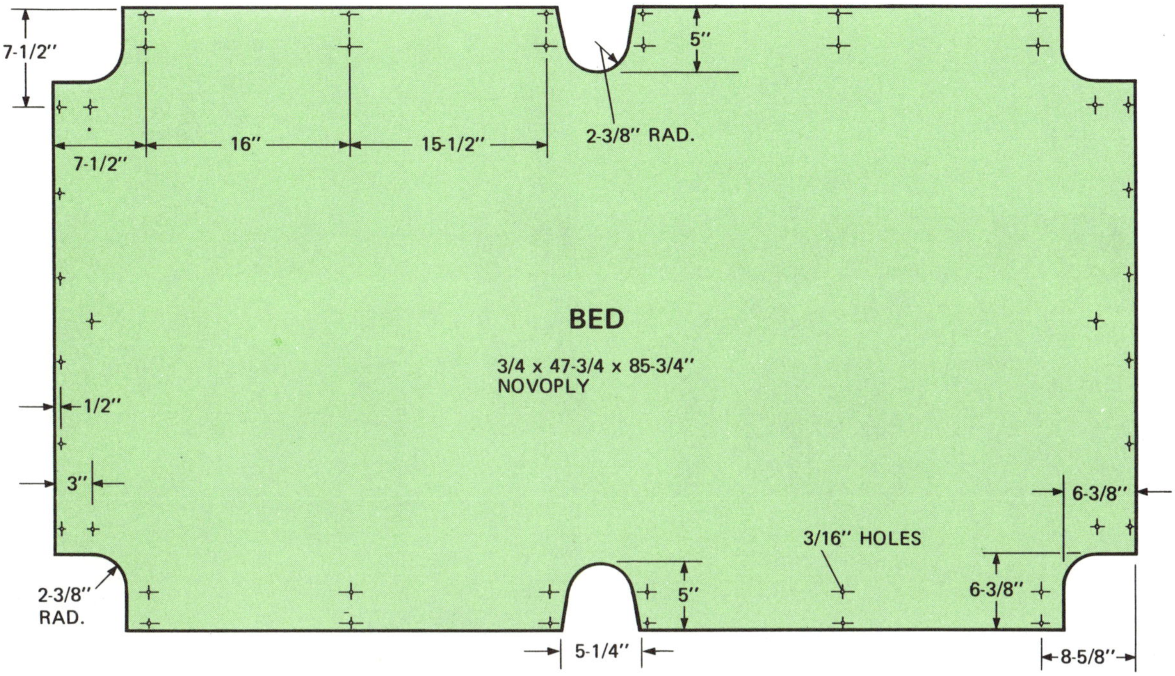

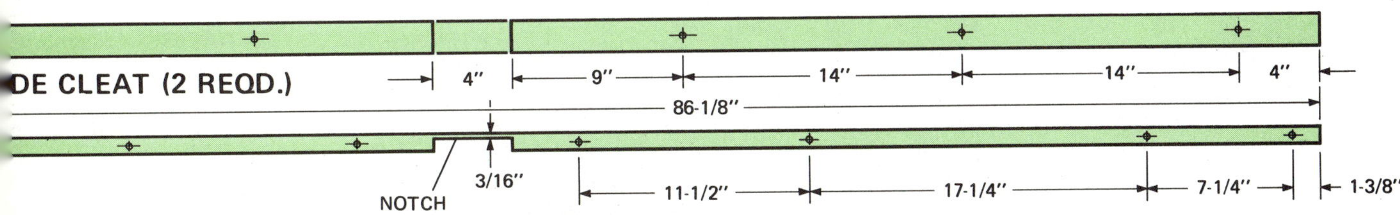

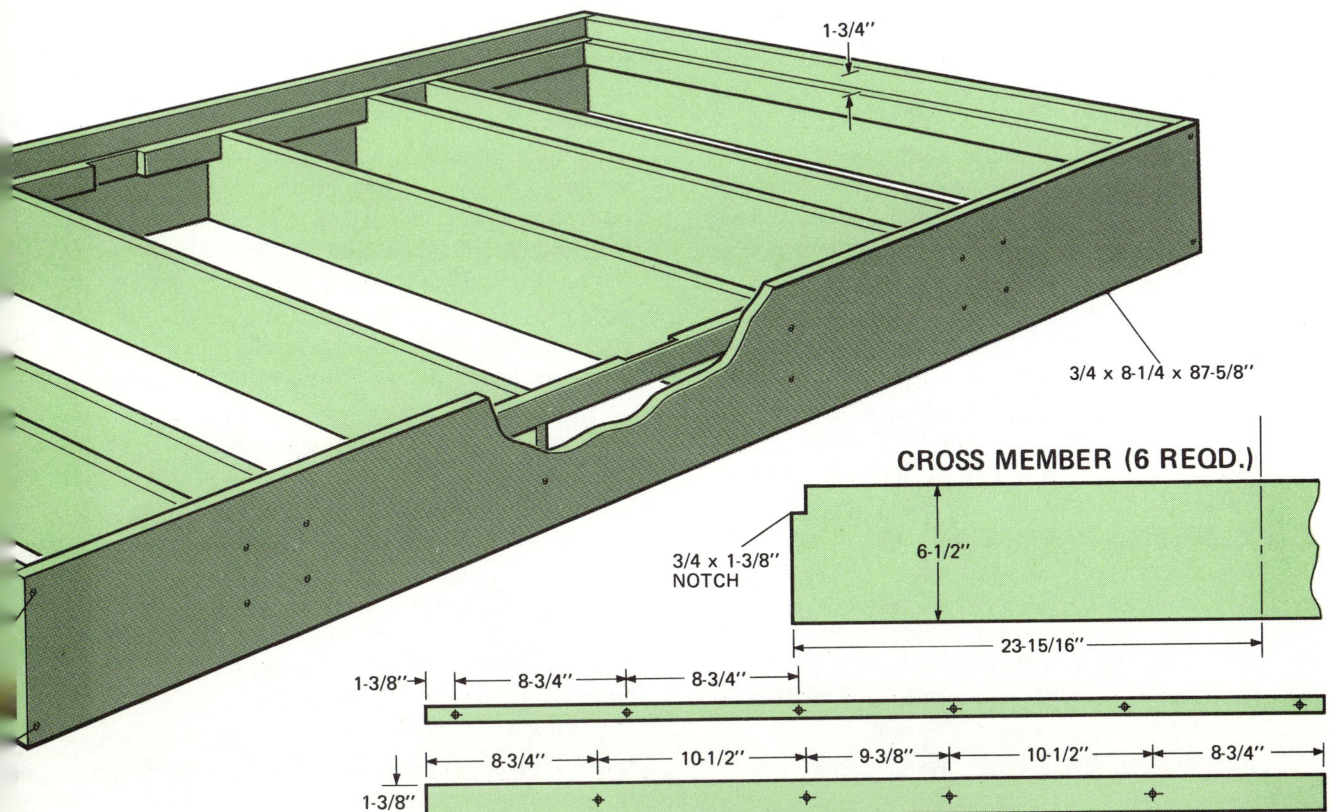

END CLEAT (2 REQD.)

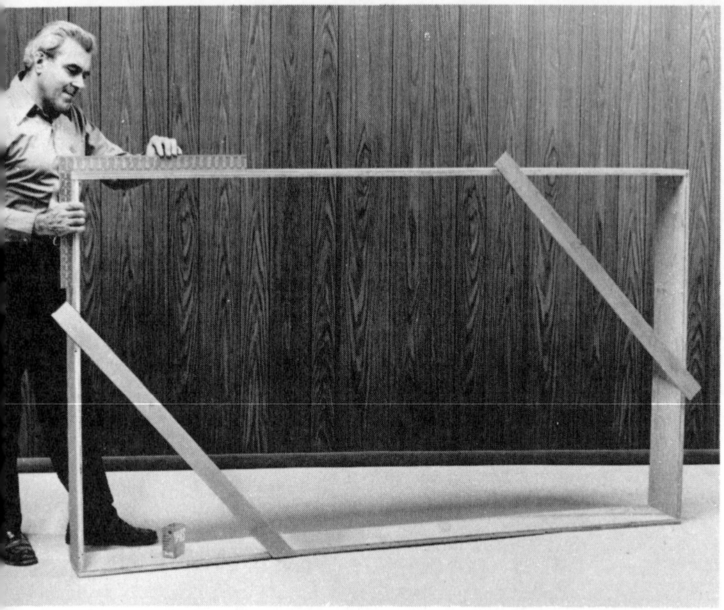

APRON ASSEMBLY is squared up with temporary diagonal braces of scrap across two corners.

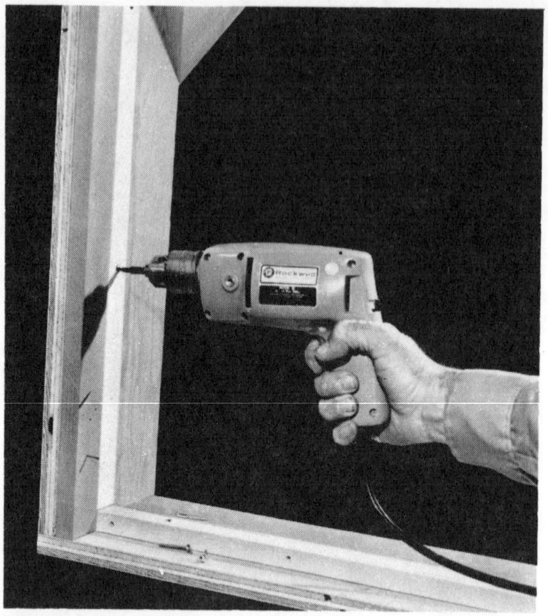

SCREWDRIVER BIT in a variable-speed drill makes quick work of driving home the many screws needed.

with care, it can prove to be very strong and durable. It features a sturdy pedestal base, plastic-laminated aprons, drop pockets which simplify the construction, and padded rails—an extra usually found only on more expensive tables.

The table is standard size (3½ x 7 ft.) and uses 2¼-in. balls.

materials readily available

• **Base.** All materials used in the table are readily available. Except where noted, ¾-in. plywood is used. Even the pedestal legs and base are made of plywood, using box-type construction which adds much to rigidity and sturdiness. Leg uprights are rabbeted to minimize edge grain, and base sections are butt-joined.

To insure accuracy and to simplify assembly, the uprights should be temporarily mounted to the pedestal *before* the scallop at the bottom of the pedestal is cut. Mount the uprights individually before they are "boxed." You will note in the material list that extra length has been allowed for this reason.

Miter the uprights at 14° from the vertical, top and bottom, then at the center of the pedestal mark two lines 8$^{15}/_{16}$ in. apart. Align the uprights on these marks, keeping the bottom even with the bottom edge of the pedestal. Tack the pieces in place with 1¼-in. brads, then drill pilot holes for the screws. Use four screws in each upright for added strength. Once located, you can remove the uprights and cut the scallop in the pedestal and recut the bottoms of the uprights to match the scallop. Uprights now may be permanently glued. The leg filler pieces are rabbeted, leaving ⅛ in. of stock as indicated. These are glued just short of the top and extend slightly into the base.

Note: When gluing edge-grain stock, glue-size the edges. Apply thinned glue (thin with water if white glue) to edges and allow to dry before regular application of glue. This seals the edge, preventing excessive absorption of glue which would cause a weak joint. Remember, this is to be a sturdy table throughout and a good careful construction job makes that possible.

Before installing the base pads to the scallops, drill a ½-in. hole at the center of each and insert a T-nut. These are for the leveling jacks. The flange of the nut must be to the outside when the pad is mounted.

When the pedestals are completed, add two furring strips to the upper ends; these will help support the table and simplify mounting the pedestal later.

now make stretcher

The stretcher can be made now and the two pedestals connected to it. Lagscrews are driven from the inside to join the pedestals. Do not use glue as you may need to disassemble the table to move it to its final destination. Lagscrews can

LAGSCREWS attach table to base. Do not use glue so the table can be dismantled easily for moving.

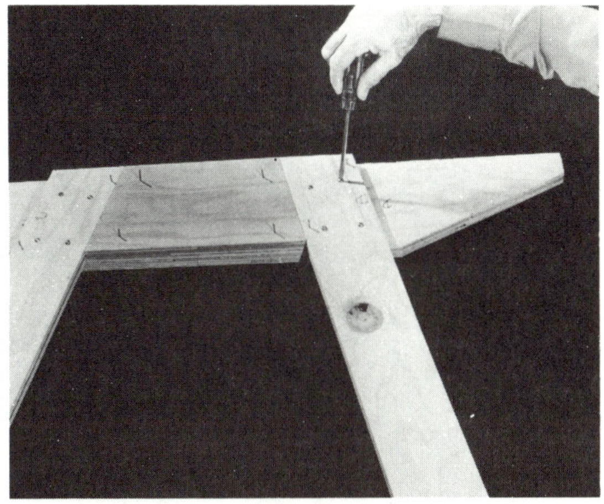

TEMPORARY JIG nailed between uprights of base assures accuracy during assembly.

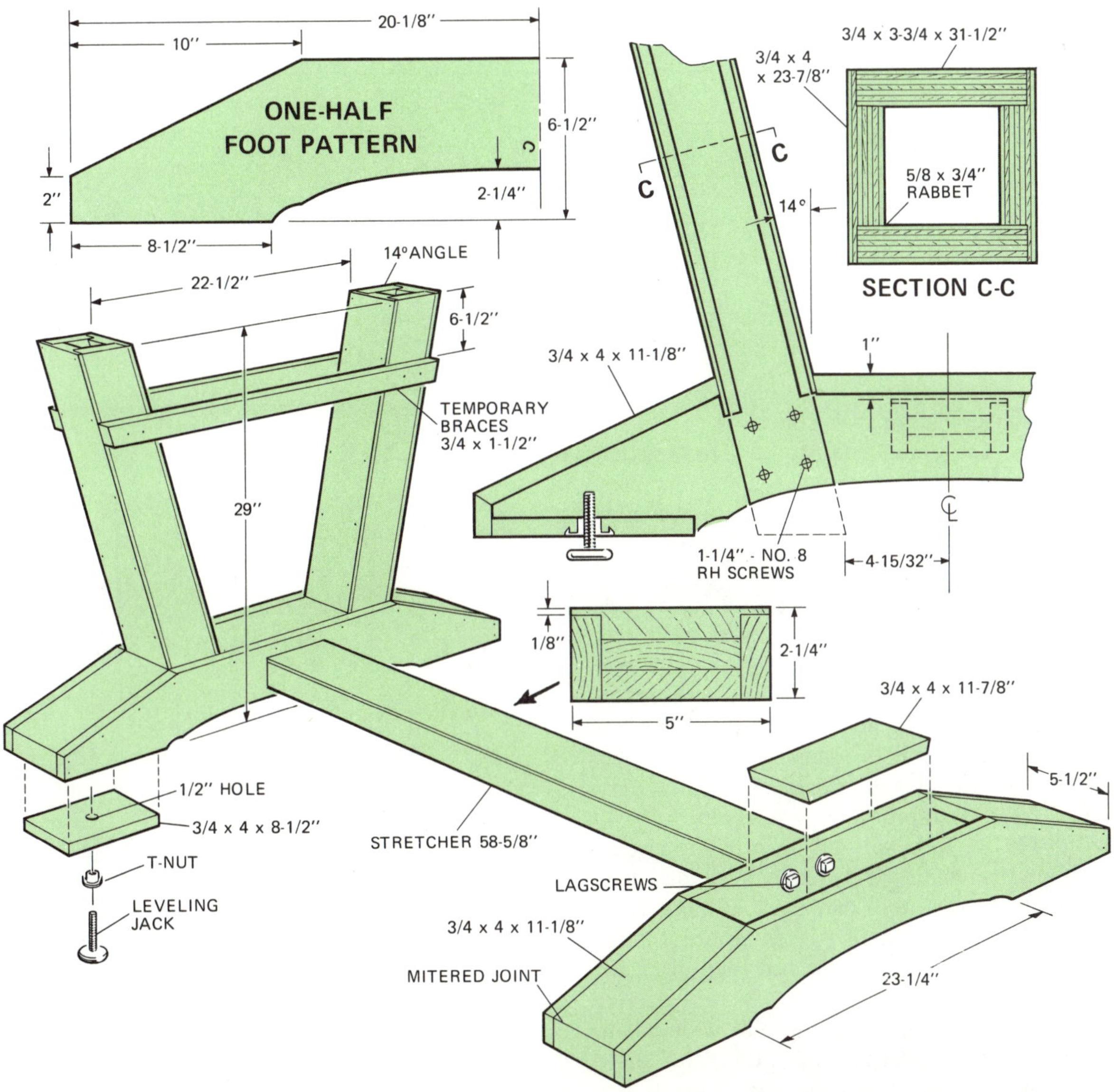

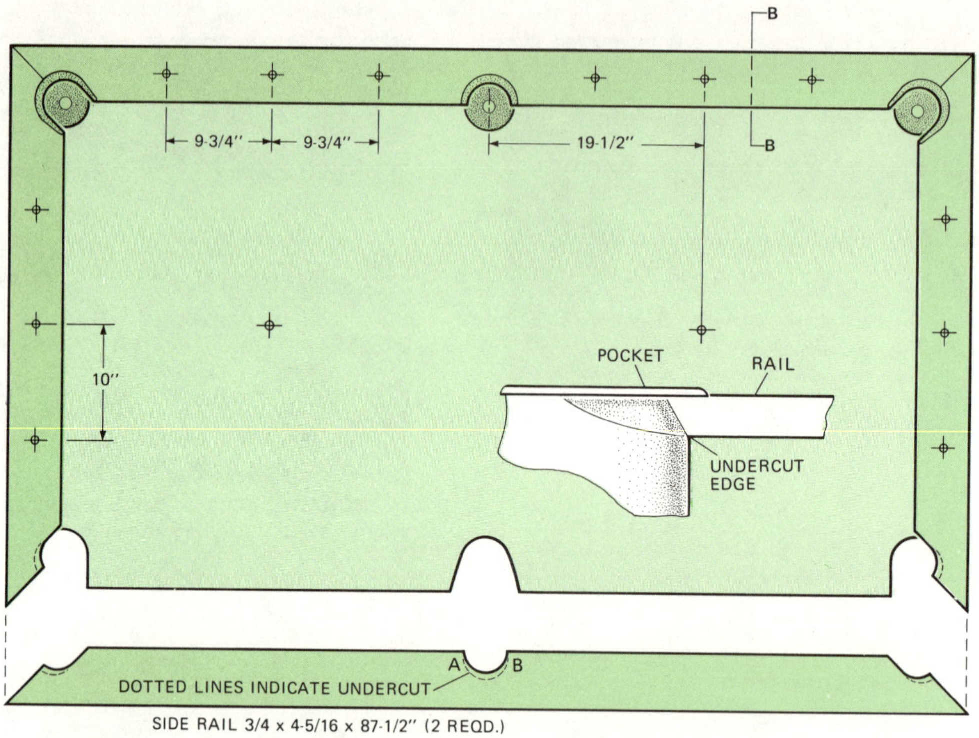

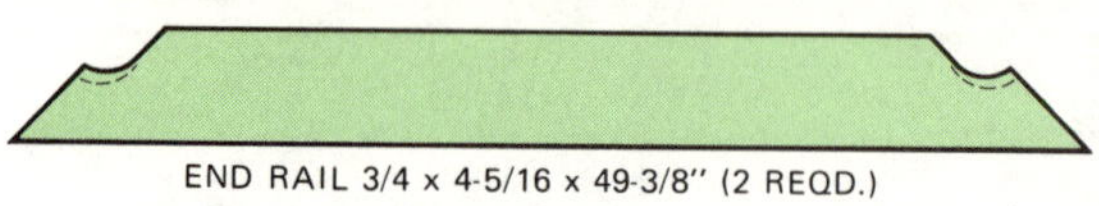

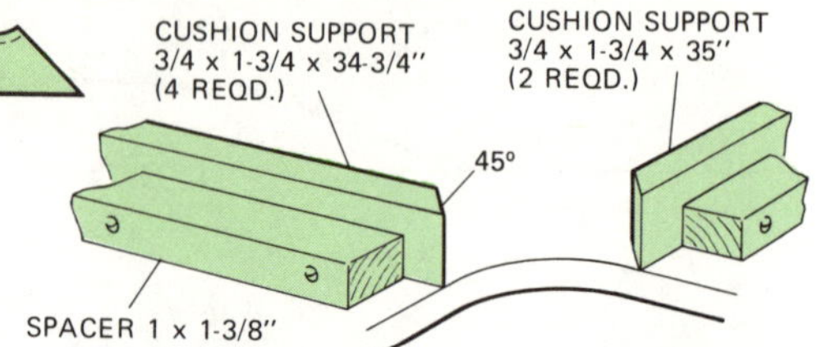

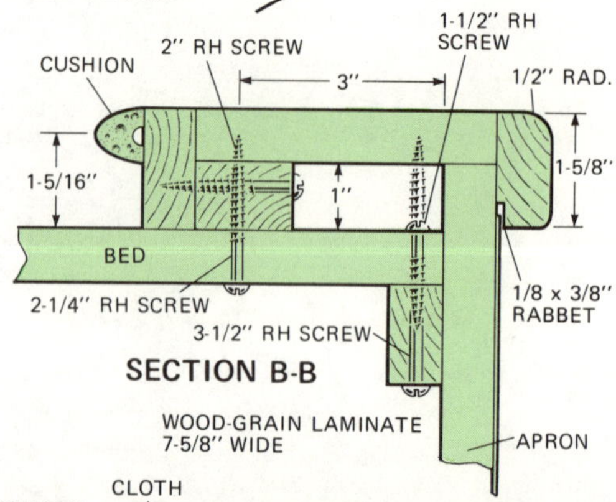

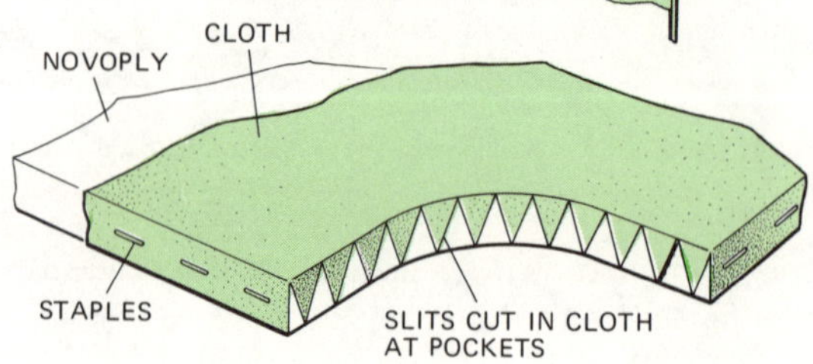

easily be taken out for such a move.

• **Apron.** The apron consists of a rectangular frame to which the bed, cleats and cross members are attached with screws. To maintain accuracy of the frame, use diagonal strips while the glue sets.

The bed support cleats are drilled for screws before mounting. Locate the holes as indicated and drill the holes straight and square. The two side cleats must be notched to allow clearance for the side pockets. The notch may be made with a router or by several overlapping passes on the radial-arm saw. Install cleats exactly 1¾ in. down from the apron's top. A scrap strip of wood 1¾ in. wide will aid in installing cleats. Temporarily nail the strip even with the top edge, then butt the cleat to it and screw in place after gluing. Top edge of the six cross members must be flush with top edge of the bed support cleats as shown.

I covered the aprons on my table with an inexpensive, wood-grained laminate called Conolite, which is applied with contact cement. It's

SLIT FABRIC at drop-pocket cutouts and staple it to the underside of the rail, then along rail edges.

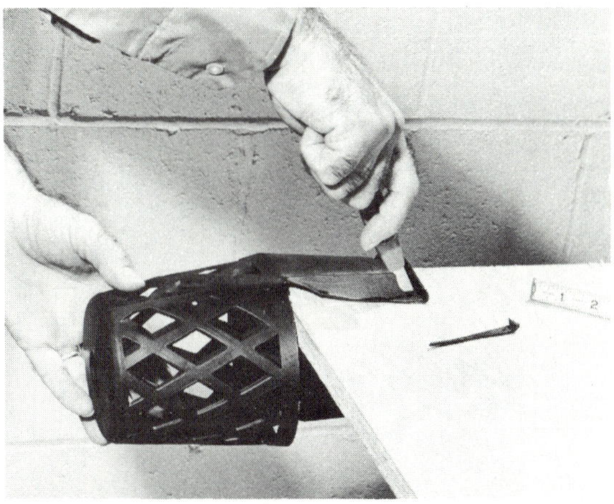

TRIM POCKETS to fit—differently at the sides than at the corners. See the drawing, above right.

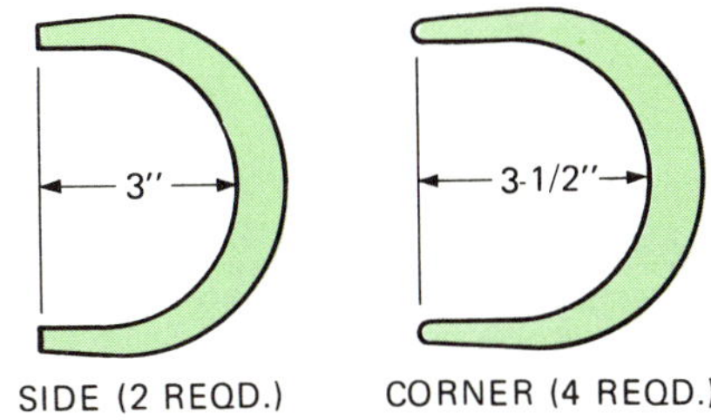

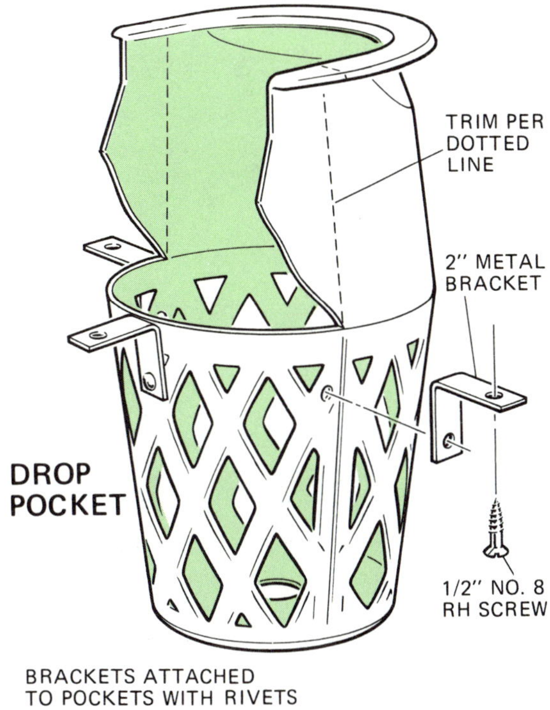

METAL ANGLE brackets are used to attach drop pockets in cutouts after trimming the pockets.

offered in rolls 36 in., wide and sold by the foot. It is easy to install and gives the table a nicely finished look. Various colors, patterns and grains are available. It can be cut with scissors, but you may find it easier to score the surface with an awl and snap it along the scored line.

Cut the laminate slightly oversize and apply contact cement to it and to the wood surface. Allow the cement to dry until it loses its tackiness, then apply carefully. Once in place, it cannot be moved. The top edge of the laminate is set 11/16 in. below the top edge of the apron. The sides and bottom should overhang slightly. Trim excess with a router fitted with a laminate trimmer or by hand with a plane. Cover the end aprons first, then the longer sides.

• **Bed.** The bed is cut from a sheet of ¾-in. particleboard. Notice that ¼ in. is trimmed from the 48-in. dimension. The length of the bed is 85¾ in. The material is dense and tough, but it is easily cut with ordinary tools such as a portable saw, sabre saw, or even a handsaw. Lay out the corner and side-pocket cutouts according to the diagram. After cutting, break all sharp edges with sandpaper. Drill the mounting holes, then cover with billiard cloth. The cloth is stapled to the underside of the bed. Do the long sides first, then the ends. Slit the cloth at the pockets, stopping the slits just short of the cutouts. Pull the cloth evenly around the pockets and staple to the underside of the bed. (Before installing the cloth remove wrinkles with a steam iron.) The bed and the felt on it are two of the most critical parts of any pool table.

• **Rails.** The rails require some tricky sabre-saw cutting. Cut the sections to size and miter the ends 45°. Place the four pieces on a flat surface and lay out the 4⅛-in.-dia. cutouts.

Make cutouts in the usual manner using a sabre saw. After all corner and sidepocket cutouts have been made, tilt your saw's base to 30° and recut the section of the cutout from points A and B. Undercutting is needed to clear the drop pockets.

The outer edging for the rails is cut and rabbeted as in the drawing. Two passes on the table

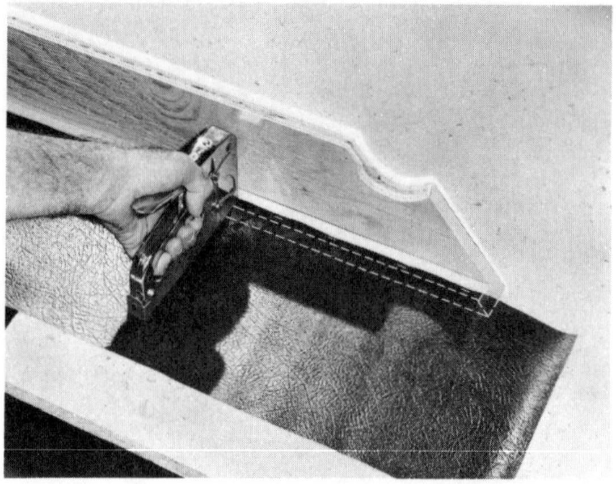

FABRIC-BACKED vinyl is stapled to the underside of rails with 5/16-in. staples spaced about 1 in. apart.

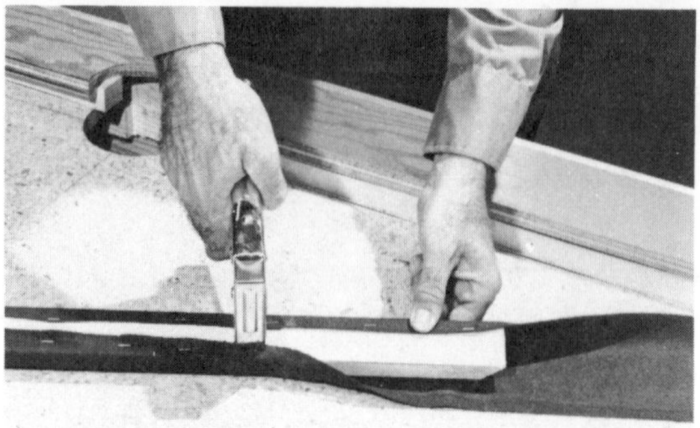

COVER CUSHIONS with 5-in. wide strips of billiard cloth, pulled taut and stapled to the rear side.

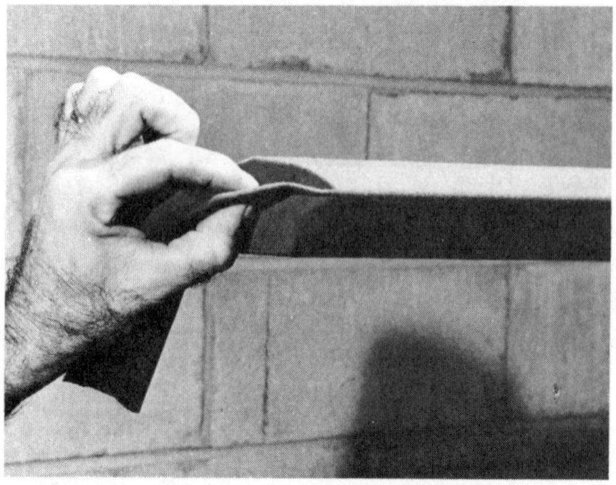

CUSHION ENDS are glued as shown, then cloth is pinched and trimmed neatly with a razor blade.

HERE'S HOW a drop pocket fits the corner hole. Front padded rail has been removed for clarity.

saw will form the rabbet—or use a router. Round off top and bottom edges, miter the ends, then nail and glue edge pieces to the four rails.

Padding the rails is not too difficult. Glue a 5-in.-wide strip of foam to the rear edge of the rail just before the round starts. Use rubber cement or Pliobond *only*. Contact cement, white glue and animal glues destroy the foam. If you use rubber cement (sold at stationery and art stores), apply it to both surfaces and let it air-dry about five minutes before joining the parts. Apply a narrow strip of cement about ½ in. wide.

Cover the rails with a strip of fabric-backed vinyl. This is upholstery material; two well-known trade names are Naugahyde and Boltaflex. Cut it in 9-in.-wide strips and let the ends overhang the rails slightly. Staple one edge of the vinyl to the rabbeted part of the rail back. Pull this taut toward the front of the rail and staple it again on the front edge, with staples about 1 in. apart. At the cutouts, slit material and staple it to the underside as shown on page 181. At the ends of the rails, trim the excess and where impractical to staple, use cement.

When all rails are covered and mounted to the table, there will be a slight gap at the miters. This is rectified by inserting corner fillers made by folding a piece of vinyl over a foam strip. Insert in corners before permanently mounting the rails.

• **Cushions.** The rubber cushions are cemented to the wood cushion supports with rubber or contact cement. The cushion rubber is not symmetrical, but has a top and bottom. It's mounted right when the nose of the rubber is 1$^{15}/_{16}$ in. from bottom edge of the support. Miter the supports as indicated, then mount the rubber. Let rubber extend past the miter, then trim it flush with a sharp knife. It's much easier to cut if the blade is dipped in water first.

Covering the cushions is next. Cushion cloth in the kit is 10 in. wide, with a small slit at the

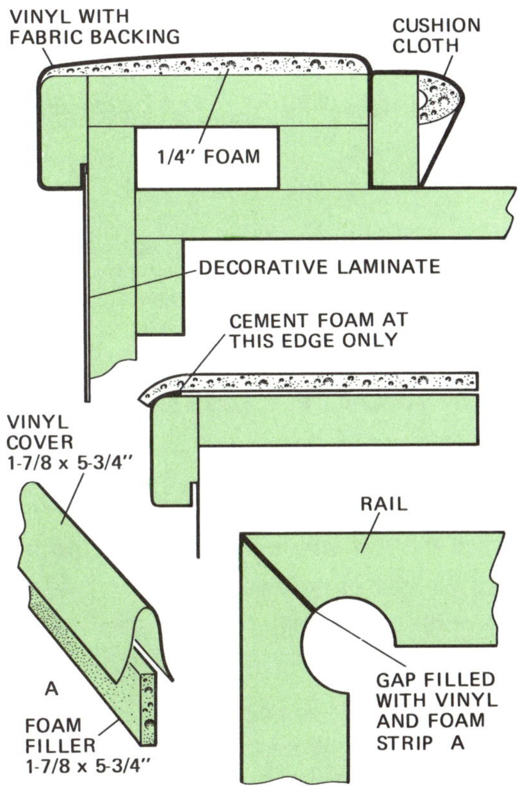

MATERIAL LIST

Note: Except where indicated, all lumber is fir plywood

No.	Size and description—Use
2	¾ x 4⁵⁄₁₆ x 87½"—Side rails
2	¾ x 4⁵⁄₁₆ x 49⅜"—End rails
2	¾ x 1⅝ x 89"—Side-rail back
2	¾ x 1⅝ x 50¾"—End-rail back
6	1 x 1⅜ x 33" pine—Support spacers
2	¾ x 1¾ x 35" pine—End-cushion supports
4	¾ x 1¾ x 34¾" pine—Side-cushion supports
2	¾ x 1⅜ x 46⅜" pine—End bed supports
2	¾ x 1⅜ x 85¾" pine—Side bed supports
1	¾ x 47¾ x 85¾" Novaply—Bed
2	¾ x 8¼ x 47⅞"—End aprons
2	¾ x 8¼ x 87⅝"—Side aprons
6	¾ x 6½ x 47⅞"—Cross members
2	¹⁄₃₂ x 7⅝ x 52"—End laminate
2	¹⁄₃₂ x 7⅝ x 88"—Side laminate
4	¾ x 6½ x 40¼"—Base
4	¾ x 4 x 8½"—Bottom pads
4	¾ x 4 x 2"—Base ends
4	¾ x 4 x 11⅛"—Base diagonals
2	¾ x 4 x 11⅞"—Base tops
8	¾ x 3¾ x 31½"—Uprights
8	¾ x 4 x 23⅞"—Upright fillers
4	¾ x 1½ x 28"—Temporary supports
1	¾ x 5 x 58⅝"—Stretcher top
1	¾ x 3½ x 58⅝"—Stretcher center
1	¾ x 3½ x 58⅝"—Stretcher bottom
2	¾ x 2⅛ x 58⅝"—Stretcher sides
18	2" angle brackets—Pockets
18	No. 8 x ½" rh screws with washers—Brackets
32	No. 8 x 1¼" fh screws
32	No. 8 x 1¼" rh screws
18	No. 8 x 1½" rh screws
20	No. 8 x 2" rh screws
18	No. 8 x 2¼" rh screws
28	No. 8 x 3½" rh screws
20	⁵⁄₁₆ x 1½" lagscrews with washers
	White glue, contact cement, staples, rubber cement

5-in. mark. Grasp the cloth at one end and pull apart at the slit into two 5-in-wide strips. Cover the cushions by stapling the cloth to the rear side, a trifle above center. Pull the opposite end taut and again staple at rear of the support. Work from the center out. Be sure the staples set flush. If not, hammer them all the way home. Do likewise with the rail. Ends of the cushion cloth are cemented. Pull the cloth toward the center, then carefully cut the excess with a razor blade. Pull loose ends to the back and cement.

The support spacer is attached to the cushion support with five 2-in. rh screws in each piece. Drive the screws tightly.

• **Final assembly.** Place the support spacer under the rail and screw rail into place with 3½-in. rh screws. Force the cushion as tight as possible against the rail and attach with the 2¼-in. screws. Have an assistant help you. If you can't get 2¼-in. screws, use 2½-in. ones with several washers under the heads to keep points from penetrating.

• **Drop pockets.** The molded-rubber pockets are made slightly oversize so they may be trimmed to fit various tables. Pockets in the kit are cut with a sharp knife or scissors. Three metal brackets hold each pocket in place, using Pop-rivets. The other end of each bracket is attached to the table with a ½-in. screw. Since bracket holes vary, no dimensions are given. If too large or too far in from edge, drill new holes as necessary. Press top of the pocket down firmly against the padded rail when positioning brackets.

Rail markers are ⅜ in. pressure-sensitive paper discs available at art and stationery shops. Peel off protective backing and press them in place. Paint the base as desired.

The kit, with four leveling jacks, 22 ft. of cushion rubber, billiard cloth, six drop pockets and a ¼ x 5 x 280-in. urethanefoam strip can be ordered from The Armor Co., Box 290, Deer Park, N.Y. 11729.

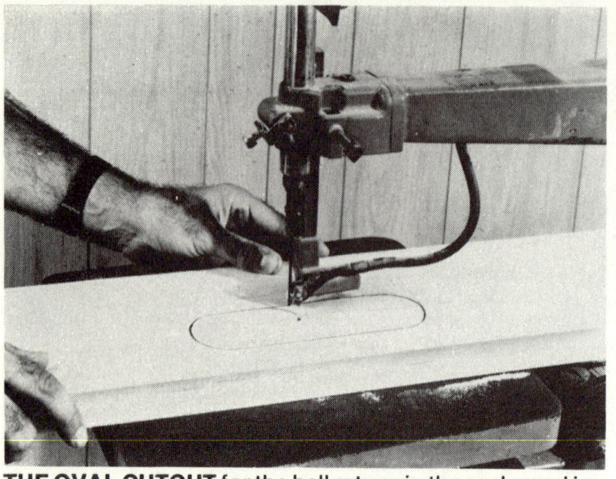

THE OVAL CUTOUT for the ball return in the end panel is made before assembly. Use a jig or sabre saw.

THE BALL-RETURN BOX is simply constructed with butt joints. The box bottom slopes slightly toward opening.

A space-saving bumper-pool table

By JOHN CAPOTOSTO

It takes approximately one-third the space that a conventional table requires. That means apartment dwellers can now enjoy pool as well as homeowners with spacious family rooms. Here's how to build your table

■ POOL HAS LONG been favored as an American family pastime, but two obstacles—cost and space—have kept pool tables out of most homes. Now, by building a regulation-size bumper-pool table yourself, you too can get in on the fun of skillful pool playing.

The most important feature of a good pool table is rigidity. Our version, with its ¾-in. particleboard bed, stacks up against good commercial tables. Also, the one shown boasts aprons and legs of 5/4 (1⅛-in.) stock. Though designed so that construction is simple, quality has not been sacrificed. And, to make shopping for materials an easy task, all the specialty pool items are available by mail order from one source.

The pool table measures 32x48 in. Some lumberyards will (and some won't) sell you the particleboard cut to size. When buying, it's important to make sure that the board is free of any warp.

Lay out the hole locations for the bumpers and drill them with a 1⅜-in. bit. Cup holes will have to be cut with a sabre saw, but before sawing them in the particleboard, check for size on a piece of scrap. When testing the cup liners for fit, drape several pieces of cloth over the holes; the fit should be fairly snug.

Apron members are cut to size next. Choice of lumber is optional but, if you plan to paint your table, a less expensive wood (such as fir) will do. If you prefer stain, consider a hardwood with an attractive grain (walnut or birch, for example). Lay out the oval ball return openings on the end panels and cut them with a sabre saw or jigsaw.

Add the cleats to the apron members, using flathead screws and glue. Position the cleats accurately as they will indirectly determine the cushion height, which is very important. Notice the counter-bored holes drilled in the cushion liner for the bed-to-liner screws.

Next, cut and assemble the legs. These are attached to the 2x3-in. frame as shown. Drill the clearance holes for the leg levelers and then drive home the special Teenuts. Use lagscrews to join the leg assembly to the bed. *Caution:* Take care when working with particleboard—overtightening a screw can strip the hole.

Cut the wood cushion liner to size, mitering the corners, then undercut the ends (see inset in

SEE ALSO

Air games . . . Chess sets . . . Cribbage boards . . . Family rooms . . . Game tables . . . Party tables . . . Shuffleboard tables

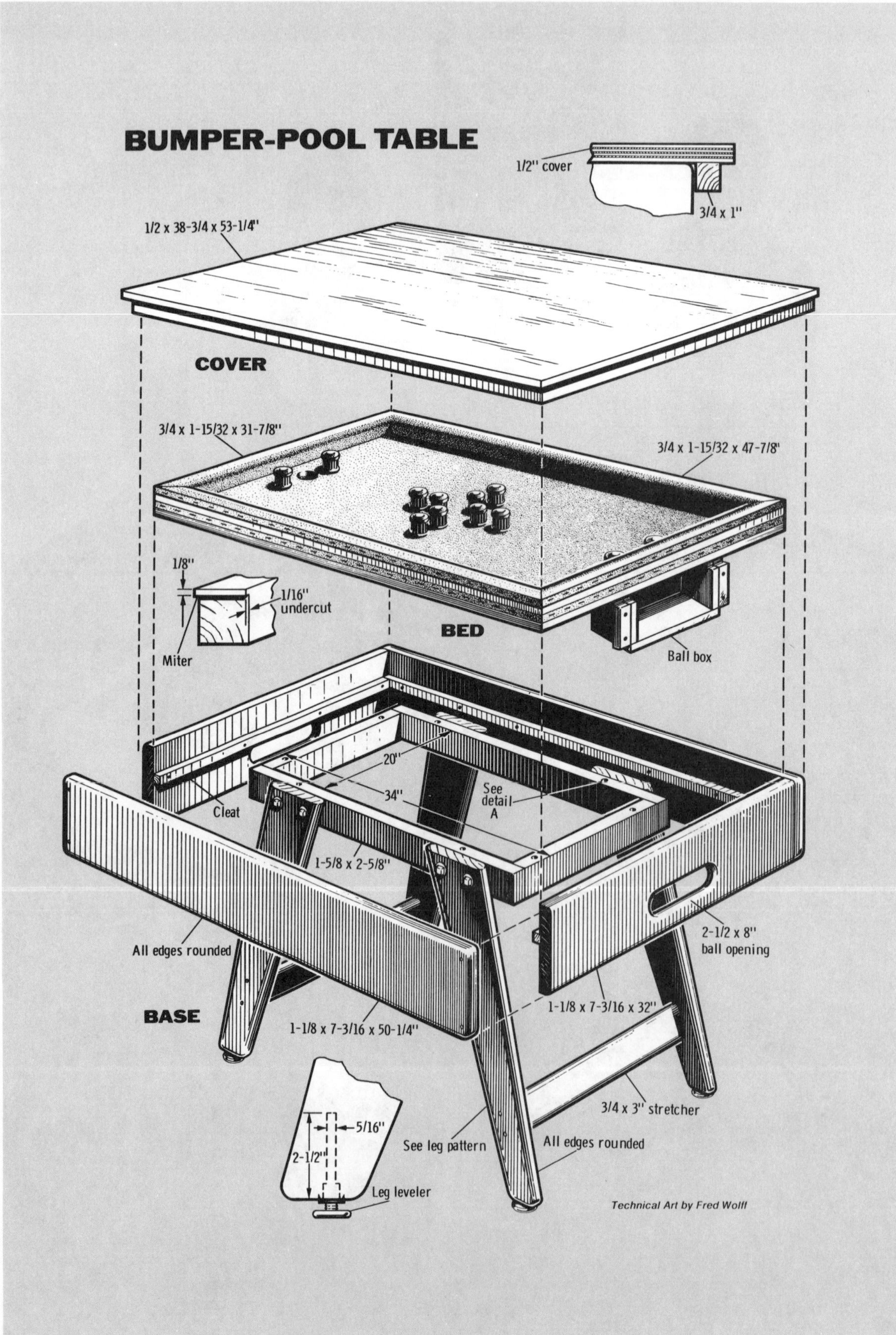
BUMPER-POOL TABLE
1/2" cover
3/4 x 1"
1/2 x 38-3/4 x 53-1/4"
COVER
3/4 x 1-15/32 x 31-7/8"
3/4 x 1-15/32 x 47-7/8"
1/8"
1/16" undercut
Miter
BED
Ball box
20"
34"
See detail A
Cleat
1-5/8 x 2-5/8"
All edges rounded
2-1/2 x 8" ball opening
BASE
1-1/8 x 7-3/16 x 50-1/4"
1-1/8 x 7-3/16 x 32"
3/4 x 3" stretcher
5/16"
2-1/2"
See leg pattern
All edges rounded
Leg leveler
Technical Art by Fred Wolff

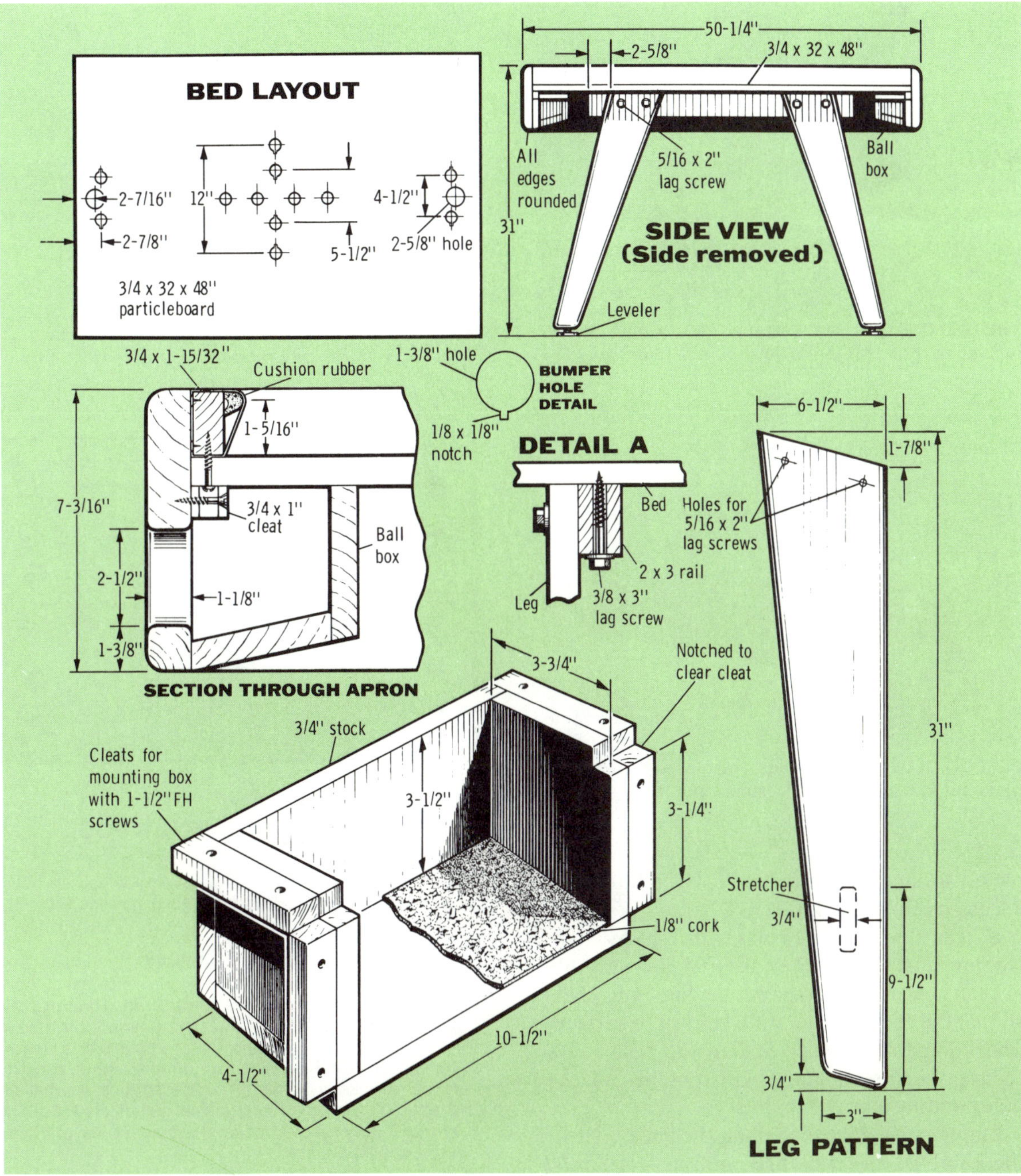

photo at top right of page 2268). The undercut is necessary to allow clearance for the gathered felt at the ends of the cushions. After mitering the lines, lower the blade ⅛ in. and recut the ends.

The cushions are now added. Cut the strips a trifle longer than the liner and apply a coat of contact cement to both surfaces. Allow this to set, then join the pieces carefully. If you examine the rubber in cross section, you'll notice it has a shallow and a deep curve. The shallow part is the top, therefore mount it accordingly to the liner. Trim ends to match the mitered liner. Use a sharp knife, after dipping it in water, to lubricate the blade or you'll have trouble cutting the rubber.

Cover the cushions and bed next. If the cloth is wrinkled, press it carefully on the *wrong* side with a steam iron set on low. Drape the cloth over the bed and tack with staples spaced 1 in. apart: first at the four corners, pulling the cloth taut before stapling; next along the ends, and finally along the long sides. After stapling com-

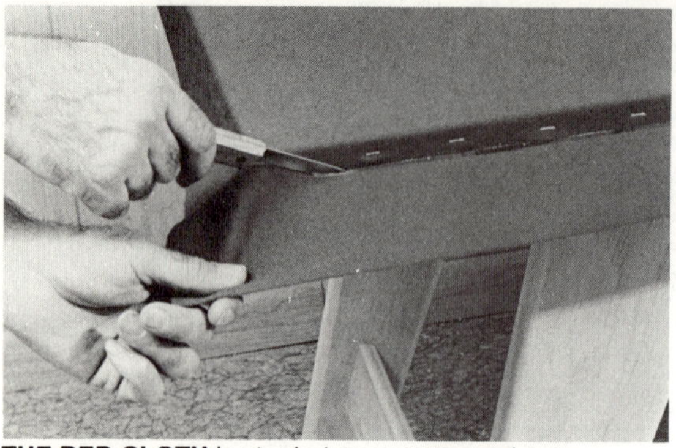

THE BED CLOTH is stapled around the perimeter every inch or so. Knife for trimming should be razor sharp.

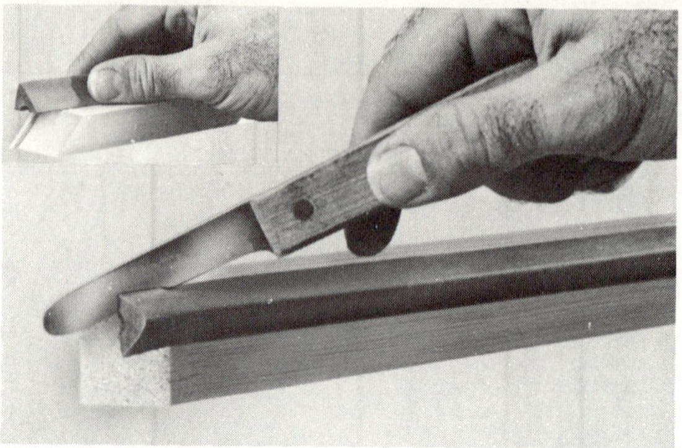

THE CUSHION RUBBER is cut a bit oversize and attached with contact cement (see inset). Next, trim,

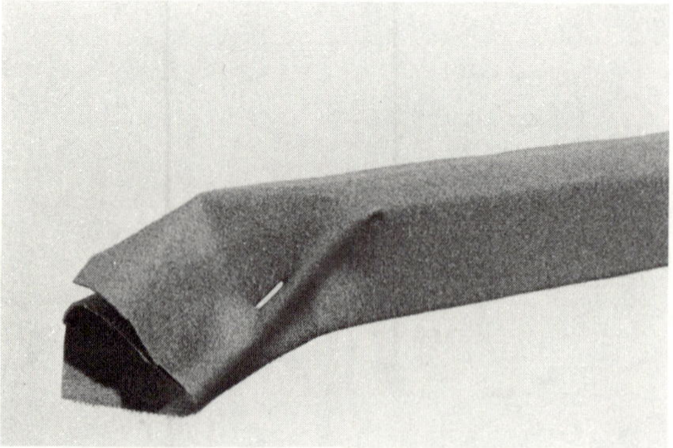

FELT IS FOLDED over the ends, and tucked beneath the undercut in the liner. Finally, staple and trim.

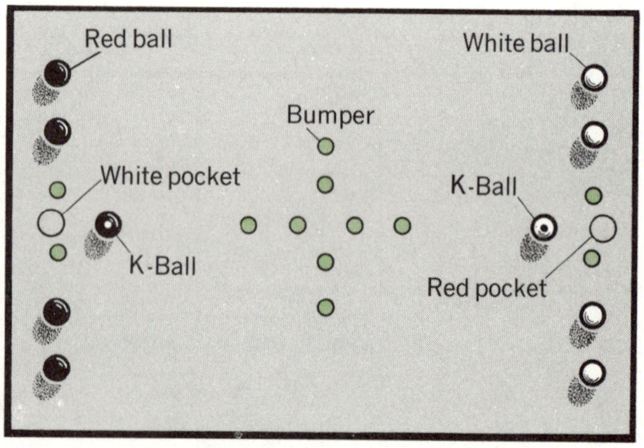

pletely around the perimeter of the bed, trim the excess cloth with a knife.

Slit the cloth over the holes with a sharp blade, stopping just short of the edges. Make eight slits in each hole area. Tap the pocket liner into place so that the edge is just a trifle below the surface. The bumpers are inserted into the holes with their projections aligned with notches of the holes and fastened with nuts.

Staple cushion covers along the back edge of the liner. Do the ends first; pull material taut, then staple at 1-in. intervals all along. Pull cloth around cushion and repeat the procedure on other edge of the cloth. Fold ends over as shown and staple gathered felt in the undercut section. Cut off excess cloth, and attach cushions to the table with roundhead screws driven from below.

Make and attach the ball boxes as shown. A plywood cover with attractive decals protects your table and completes the job.

Specialty items are available from Armor Co., Box 290, Deer Park, NY 11729. Write for free price list, with parcel-post rates and state taxes where applicable.

HOW TO PLAY BUMPER POOL

Number of players: two to four. Each side has five balls: one side red, one white. In each set ball marked with spot is called the king (K) ball.

STRATEGY OF PLAY

Balls are spotted as shown above; white balls shoot toward white pocket and red toward red. To start play, both players shoot their K balls simultaneously toward their respective pockets. The player whose ball is closest to his pocket has the right to continue to shoot. After he "makes" (pockets) his K ball, he may shoot at *any* ball on the table. *Important:* Until a player makes his K ball, he may shoot only for his pocket; he may not try to hit his opponent's ball.

SKILLFUL PLAY

The strategy is to keep your opponent from having an open shot at his pocket while you leave yourself open to shoot at your pocket. This is usually done either by knocking your opponent's ball out of position, or by positioning your own ball in such a manner as to block his shot. The player who pockets his five balls first wins.

PENALTIES

If a player sinks one of his balls before the K ball, opponent pockets any two balls and shoots.

If a player causes a ball to jump the table, his opponent places the jumped ball wherever he chooses (including in the center of the eight-bumper cluster), pockets any two balls and shoots.

If a player pockets an opponent's ball, it is a scratch and he loses his turn. The pocketed ball stays in the pocket.

Overtreated wood?

For 16 years we have struggled with the 6×14-ft. deck on our church parsonage. When it was new we stained it with several coats. Finally, as a last resort, we painted it. Nothing we have tried will adhere to the wood. The paint seems to be oily on the wood side when peeled back.

Besides the fact that it is an eyesore, we are constantly replacing wood that is rotting, because the deck has no protection from the weather.

Someone said our wood may have been "over" treated. Is that possible? Will we have to tear it all down and start over?—James E. Conner, Belmont, Mich.

The initial stain and paint jobs most likely didn't cover the sides and bottom of the wood decking, allowing moisture to penetrate the pores of the wood.

When there is sunshine following rain, the warmth draws the moisture to the surface and from the wood. The painted surface is flaked off in the process. The fact that you also have rotting wood indicates that pressure-treated wood wasn't used.

Replace all rotted wood with pressure-treated, dry wood. Check your decking supports (joist and girders), too. If they have rotted, I'm afraid you'll have to tear down and start over, using dry, pressure-treated wood.

There are several brands available. Check with your local lumberyard or home center to learn what they carry.

Smoke gets in your eyes

Last fall I cleaned my fireplace flue with a sack filled with dry grass clippings and a weight. I lowered and raised the sack up and down the length of the flue. Since the "cleaning," my fireplace smokes. It had given me no such trouble before. What could be wrong?—R. Weston, Boston, Mass.

You didn't finish the cleaning. Much of the debris you loosened when cleaning the flue lodged on the smoke shelf, which deflects the downdraft and is standard in most masonry chimneys. When the shelf is clogged with debris as in the exaggerated detail, an eddy occurs with the result that smoke enters the room. Removing the damper is, in most cases, impossible. You'll have to snake your vacuum cleaner hose past the open damper to remove that debris. Experiment with your damper setting; close it as far as possible without the fireplace smoking. You'll get more heat in the room.

Low-radiant heat for doghouse

The plans I have for building a doghouse state that low-radiant heat can be used during the cold winter months. Just what is meant by low-radiant heat and where can I get the required parts?—C. Maynard, Carteret, N.J.

This type of heat radiates directly to objects; it doesn't have to heat the air surrounding them. Low-radiant heat is usually supplied by electric cables in the floors or ceilings.

To protect the cables from damage by the animals, lay them in a bed of sand over polyurethane insulation and vapor barrier, followed by a minimum 3 in. of concrete.

Some cables can be laid directly in the concrete, but insulation is still required to keep bottom heat loss to a minimum. (Use Styrofoam panels.) Temperature controls are required. Protect all wiring in the conduit so your dog won't chew it.

Choosing a roof color

When I reroof my house this spring should I choose a white roof to reflect the sun's rays and lower airconditioning costs or a black roof to help melt the snow?—Dave Lindman, Minneapolis.

Actually with today's drive on energy conservation, which includes venting the attic space and adding up to 12 in. of insulation in the ceiling, the emphasis on color is not too important. A layer of snow will act as an additional insulator against cold.

In summer, white will certainly reflect the sun's rays. I would choose a color compatible with the color scheme of your home. Keep in mind, though, that the light colors tend to stain from the acids in leaves and pine needles.

Rust stains on concrete

The weep hole in the tailpipe of my 1977 car is causing quite a rust stain on my garage and driveway concrete. Any ideas?—J.W. Meyers, Weleetka, Okla.

Many contemporary buildings are built of steel such as "Corten" that has a controlled-rust characteristic. This steel rusts over a period of 3 to 5 years until it reaches a handsome patina. During the process, some rust stains appear in unwanted areas. The larger building suppliers carry an agent that removes these stains: Iron and Manganese Stain Remover, from Price Research Ltd., Kansas City, Mo. This can solve your problem. Cost is about $10 per gallon. Follow instructions on the can. Briefly, you'll be directed to apply remover to the stain and wash it off after 3 to 5 minutes. Reapply if necessary.

Build a cabana for your pool

You can use this standard-built structure all year long. In the summer it makes a great changing area and in the winter it can be used for storage of yard equipment

By DON SHINER

SEE ALSO

**Cabanas . . . Carpeting, outdoor . . .
Garden shelters . . . Gazebos . . . Playhouses . . .
Pools, swimming . . . Summer houses**

■ THERE ARE two distinct advantages to be gained from erecting a small structure adjacent to your pool. For one thing, you'll keep wet bathers from dripping water throughout the house because they'll have a convenient place to dry off and change. And when the pool is closed down at the end of the season, the little house can be put to good use for winter storage of seasonal items such as tractors, lawn furniture and the like.

The handsome cabana shown to the left gives 84 sq. ft. (it measures approximately 7 x 12 ft.) for year-round use to suit your family's needs. Construction is conventional as can be seen in the drawings that follow. Our experience has proven that it is far more convenient if it is located close to the pool. If the apron around your pool is too narrow to accommodate the house, it is well worth the slight extra effort and investment to increase the apron on one end, or, if you would rather have the house located elsewhere, simply add a connecting flagstone walk between the new slab and the existing apron next to the pool.

The house is built following standard building procedures. First, stake out the desired location and remove all topsoil. Dig and pour footings around the perimeter to meet local area requirements and then pour a 4 to 5-in.-thick slab. *(Editor's note:* Before starting actual construction, check with your local building department; you may be required to obtain a building permit.) In my case, the existing pool slab was wide enough to accommodate the little house so I simply laid a double bead of caulking on the concrete over which the sole plates were laid. Use screws and lead anchors to secure them.

The 2x3s used for the studding provide more than adequate strength because there is a rather steep roof pitch to eliminate snow (load) ac-

CABANA PROVIDES SPACE for bathers changing to swim togs and, as a bonus, there is extra storage for all of your lawn equipment and a tractor rider-mower.

TYPICAL FRAMING

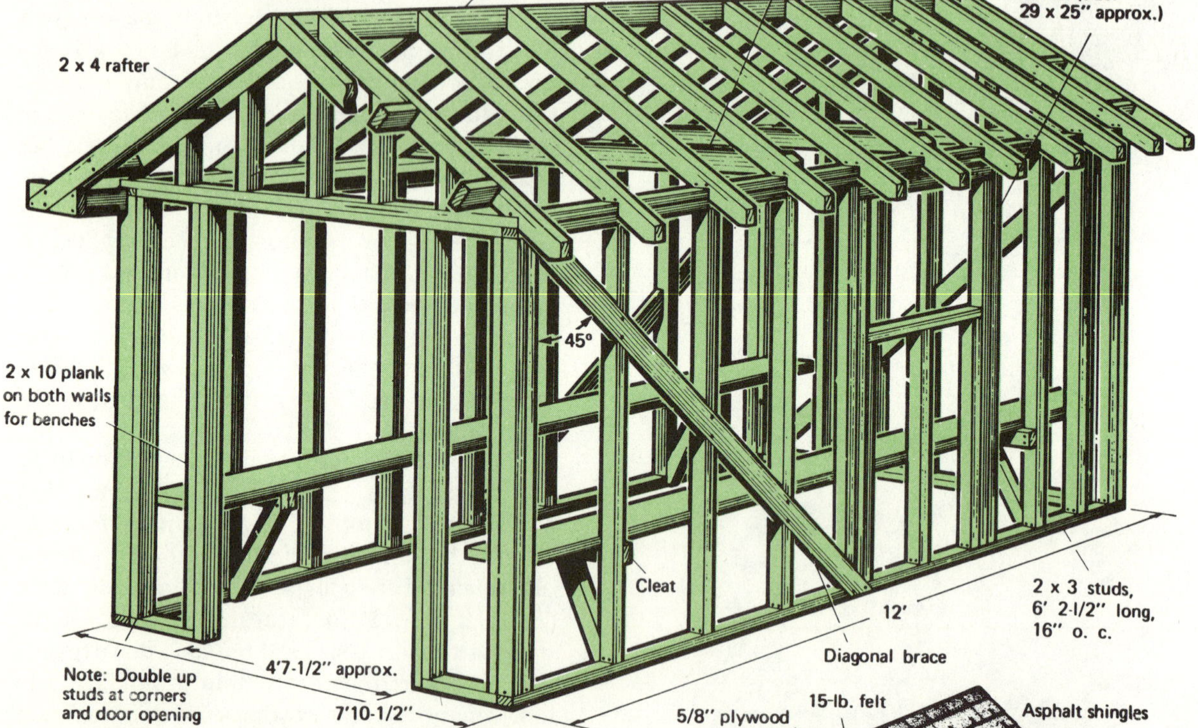

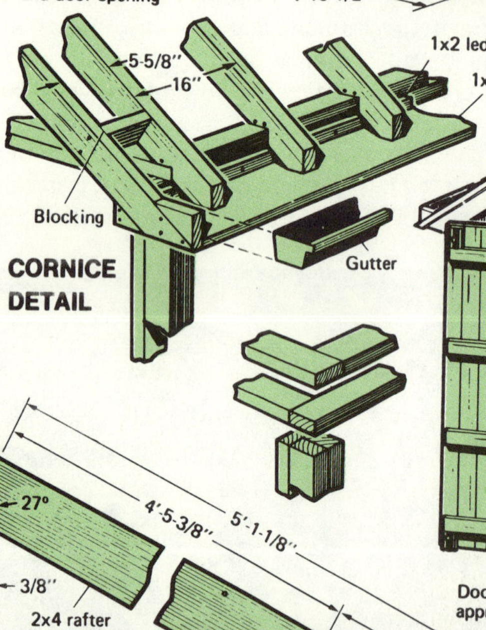

CORNICE DETAIL

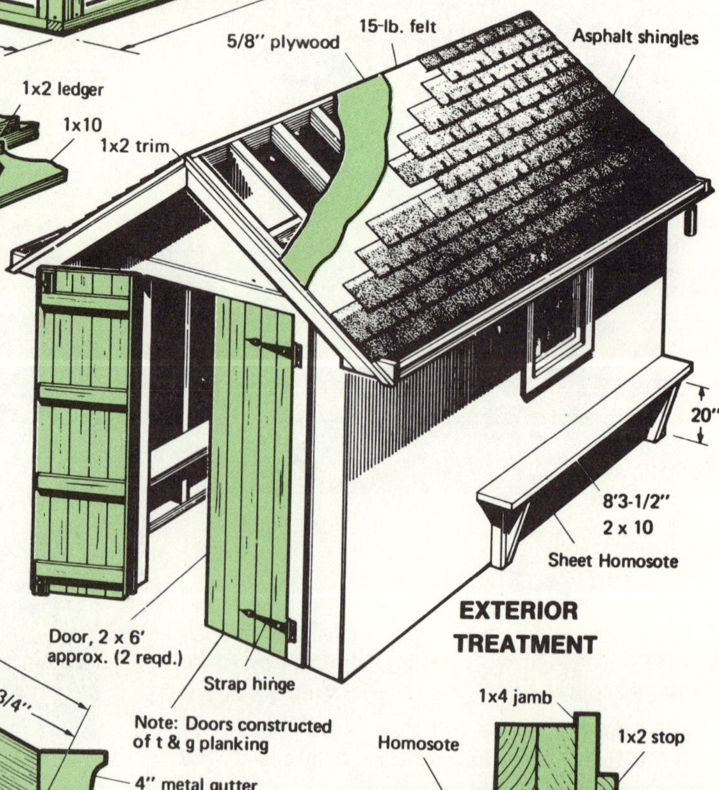

EXTERIOR TREATMENT

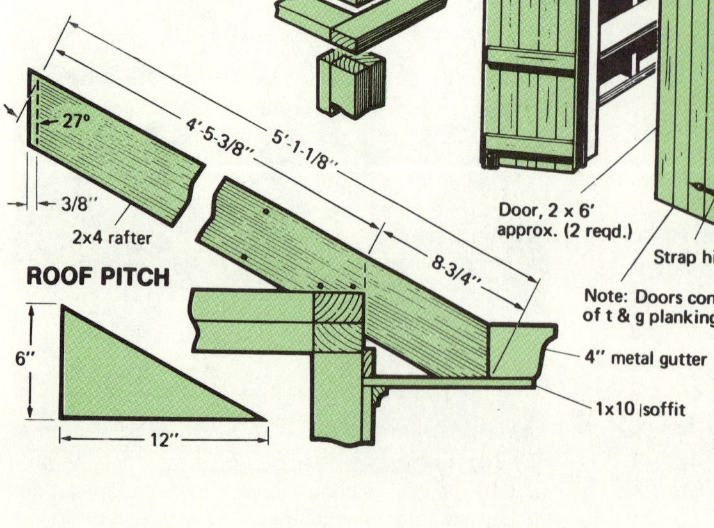

ROOF PITCH

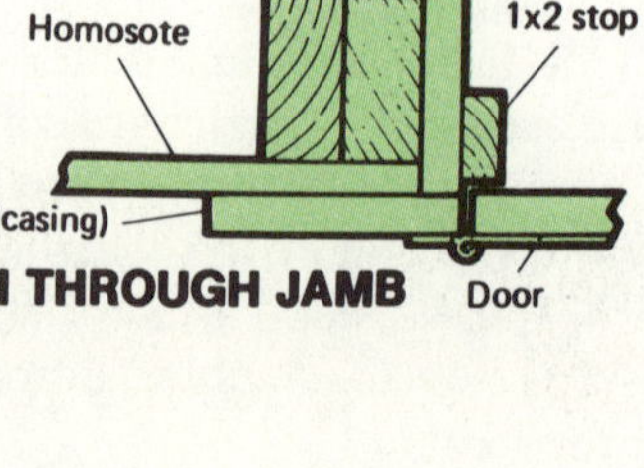

SECTION THROUGH JAMB

2-FT.-WIDE DOORS open up to make way for a riding tractor. If you don't have a tractor, a single door will do.

cumulation during the winter months. The rafters are nominal 2x4s nailed 16 in. o.c., each directly over a stud. For ventilation, I installed a window on each side of the house. Window size can be determined by personal choice or by what windows might be on sale at the local lumberyard. The rafters are covered with ⅝-in. plywood, followed by 15-lb. felt and asphalt shingles. Wall construction was kept simple (and economical) by using 4x8-ft. sheets of Homosote, which stands up well against the weather. It can be painted at first, and, as funds are available, covered with siding or shingles to match your home.

If desired, the cabana can be partitioned inside to provide individual dressing rooms. We chose to leave it as one big room so that the winter storage would not be cut down or made impractical.

The doors are constructed of boards held together with horizontal strips nailed on the inside. Barrel-type door bolts are fastened to one door at top and bottom to enter holes drilled in the slab and header. Add a standard doorknob and strap hinges to complete the door hardware.

We chose to install two 2-ft.-wide doors because of a riding tractor. If you don't own one, or will never have the need for one, you might prefer to install a standard 2½ to 3-ft.-wide single door in the conventional manner.

Since there was no reason to do any fancy finishing, I chose to leave the interior unfinished. For convenience, however, I installed two 2x10-in. benches the full length of both walls. The diagonal bracing (as shown on the facing page) provides more than adequate strength and there has been no noticeable sagging. Because the house is next to the pool, a short bench was fastened along an outside wall. Thus, whenever our youngsters have a gang in, there is more than enough seating for everybody.

DOORS ARE held closed by a pair of sliding bolts on one, and a latch and pull combination on the other.

Vacation all summer in a low-cost pool

INVEST A FEW DAYS this summer and bring a piece of the ocean into your back yard. Above-ground pools are dotting lawns all across the country, and with good reason. Most are small enough to bring home in a station wagon, and big enough to keep your family and friends wet, happy and cool all summer long. Pool designs are pretty much the same, either round or oval, although different manufacturers offer a variety of finishes and assembly hardware. After you've shopped around, you should base your choice on two factors—quality and safety. Here are some guidelines:

POOLS are great for keeping your family cool and calm on blistering summer weekends. You can take a quick dip before dinner or spend all afternoon splashing with the kids. Young children will learn to swim here faster than at the beach, and you'll be able to supervise them properly. The most common complaint about above-ground pools is the stark appearance of the side walls. Good landscaping (above) is the answer. Picture yourself (lower right) catching up on your daydreams, floating lazily under the summer sun

Select from reputable makers. They will offer guarantees on filter tanks and warranties on pool liners. Stay away from pools with electro-galvanized steel walls. They look all right, but they're not durable. For a good-quality, economical pool, look for roll-formed aluminum or hot-dipped, galvanized steel walls. Extruded aluminum or steel walls with a copper additive are excellent quality but more expensive. Finishing should include a two or three-coat paint process with a final bonderizer application. A simple guide to quality is that aluminum pools should be embossed for strength and painted to resist corrosion. Steel pools should have corrugated walls, not flat sheeting. If you can't get this kind of information from a salesman, watch out.

The major responsibility for running a safe pool rests with the owner who must supervise who goes in and how they act. But there are areas you can't control and here's where a good manufacturer should step in to help. Most pool ladders can be easily climbed by children who can't swim once they get to the other side. When you're not around, this is a danger. To prevent it, safety ladders were developed. The outside steps and frame are hinge-mounted so they can

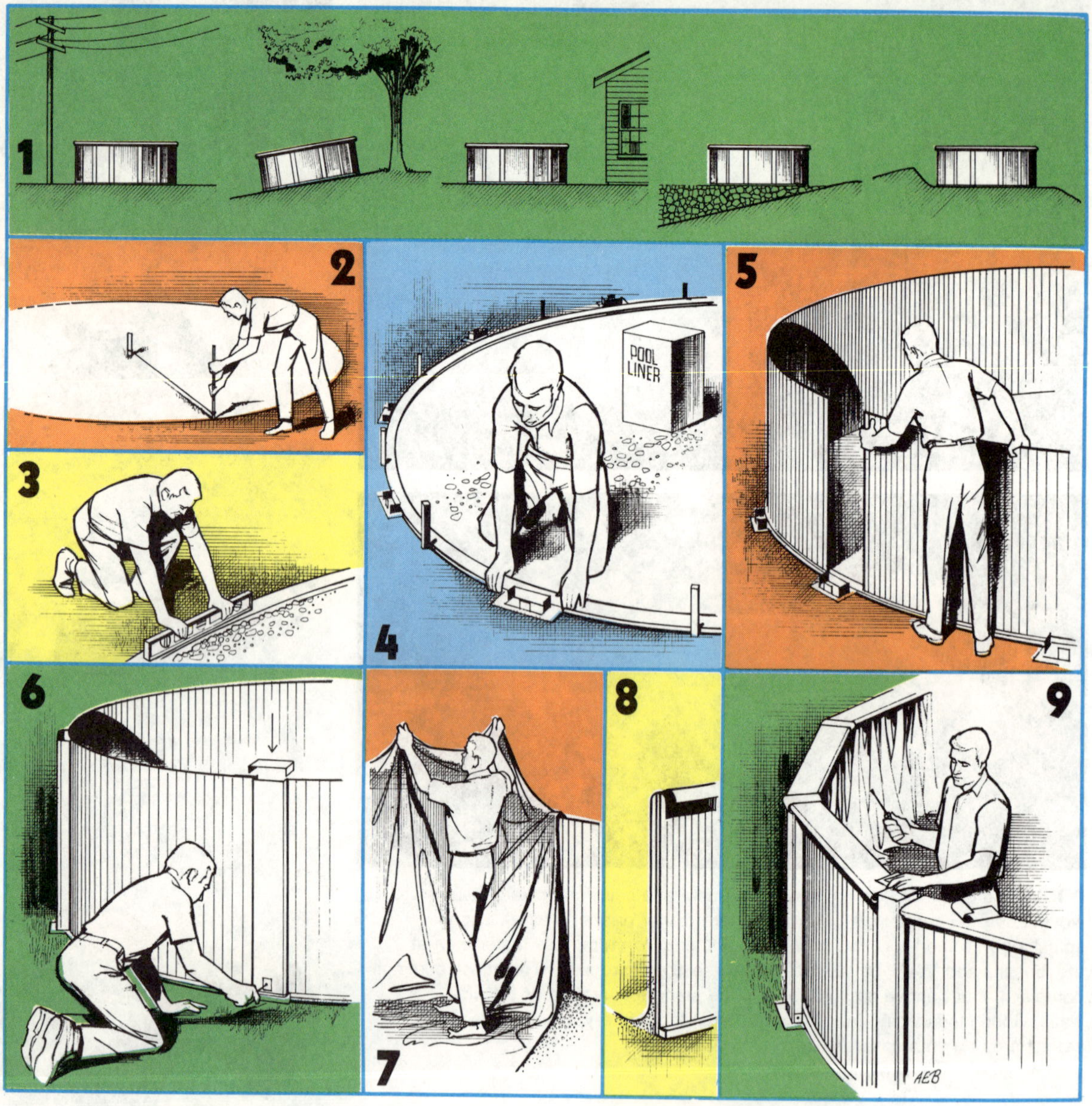

Putting in your pool

1. Pick the right site. Stay away from overhead obstructions, especially electrical lines. A level site with good drainage is best

2. Drive a stake in at the center of your site. Use string to scribe a circle two feet larger than your pool size. Note: avoid areas where chemical weed killers have been used

3. Check for level thoroughly. Use a level on top of a straight 2x4 to increase accuracy. Water in the pool will be level no matter what you do. But if the rim turns out to be uneven, you'll be wasting space at one end of the pool that could have been filled

4. Use temporary stakes between the support pads to keep the bottom rim in line as you work. Follow the manufacturer's instructions carefully—you're building the foundation for a large and heavy amount of water

5. Take my advice and get some help for this step. The one-piece steel wall can be as wriggly as an eel. Use 1x2 stakes to keep the wall steady while you're fitting the rim

6. Get a good, tight assembly on your uprights. They're the backbone that keeps the wall rigid

7. Take off your shoes—they'll wreck the liner. Try for no wrinkles (you'll get a few anyway) and leave an overlap (check the specs for how much) at the top edge of the pool wall

8. Make sure you've built up a round cove of earth at the inside bottom edge of the pool wall. If you don't, the tremendous water pressure may force the liner under the wall and tear it

9. Installing the rim locks up a job well done

COMMON POOL SIZES

Rounds

15′
18′
21′
24′
27′

Ovals

12 x 24′
15 x 27′
15 x 30′
15 x 41′

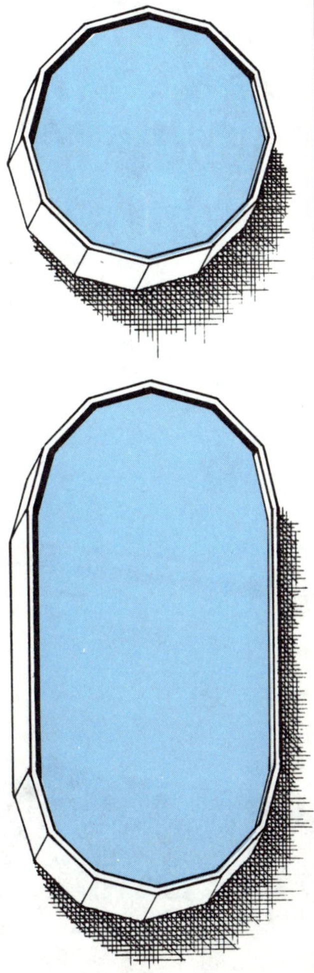

Tools of the trade

Tamper	Packing down fresh earth
Shovel	Removing the sod
Wrench	Bolting the frame
Hammer	Driving rim stakes
Screwdriver	Assembling the uprights
Level	Checking the grade
Tape measure	Laying out the site
Rake	Clearing the dirt floor
Masking tape	Protecting the liner rim
String	Scribing the circle
Clothespins	Holding liner as you go

be swung up off the ground out of reach. This is good protection against a child's wandering over to take a dip when no adults are around.

Safety ladders will also help prevent accidents as swimmers get in and out of the pool because they are anchored, usually by two chains, to the edge of the pool wall. Most of them bear a sign saying NO DIVING, a caution that goes for the rim of the pool, too. A ladder without chains is likely to tip with the weight of a swimmer pulling himself onto the step.

When electricity and water come together, accidents happen. You must decide how to run the electric cord to the pool (don't run the lawnmower over it), but the manufacturer should provide built-in protection against shock hazards. You can help by using a GFCI on the circuit. Another safeguard is to look for a UL-approved label. This means that Underwriters Laboratories has inspected the electrical system. Some dealers may show you a UL tag on the wire, but that's not enough. Make sure the filter pump is tagged as well.

Most makers provide clear and complete installation instructions. A typical job is shown here to let you know what's involved. Twelve or 15-foot pools can be set up in a day. For larger ones you'll need a few friends and a weekend. Select a site that's as flat as possible. Dig down to create a level surface if you have to. Freshly built-up earth will compress and settle, causing part of the rim to sink with it. Enlist as much help as possible when you're fitting the steel wall into the bottom rim. It's like trying to hold five slippery eels by the tail—as you grab one, another slides away. Try a few 1x2 temporary stakes to brace one section while you're fitting the opposite side.

smooth as silk

Before you fit the liner, go over all of the ground with a fine-tooth rake. A small pebble or sharp twig can work its way through the liner and cause a leak. Any hard edge will be extremely uncomfortable underfoot. Fit the liner carefully and be sure to provide enough fill to create a soft corner where the liner meets the bottom edge of the pool wall. Bare feet are mandatory during this operation. Get the liner as wrinkle-free as possible and leave a healthy overlap on the rim. A 16-gauge material, standard on most pools, doesn't have much of a tolerance for stretching. Twenty-gauge liners are available and will adjust to a stress without ripping.

A new product worth noting is the solar pool cover panel, available through Wards (about $30 for a package of 4). The polyethylene bubble pads can raise the water temperature 10 to 15 degrees when floated on the surface and roll up for easy storage.

Choose the right pool and invest in quality equipment. It will pay off in years of summer fun for your family.

Shape up your pool

WHEN WARM WEATHER is on its way, the time is right to tune up your swimming pool so you can enjoy it during those hot summer days. To help you get started, we suggest steps you can take for properly opening your pool.

The basic strategy is to get your pool to the point where you can follow a simple, regular maintenance schedule. There are six steps involved in opening your pool, according to experts at the Sun Swimming Pool Products Div. of FMC Corp. The steps take two to four days to complete, depending on such considerations as how well you protected the pool during the winter and how large it is.

Make sure that you perform each step successfully before continuing to the next.

1. Fill the pool

If you've properly winterized your pool, cleanup is a minimal task. The recommended level for filling most pools is to the middle of the skimmer, the built-in device that traps surface debris.

Pool water evaporates and is dragged and splashed out by swimmers. You'll have to add water periodically to maintain proper level.

SEE ALSO

Cabanas . . . Carpeting, outdoor . . . Poolhouses . . . Swimming pools . . . Yard lighting

2. Check equipment

Check the pump, filter and circulating system. Refer to the owner's manual for reinstalling parts removed for winter storage. Make sure mechanical components are clean and in proper working order.

To reinstall the pump/motor, first turn off the power at the control panel. Replace the gasket between the pump's tank and seal plate if it is damaged. Reinstall the drain plugs. Check the pump shaft for free movement. With power on, prime the pump following instructions in the owner's manual.

3. Adjust pH level

The pH level is a measure of the acidity or alkalinity of water. Unless your pool is within a certain pH range indicated by a test kit, chlorine disinfectant won't kill the bacteria that it's supposed to.

The level at which chlorine optimally sanitizes ranges from 7.2 to 7.8. To get an accurate measure, follow the manufacturer's directions in your pool kit.

If pH is too *low,* chlorine dissipates rapidly, pipes and fittings can become corroded, plaster can become etched and swimmers can get an irritating eye burn.

If pH is too *high,* scale forms, pool water turns cloudy and swimmers get eye burn just as they do when pH is too low.

If the pH level is too low, add a pH plus chemical; if the level is too high, add a pH minus chemical.

Note on water testing: To properly care for your pool, you will need a complete kit or individual kits to measure pH level, total alkalinity, chlorine level and water stability. Each year change test chemicals (reagents) that are in your kit.

4. Adjust total alkalinity

After you've adjusted the pH level, adjusting total alkalinity helps *keep* the pH in the proper range. The three main alkaline chemicals—carbonate, bicarbonate and hydroxide—dissolved in the water in proper proportion act as a buffer preventing pH change.

Use a kit to test for total alkalinity. Test it weekly and maintain it between 80 and 150 parts per million (ppm, the standard measure of concentration in swimming pools). Your pool-supply dealer can also tell you if an alkalinity problem exists in your area and can provide formulations needed to correct it.

5. Superchlorinate the water

Superchlorinating means applying 5 to 10 times the regular daily dose of chlorine to water. The two primary reasons for adding chlorine are: 1) to disinfect—kill water-borne organisms and algae; 2) to oxidate—burn out undesirable solids, colors and odors. While all pools must be superchlorinated from time to time, it is definitely needed when opening your pool for the season.

Before you superchlorinate, determine the capacity of your pool in gallons; then determine the needed dosage of superchlorinator following directions on the package. Wait until the residual chlorine is at the recommended level of 1.0 to 1.5 ppm according to the kit before continuing to the next step. You might want to superchlorinate at night and then test the water the following morning.

There are several types of chlorinating products on the market. Among them are liquid chlorine and calcium hypochlorite, which tend to lose effectiveness after a few hours due to the action of sunlight. On the other hand, chlorine concentrates in tablets or granular form contain a built-in stabilizer that resists chlorine decay induced by sunlight.

6. Stabilize the water

The final step in getting your pool ready is to stabilize or condition the water. This process minimizes the loss of chlorine due to ultraviolet sunrays. It also makes sure that the chlorine disinfectant will keep working around the clock.

To complete this step, you'll need a test kit and a conditioner chemical. Results from the kit will tell you how much conditioner you should apply. Each time you refill the pool, you should also stabilize the water.

Computerized analysis

To make pool maintenance somewhat easier, computer systems that can identify potential problems in the pool water are available. The water can be tested before the pool is filled, after it is filled or during the season.

Basically, a water sample is run through tests to analyze and balance it. The results, along with information about the specific pool, are entered into a computer that completes a data sheet telling *what* chemicals are needed and in what *order* and *quantity* to apply them to maintain your pool water safely.

The service is available at pool dealers. However, it doesn't take the place of careful monitoring by pool owners. Before you purchase a large amount of chemicals based on the results of such a test, it pays to satisfy yourself that the chemicals are needed.

Turn your above-ground pool into a back-yard resort

By HARRY WICKS

POOL VIEW from existing house deck is enhanced dramatically by the use of woods left to weather naturally. Western pine and fir were used throughout the deck and activity area.

■ YOUR ABOVE-GROUND pool will nestle beautifully into this enchanting back-yard entertainment center. It makes your yard into a outdoor living resort but the pool still remains the focal point.

The decks and privacy walls were designed to take full advantage of the beauty of such common woods as western pine and fir. When this wood is left natural (and treated for extra protection with a clear preservative), it will eventually weather to a subtle silver gray. This soft and pleasing tone works to achieve an even greater harmony with its surroundings.

The pool shown is owned by the Benjamin

Mark family on Long Island, NY. The challenge that was given architect Ira Grandberg, AIA, was to create an exciting new look for above-ground pools. Traditionally, these pools have been surrounded by a wrap-around, doughnut-shaped deck. Grandberg's solution was a two-level deck. One area would be reserved for bathing and the other for a variety of entertaining. The finished product is the result of a joint effort by Western Wood Products Assn. and *Popular Mechanics.*

where to start

Using stakes and mason's line, carefully lay out the entire deck to suit your property and pool size. Before you go any farther it would be a good idea to make a visit to your local building authority. Make certain that your intended structure conforms to local building codes before you begin turning the first spadeful of earth. Start by staking out what will be the upper level to suit your particular pool and needs. Next, work up a scale drawing of deck elevations—and an elevation for a fence around the upper deck. The fence should be no less than 1 ft. above the upper deck and no more than 3 ft. higher than the flooring.

Elevations for both levels as well as the fence are determined by several factors, including pool height, land contour and existing plantings. All three elements should be taken into careful account before you begin.

securing deck to footings

The lower deck rests on cylindrical footings. These are made by pouring concrete into standard Sonotube forms. The deck joists, in turn, are secured to footings using commercially available hardware. Another technique is to use drift pins embedded in the concrete. Decking is nailed to the joists with 8d hot-dipped galvanized nails. Be sure to leave a uniform space between the 2x6 planks to allow rain to drain off and for swelling and shrinking of the wood.

The near side of the upper level is built directly over the edge of the lower level. For that reason,

FOOTING DIAGRAM

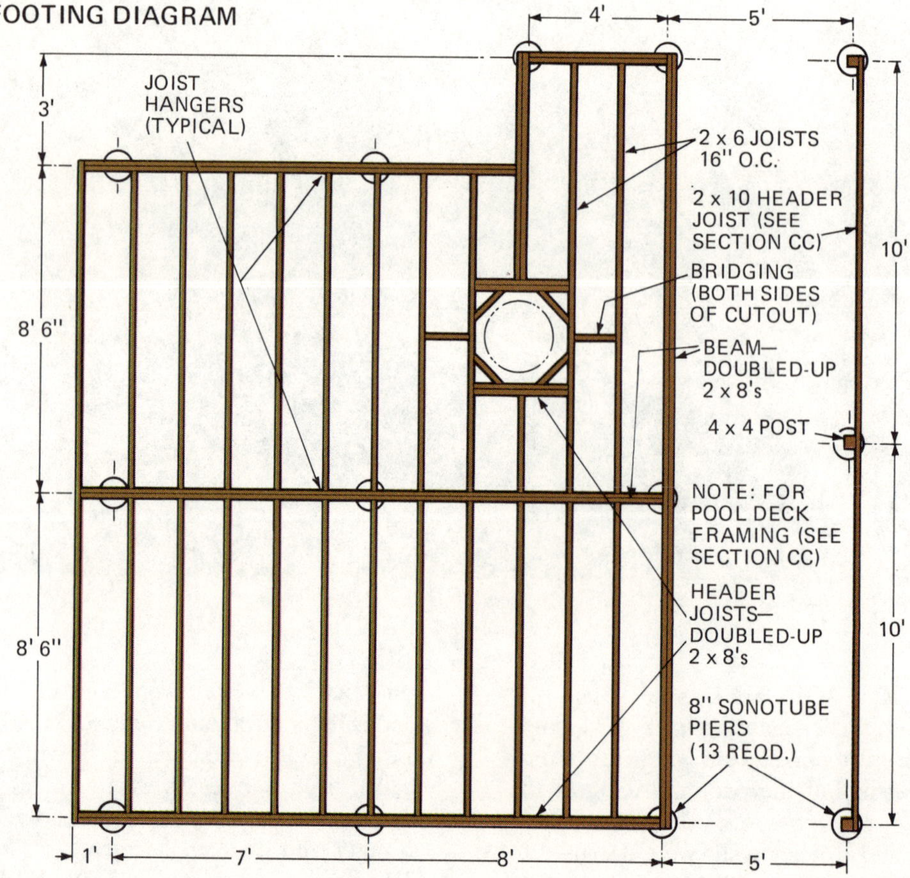

the joist along that edge of the lower level is doubled up to create a beam. The pool side of the upper level is supported by three 4x4 posts secured atop cylindrical footings with drift pins.

Metal joist hangers are used throughout the entire project. They are readily available at lumberyards and homebuilding centers. Use of such hardware makes the task a lot easier, yet assures excellent structural stability. If you frame around any existing plantings, as we did with the tree at stage center, you will inevitably have to cut at least one joist and install headers. And don't forget to take into consideration that a tree such as this will grow larger through the years.

To minimize deflection (bounciness) in that area, you would be wise to install bridging between pairs of joists flanking both sides of the framed opening (see drawing). To create the round opening, simply install decking over the joists in a conventional manner, but leave a goodly amount to overhang the opening and cut the decking with a sabre saw.

The high point of this deck design is the privacy screen. This is established by installing the built-in seating planter wall. This line continues the line of the upper deck with the installation of the fence.

Note that the half-cylinder at the right end of the seat is supported by being cantilevered on extended decking in the corner, and by being tied into the wall behind the seat. Since the half-cylinder doesn't weigh very much, this procedure is structurally sound.

When building the steps to the upper deck, lay them out so that the riser height falls in the comfortable-to-navigate 6- to-7½-in. range.

construction hints

■ Make certain that all lumber that comes in close contact with the ground is thoroughly protected by wood preservative. Though joists rest on concrete piers, you are well advised to coat them immediately after they are installed. An alternative to this might be to purchase wood that

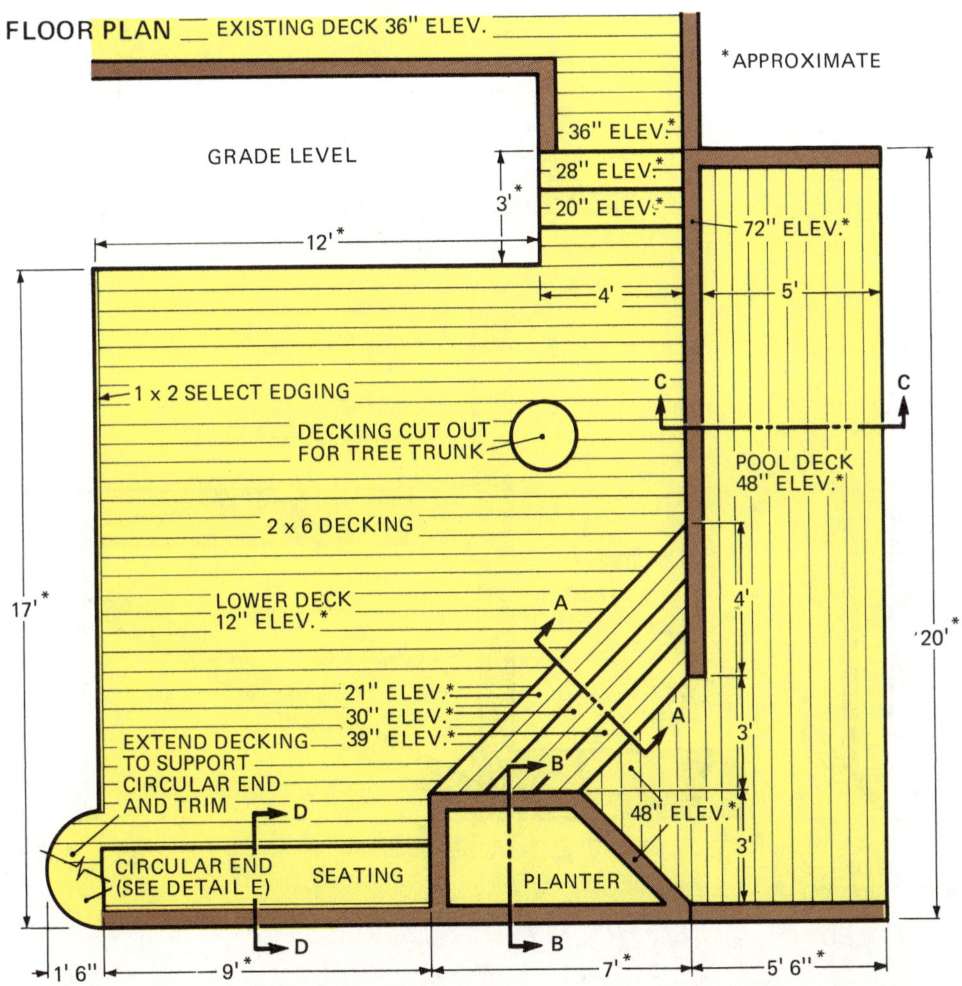

has been pretreated at the mill to be "all-weather" stock.

■ To prevent water problems or rot, the planter is fitted with a sheet-metal liner. To guarantee against water seepage, solder the corners with the box securely in place. Note that the liner folds over the planter sides and is capped by the top trim detail on the planter.

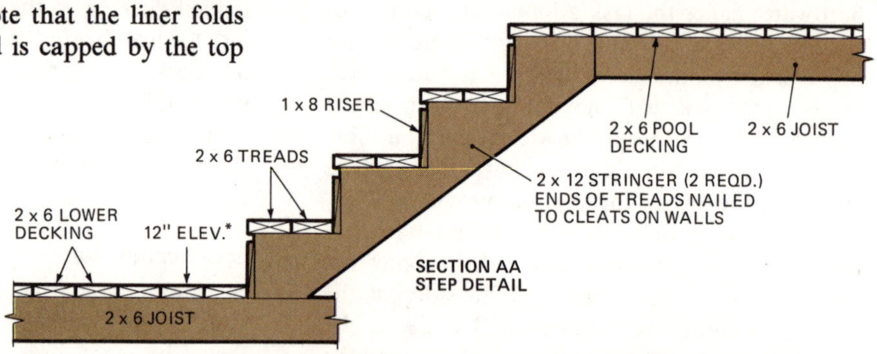

SECTION AA STEP DETAIL

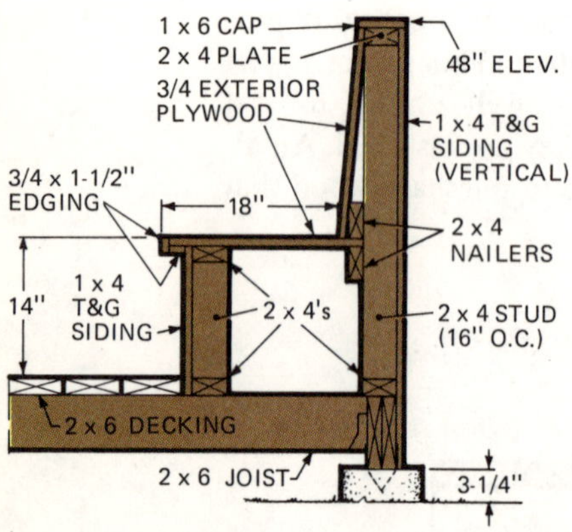

SECTION DD—SEATING

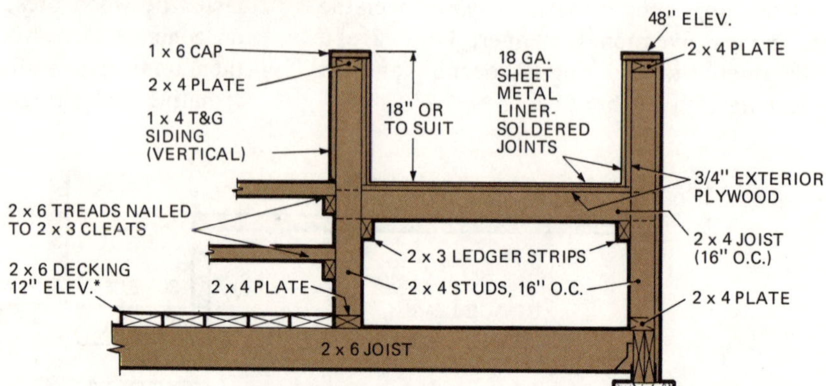

SECTION BB—PLANTER

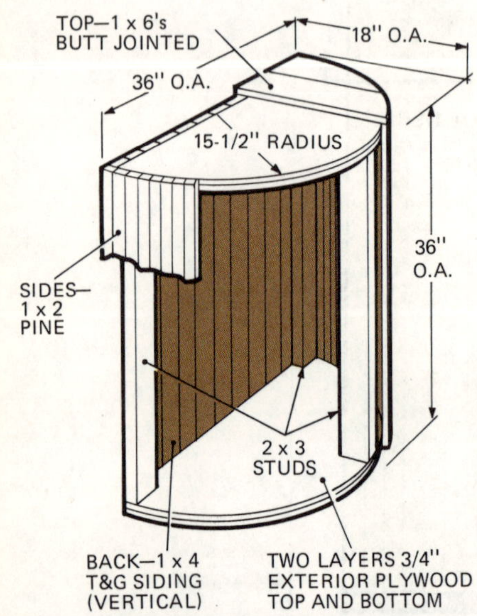

DETAIL E CIRCULAR END

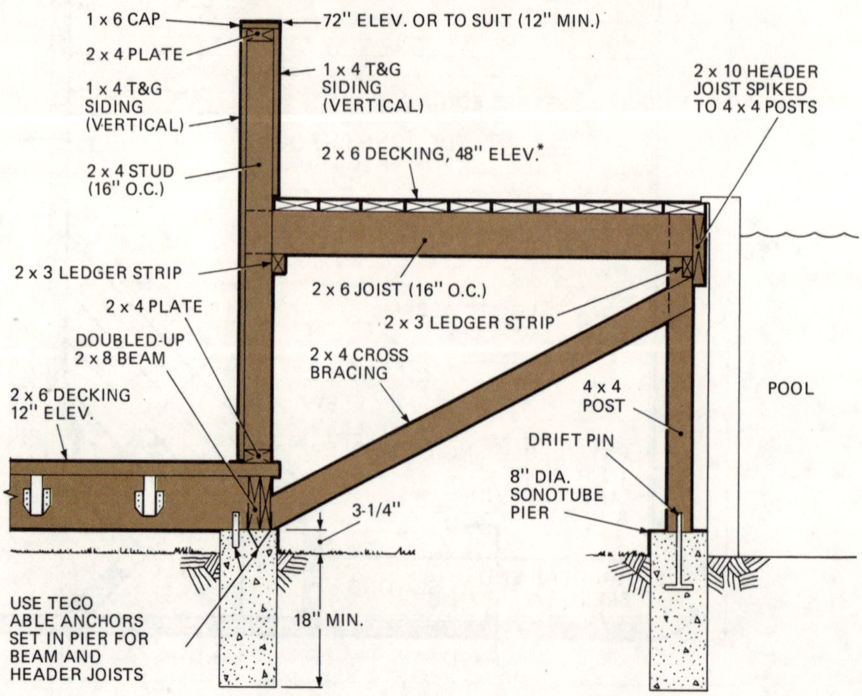

SECTION CC—LOWER AND POOL DECK

Build an old-time porch swing

■ THOUGH YOUR MEMORIES may not include spooning in a porch swing, your entire family from grandparents to toddlers are sure to enjoy sitting and relaxing in our version of the old-fashioned, front-porch swing.

Of contemporary design, simple construction

SEE ALSO
A-frame swing sets . . . Playgrounds . . . Swings

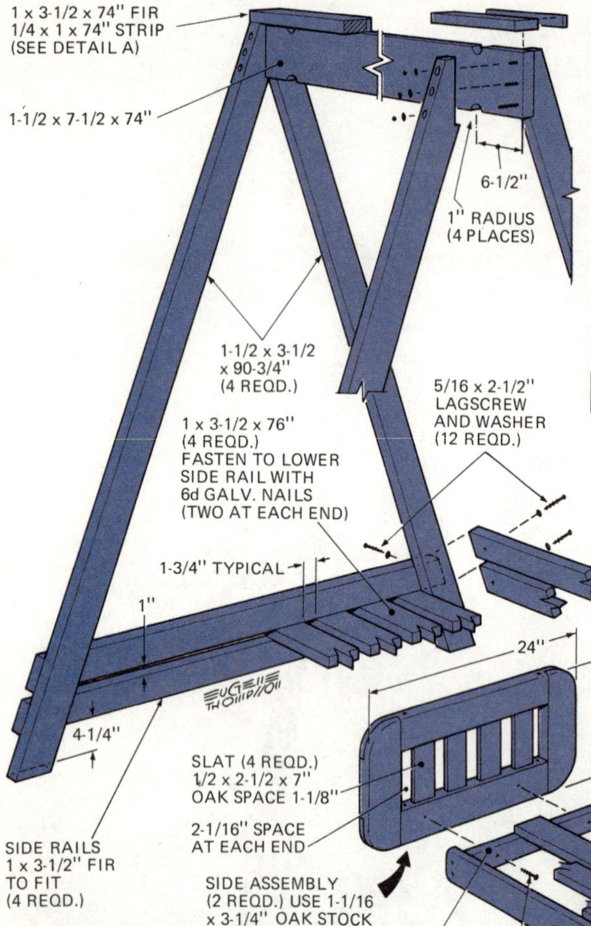

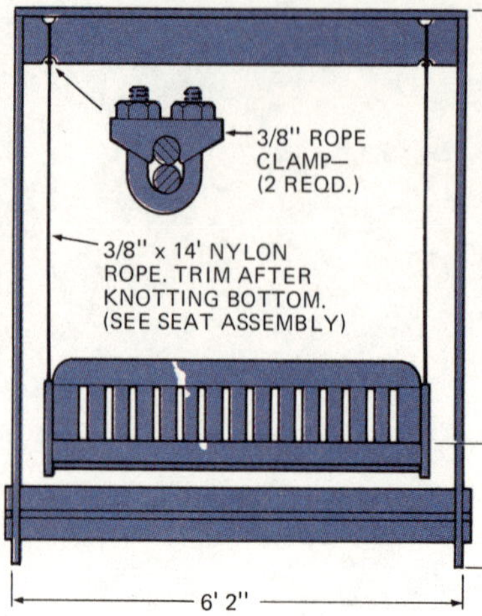

FRONT ELEVATION

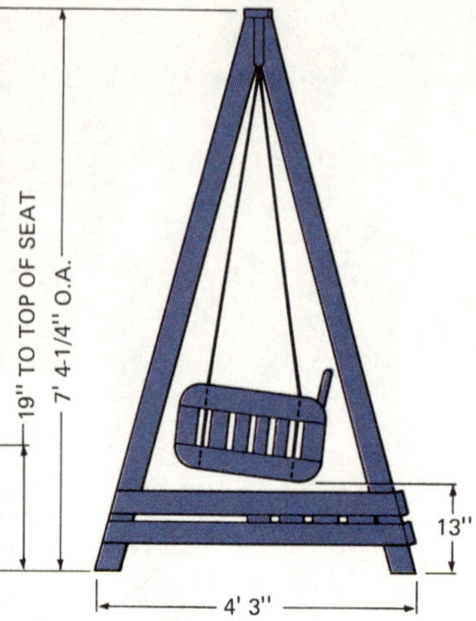

SIDE ELEVATION

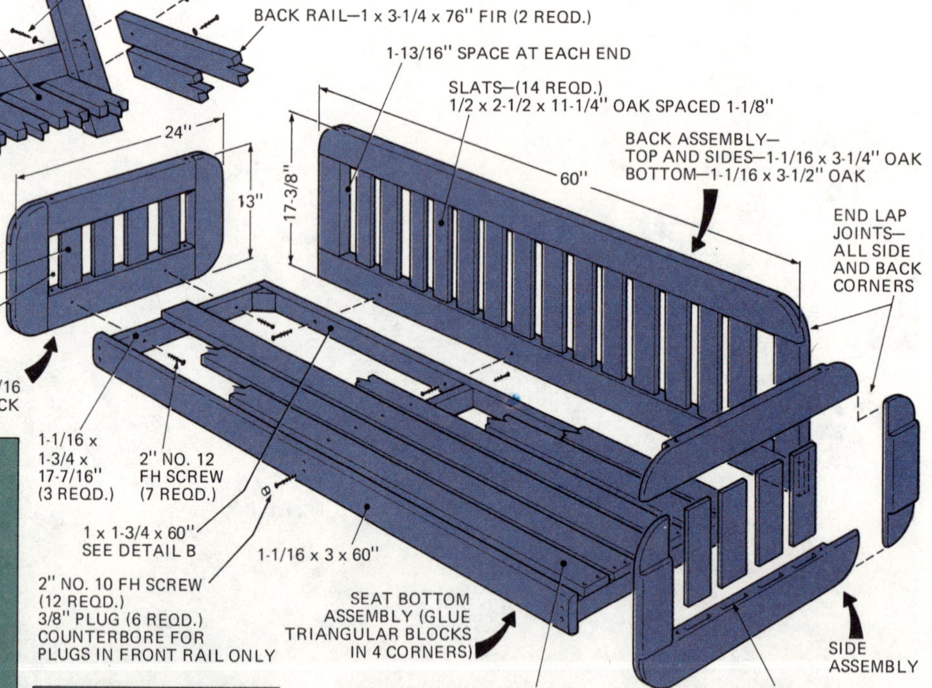

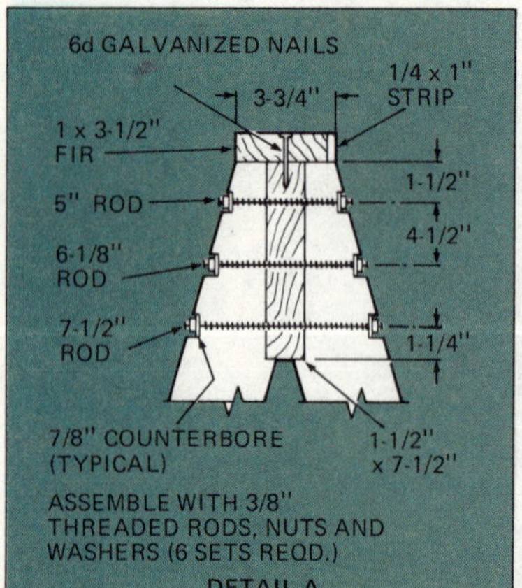

DETAIL A

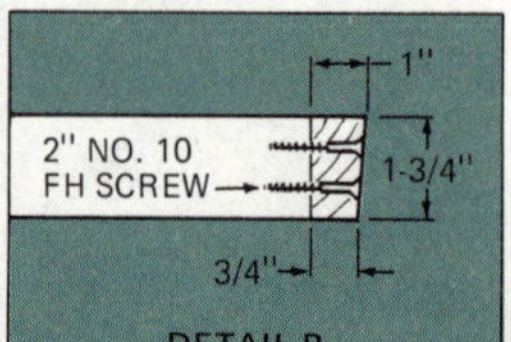

DETAIL B

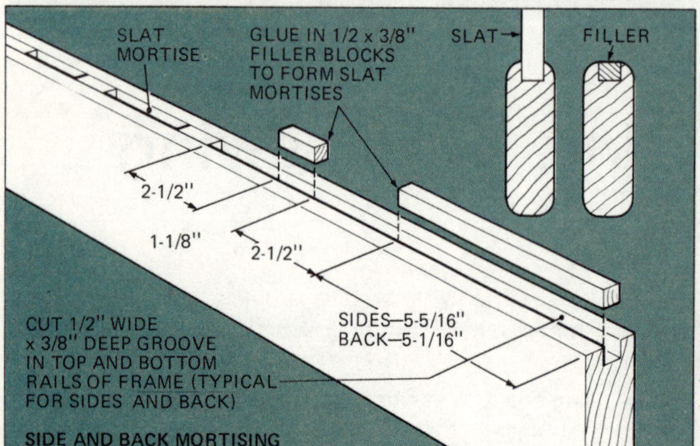

SIDE AND BACK MORTISING
DETAIL C

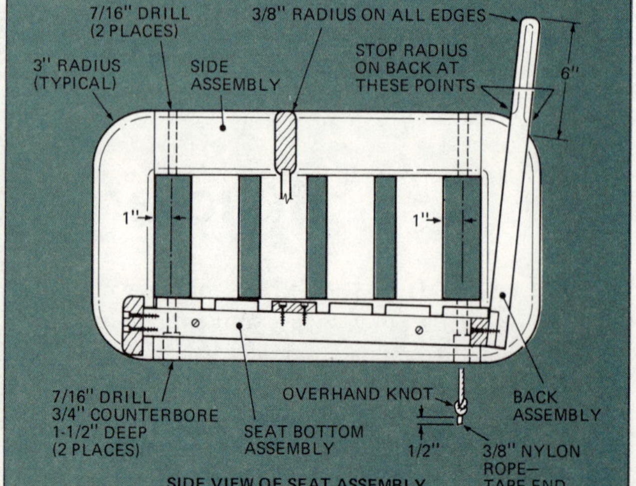

SIDE VIEW OF SEAT ASSEMBLY

details for readers to follow were worked out by Rosario Capotosto, based upon an original sketch by designer Tom Fung. If you own a porch you can suspend the swing from stout hardware anchored in the porch rafters or joists. Happily, those who live in today's modern porchless houses can enjoy this swing too because we've created an alternate suspension system—a sturdy A-frame whose design blends beautifully with that of the swing. This frame allows you to set up your swing in a garden, on a patio, or anywhere in your yard the family gathers.

starting construction

The seat section of the swing has been designed and constructed like a fine piece of furniture—quality joinery, weatherproof glue joints and plugged-over screwheads are used throughout. The seat is built of 5/4 and ½-in. oak while the A-frame is built of lower-cost 2x4 and 2x8 construction-grade fir. We selected clear 1x4 flooring for all horizontal frame members because it measures a full 3½ in. wide and its thickness gives more rigidity than does ¾-in. stock.

More often than not, you will find that hardwood comes from the lumberyard surfaced on two sides only (S2S). When the lumber comes this way, you must use either a plane or jointer to joint one edge perfectly smooth and straight. You can then rip the boards (using either a radial-arm or table saw) to the widths required for the seat back and side sections. We used red oak for the seat—5/4-in. stock for all parts except the slats, which are of ½-in. stock.

Caution: when you go to buy your lumber, be selective; it is almost impossible to perform accurate grooving and lap-jointing on stock that is warped.

cut scrap slats

Use your saw and a dado cutterhead to cut the grooves in the back and side section rails to receive the slats. Notice that we installed filler blocks in the grooves to get accurate and neat mortises for the slats. Cut several scrap slats to act as guides to mark the spacing for the actual slats. Cut the filler blocks out of ½-in-sq. stock—which will project a hair above the surface after installation to permit flush trimming later, after gluing. Set the blocks in place with dummy slats and mark the glue border-lines (Photo 2). Mix some resorcinol (waterproof) glue and apply it sparingly to mating surfaces—don't make it too watery or it will ooze into the grooves and require difficult cleanup later.

If the blocks are snug fitting as they should be, clamping will not be necessary. Proceed down the rail installing blocks, with the aid of dummy spacers, as you go. Next day when the glue is dry, trim off the ⅛-in. projection by ripping with a smooth blade in the table saw.

holes for the ropes

At this stage you should bore the holes for the nylon rope. The top racks get 7/16-in.-dia. holes while the lower members are counter bored to receive the knots. Make certain that you bore the larger, ¾-in.-dia. hole first and then the 7/16-in. hole. If you reverse this order you will have great difficulty centering the holes. A drill press is almost essential for this operation to ensure that the holes pass straight through the sides.

To mark the frame members for end lap joints, clamp the sections together. Then use either a knife or a very sharp pencil to mark the cutting lines. Set the saw's dado head for a wide cut and its elevation so that the cutters will penetrate half the thickness of the stock. It's a good idea to check a test joint in scrap stock so that you are certain to produce perfectly mated end lap joints. For greatest accuracy when you're making an end lap joint, cut the first one completely and then use it as the marking guide for its mating cut.

Next, you should assemble the units temporarily to check the distance between the mortise bottoms and cut the slats to suit. Make it a point to cut the slats about 1/16 in. shorter than the actual distance to allow for the glue. Cut the slats, and then break all sharp corners on them using a Surform plane and fine sandpaper. Set the slats aside.

rounding the edges

Before you can glue the slats in place you must round the inside edges of the frame sections with a router; this cannot be done once the slats are installed. Since the mortised inside edges will not give the router cutter's pilot guide a true surface to ride against, a simple woodworking trick is called for. Temporarily assemble the sections without slats (using tacks only at corners in the waste area, where the outside corner radius will be cut). Then cut strips of ⅛-in. hardboard equal in width to the thickness of the stock and place them around the frame inside to provide a smooth, flat surface for the router bit (Photo 7). You would be wise to set up a test strip and make a trial cut using a ⅜-in. rounding-over bit. Adjust the depth-of-cut so that it doesn't reach the mortise.

1 **TOP** and bottom rails are grooved to receive slats.

2 **USE DUMMY** slats to locate filler blocks; mark glue border lines.

3 **AFTER GLUE** dries, trim the rails slightly on the saw.

7 **TACK FRAME** together; insert ⅛-in. strips for router guide.

8 **ROUND** corners using ⅜-in. bit set not to reach mortises.

9 **PUT SLATS** in grooves using glue; apply glue to lap joints.

13 **CUT** mitered ends with saw miter gauge at 15°.

14 **TO CUT** the long notch, clamp a 2x4 to the saw table.

15 **USE** holesaw in drill and a scrap block to bore notches.

sand all edges

While sections are still temporarily assembled, sand the insides as well as all the rounded edges. It's easier to do this before the slats are in place. Make light match marks on the mating parts and then disassemble the units.

To install slats, apply glue sparingly in recesses and to the end surface of the slats. Insert all slats into one rail, apply glue to the second rail and push it onto the slats. Apply glue to the lap joints

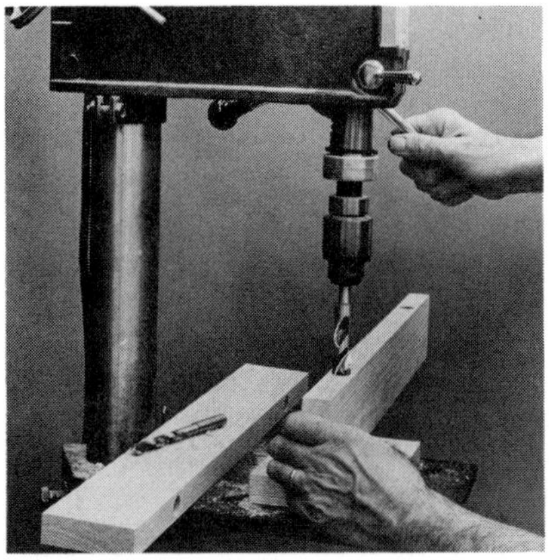

4 **BORE** holes for rope. In bottom, drill larger holes first.

5 **CLAMP** parts to find exact dimensions for end lap joints.

6 **CUT LAPS** with dado head in radial or table saw.

10 **USE** sabre saw to cut radius on corners and round with a router.

11 **CLAMP** seat frame to side and back while you bore pilot holes.

12 **LAY** frame members on floor. Mark at 105° for miter cuts.

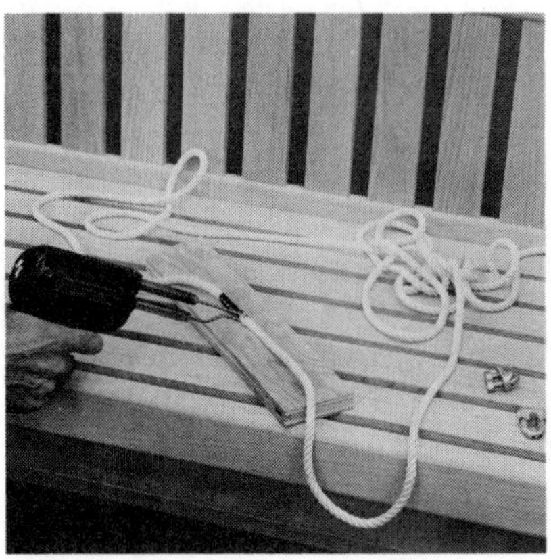

16 **TO PREVENT** unraveling, cut rope with a soldering gun.

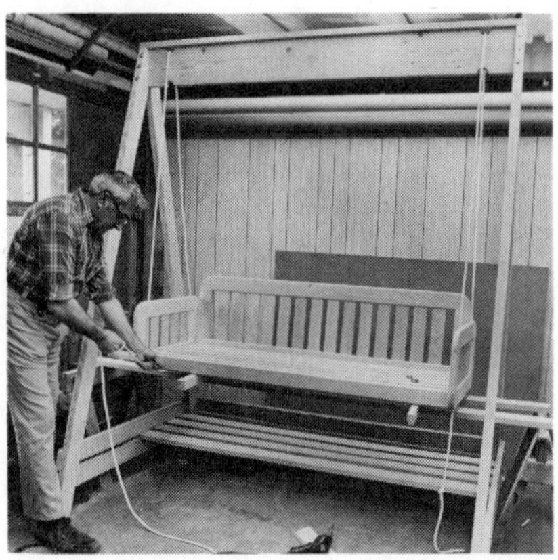

17 **PROP SEAT** on horses to install the rope.

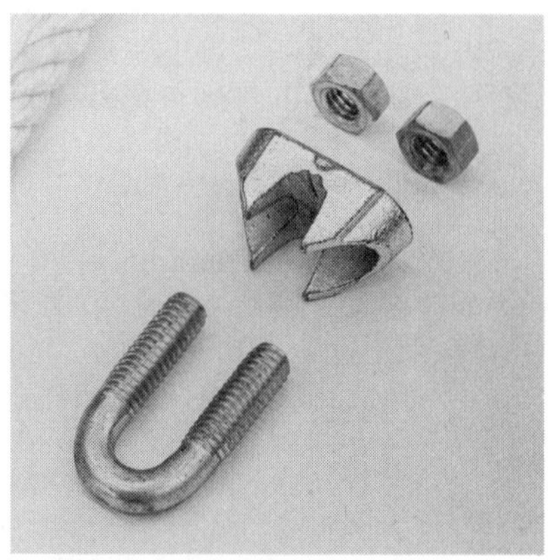

18 **WEATHERPROOF** clamps are available from marine houses.

and complete the frame assembly. Hold the sections secure and square with bar clamps until the glue dries.

The seat frame is made separately. Cut the parts to size and assemble them with glue and screws as shown. Counterbore the screwholes at the front so that the screwheads can be concealed with plugs cut from the oak stock. If you don't own a plug cutter, you can use maple dowels. Before you glue the seat slats in place, clamp the seat frame to the back and sides and bore the required screw holes. Two screws go into the sides from the end of the seat frame, three from the back and two from the outside of the side panel into the side of the seat back. These are sunk and plugged. Refer to the drawing on page 2286 for details.

making the A-frame

Start with the 2x4 verticals. Lay them out as shown in the photos and mark the miter cuts. Cut the miters using a radial or portable circular saw. Next, cut the 2x8 to length and cut the half-circles for the rope near each end. For perfectly accurate notches, use a hole saw as we did (Photo 15). Since the standard hole saw only penetrates to about ¾ in., you will have to drill from both sides and then complete the cut with a sabre saw. Use a drum sander to smooth the cut. Mark locations for the ⅜-in. bolt holes, then use a 1-in. bit to bore a partial hole parallel to the flat surface of the notch, just deep enough to seat the washer. Then bore 7/16-in.-dia. holes through the assembly. This is best accomplished with a helper. Lay the 2x4s on the side with the 2x8 held vertically in place between the notches. Do this on 2x4 scraps on edge to permit access with your electric drill. But, if you mark the bolt holes carefully and then support each member in proper position on the drill press, you can bore the holes individually on the separate pieces.

Since lagbolts are not available in the size required, you will have to use threaded rod cut to size, with nuts and washers at both ends. (Oversize lagbolts will not have sufficient thread to allow cutting to length.)

assembling the frame

Assemble the frame by bolting the tops, then attach the three lower outer rails. Before you add the second rails, nail in the four horizontals using two hot-dipped galvanized nails at both ends.

To hang the seat, set it in place on high sawhorses or other support. Pass the nylon rope through the 2x8 half hole, then through the chair sides. Make an overhand knot at each end, then wrap a piece of plastic tape tightly around the rope just below the knots. *Do not cut off the waste with a knife or scissors or it will unravel.* Instead cut by burning it through with a soldering gun or heat knife. The heat will melt the end and prevent unraveling. Melted nylon will mess up the gun tip a bit, but can be cleaned off with a light sanding after the gun cools.

adjusting the seat

The knot will seem too big to fit the ¾-in. hole, but can be forced in if you pull hard enough. The fit will be good and snug so you won't need a washer. Remove the supports and let the seat hang, then attach the special rope clamps at the top. The seat can be adjusted to any angle you want and locked in position by tightening the clamps. Most people prefer to have the seat of the swing tipped slightly to the back. Although this makes it a little harder to get out of the swing, you don't have the feeling you will be sent off the front edge when you start swinging. Do some experimentation to determine which position is most comfortable for you.

finishing the swing

Very little work is required for finishing the swing; we simply applied three coats of Flecto Varathane Liquid Plastic (Exterior) to the new wood following the manufacturer's instructions on the can. Since the swing itself is of oak, however, its parts must first be rubbed with natural paste wood filler to fill the wood's open pores. Using turpentine, thin the filler to a creamlike consistency and brush it on—first against and then with the grain. Let the filler set until it turns flat, then rub off all excess filler with burlap or other coarse-textured cloth. Wait 24 hours before applying the first coat of Varathane. (Note: *You do not need to use the filler on the close grain fir used in the A-frame*).

alternate suspension method

Those who have a porch will want to hang the swing from its ceiling rather than build the A-frame. You can suspend the swing from two ⅜ x 4½-in. screw eyes turned into one or two ceiling joists. (If the ceiling joists run parallel to the swing's length, both screw eyes will be in one joist. If joists run perpendicular to the swing, each screw eye will be in its own joist.) Locate joists using a small nail. When a joist is located, bore several small holes to make certain that the screw eye will go into the center of the joist.

Some additional hardware is necessary for a ceiling installation to prevent undue wear and tear on the nylon rope. You should install an open-end wire rope thimble between each rope clamp and the screw eye above it.

The clamps and rope are generally available at marine supply houses.

HANDY SET of spade bits lets you bore ¼, ½, ⅝, ¾, ⅞ and 1-in. holes.

SAND-O-FLEX sander is fast way to smooth scrolls and irregular edges.

BIT SHOWN bores pilot and shank holes and countersinks in one operation.

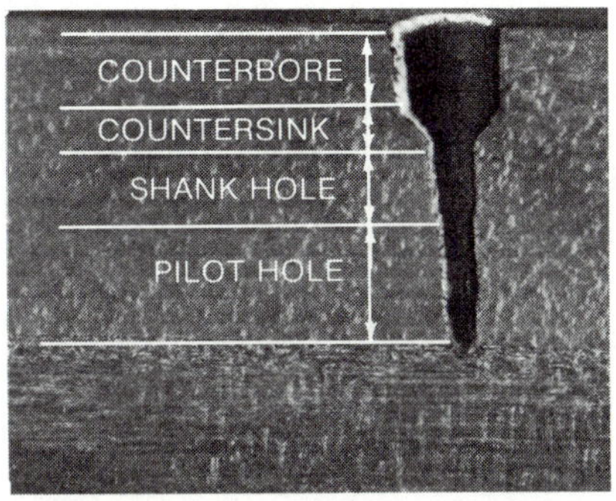

HOLE WAS bored using bit at left; note counterbore for dowel.

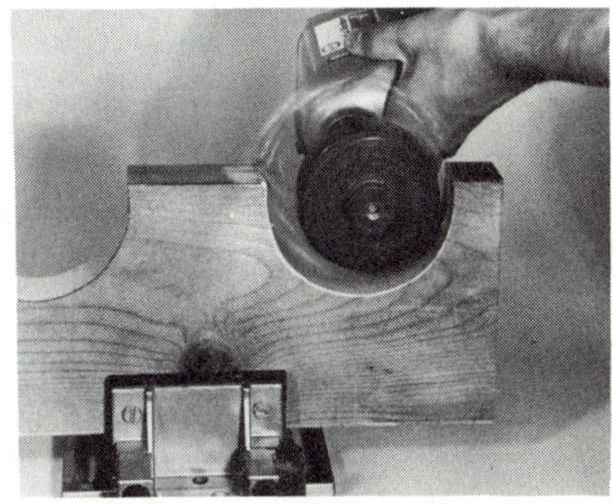

DRUM sanders come in various diameters for sanding circles.

POWER BORE bit produces a perfect circle for craftsmanlike hole.

BIT CUTS cleanly and makes hole that dowel or dowel plug fits perfectly.

Accessories for your drill

By HARRY WICKS

THOUGH I ADMITTEDLY shun so-called multipurpose tools, there are cases when a good power tool can be made even better by coupling it with the *proper* accessory. A good example is the portable electric drill: No tool around has more accessories designed for it.

After twist drill bits (for use in either wood or metal), the boring tools to buy are a set of spade bits. With these, you can bore accurate, large-diameter holes in wood with very little effort. A spade bit is ideal in construction work, such as boring through studs for electrical or plumbing lines.

Other accessories to look into:

Screw Sink. This is Stanley Tools' name for the bit that lets you bore pilot, shank hole and countersink, all at one time. Variations are also available from Sears and other tool suppliers.

Power Bore bits: Here is another winner from Stanley. These are my personal favorites for boring accurate circles.

For fine finishing of contours, nothing matches Sand-O-Flex. I keep two handy in my workshop—one fitted with rough grit, the other with fine.

SEE ALSO
Angles, drilling . . . Drills, portable . . . Motors, shop . . . Power-tool maintenance . . . Power-tool stands

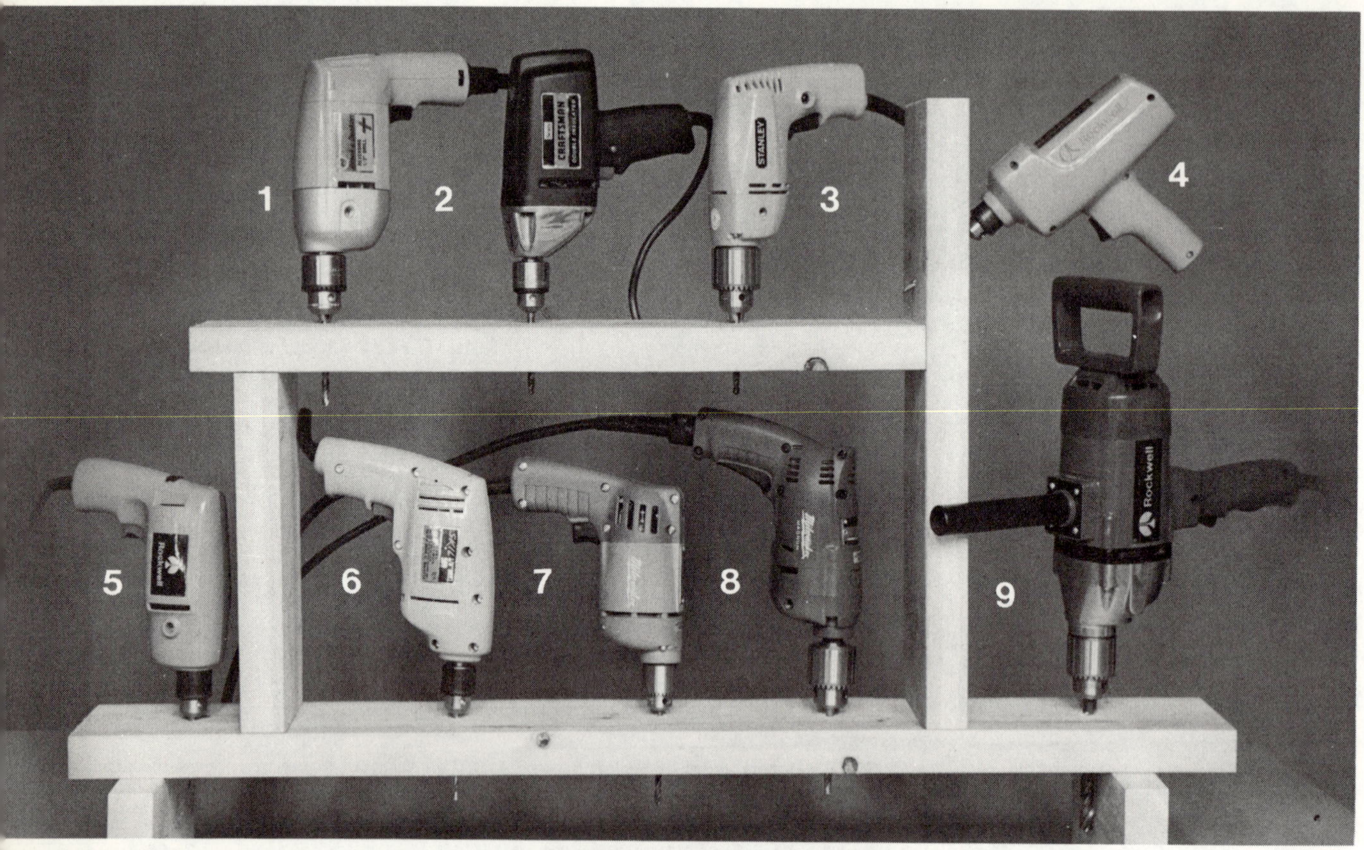

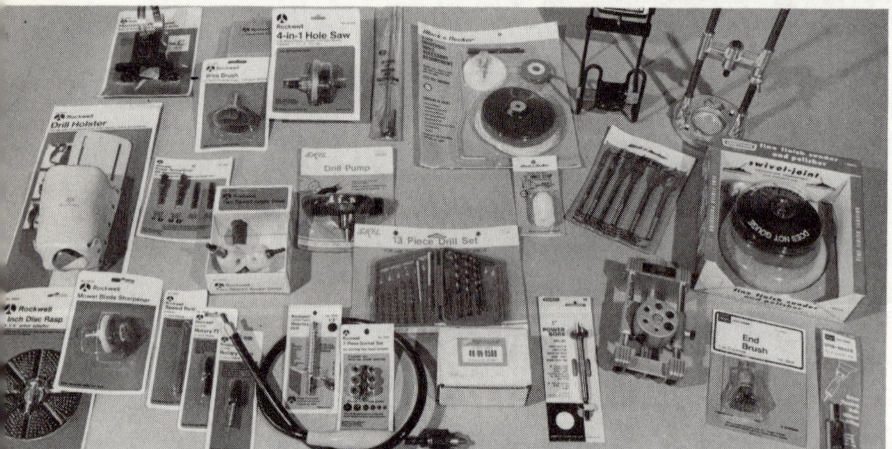

A SELECTION OF quality drills: 1—Black and Decker ½-in. Single Speed Reversible; 2—Sears ⅜-in. Variable Speed Reversible; 3—Stanley ½-in. Variable Speed Reversible; 4—Rockwell ¼-in. Cordless; 5—Rockwell ⅜-in. Variable Speed Reversible; 6—Skil ⅜-in. Variable Speed; 7—Milwaukee ¼-in. Single Speed; 8—Milwaukee ⅜-in. Variable Speed Reversible; 9—Rockwell ½-in. Single Speed Reversible.

A FEW of the vast number of accessories that make an electric drill versatile.

You can do almost anything with a portable drill

By ROSARIO CAPOTOSTO

SEE ALSO

Angles, drilling . . . Drills, portable . . . Motors, shop . . . Power-tool maintenance . . . Power-tool stands

BECAUSE IT CAN perform so many functions, an electric hand drill is one of the most useful tools you can have in your home or shop. A power drill bores holes with ease, speed and efficiency. With accessories it does much more.

Combined with the proper attachment, a drill sands, grinds, polishes, files and shapes. It also cuts sheet metal, pumps water, mixes paints, drives nails, and turns screws and nuts.

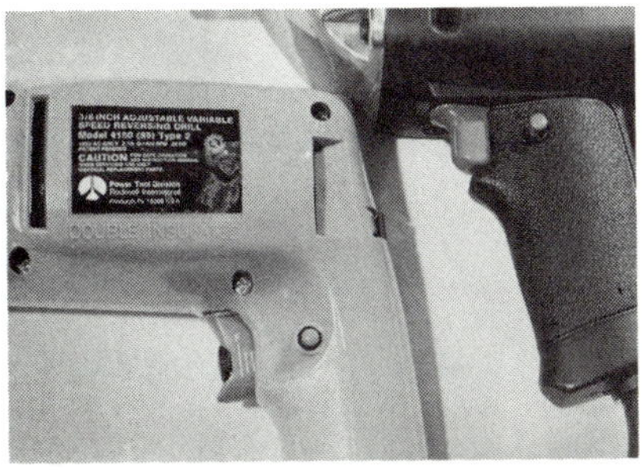

VARIABLE-SPEED triggers control rpm. Most makers offer one model with it.

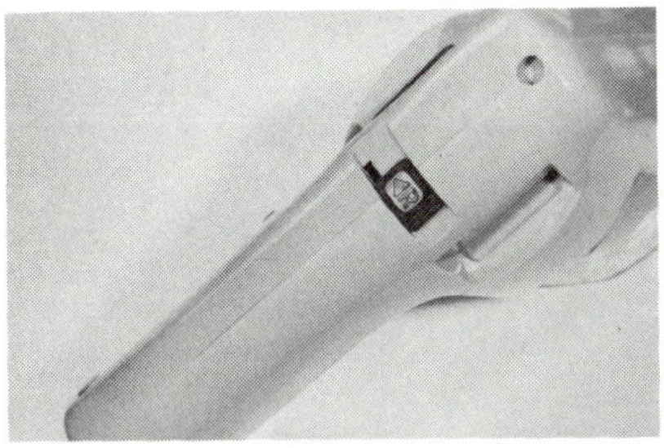

REVERSING switch lets you back out screws, nuts and frees jammed bits.

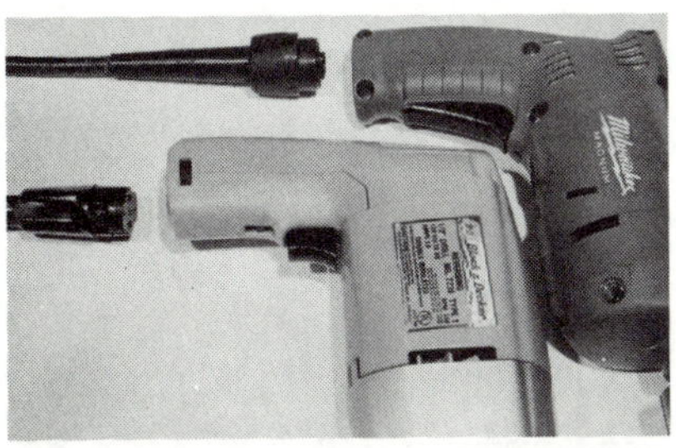

SOME DRILLS have detachable cords that are stored in your tool chest.

FOUR-POSITION D-handle on heavy-duty drills gives maximum control.

SIDE HANDLE should be used on any high-torque drill.

A drill is identified by the maximum capacity of its chuck: ¼-, ⅜- and ½-in. This is the same figure as the maximum diameter of the drill bit shank that the chuck holds. Generally, the chuck capacity indicates the maximum size hole that can be bored in steel without undue strain.

There is a direct relationship between size, speed and power of a drill. As the chuck size in-

Bits and accessories you should know about

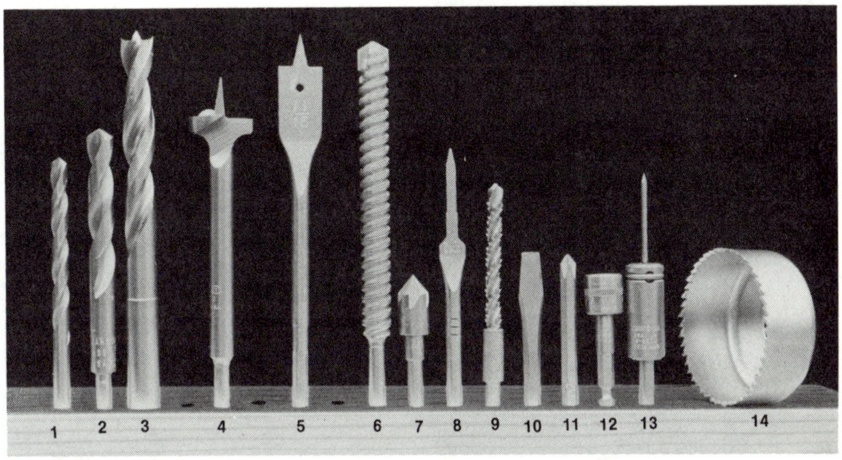

THIS LINEUP of bits and accessories is: 1—high-speed twist; 2—high-speed twist bit with reduced shank; 3—brad point spur bit; 4—flat-bottom spur; 5—spade; 6—masonry; 7—countersink; 8—wood screw pilot bit; 9—wood rasp; 10 and 11— screwdriver bits; 12—nut driver; 13— nail spinner; 14—hole saw.

FULL-CIRCLE flat bearing surface of Stanley's power bore bit gives stability, and a perfect circle every time.

TO BORE holes in metal, hold work in vise. Grasp tool in both hands to stop whip when bit breaks through.

BORE MASONRY with heavy-duty drill, carbide bit; use water to cool bit.

CUT HOLES up to 2½-in. diameter with a hole saw at slow speed.

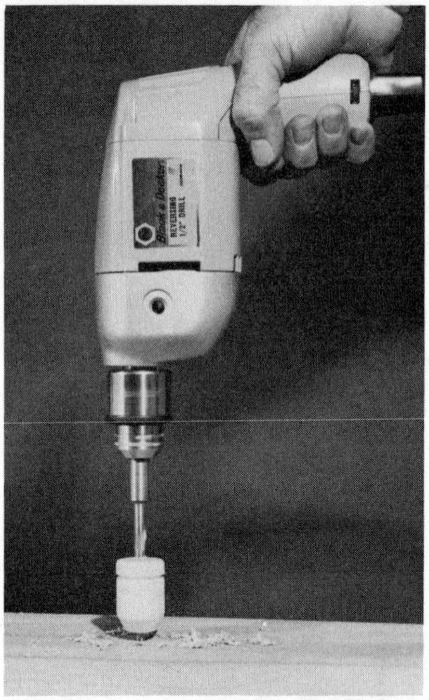

PLASTIC COLLAR tightens at any position to control depth of hole.

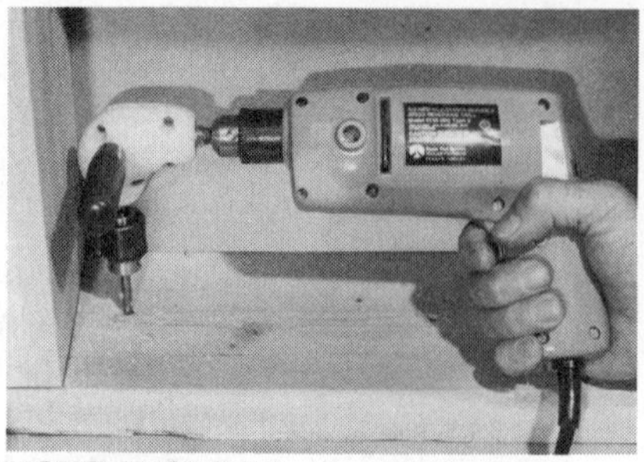

RIGHT-ANGLE drive permits boring holes in tight quarters. Auxiliary handle helps to steady the bit.

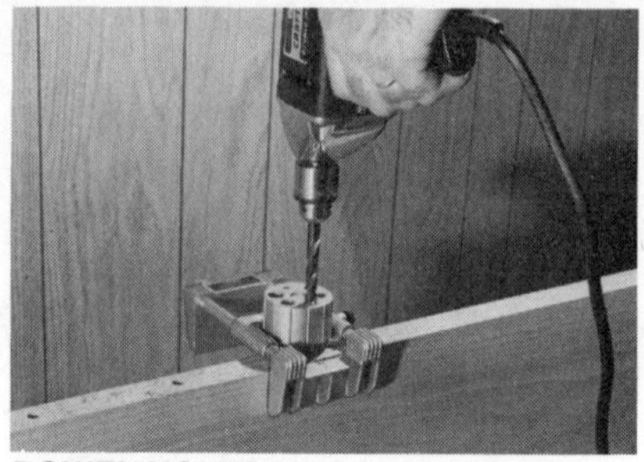

DOWELING JIG clamps on edge of board. Adjustments are locked in to assure duplication on mating piece.

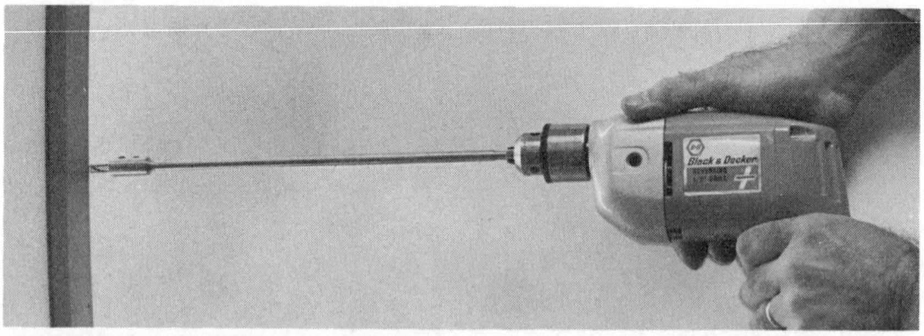

POWER BIT EXTENSION is handy for reaching otherwise inaccessible areas.

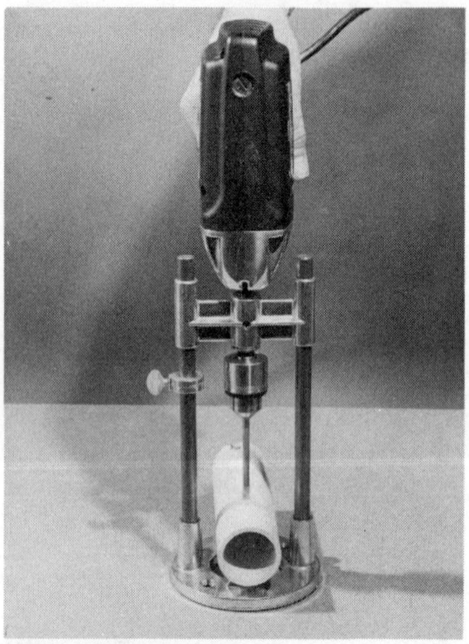

PORTALIGN drill guide provides automatic centering for round stock.

CORDLESS DRILL with battery is a must when outlet isn't available.

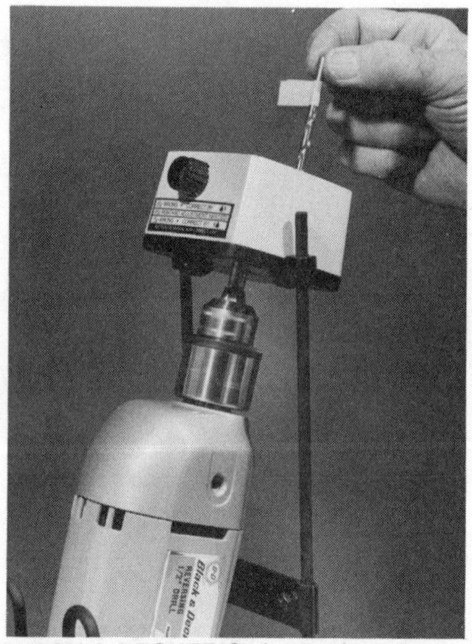

BLACK & DECKER'S sharpening attachment sharpens dull bits quickly.

DRUM SANDERS, available in several sizes, sand contours.

creases the rotation speed (rpm) decreases while torque (twisting power) increases. Therefore, a ¼-in. drill delivers more rpm and less power than a ½-in. tool. The ⅜-in. drill performs between the two—often a most desirable compromise.

Horsepower (hp) rating also relates to the workload capacity of a drill. If you plan heavy-duty drilling you would do well to invest extra dollars for a high-hp-rated tool.

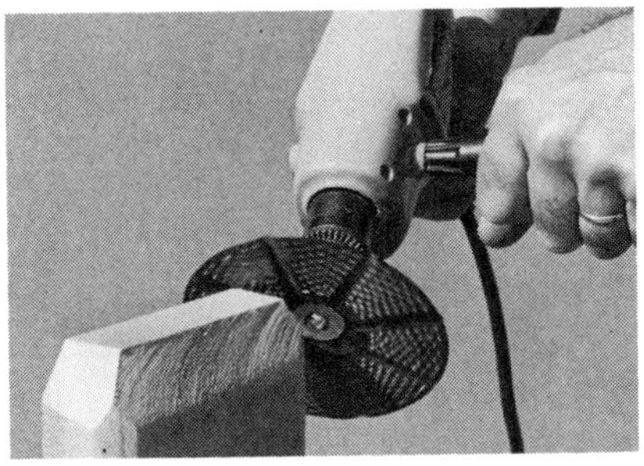

DISC RASP removes rough stock, won't clog and outlasts abrasive paper.

LAWNMOWER sharpener lets you work on blade without removing it.

HORIZONTAL drill stand with adjusting clamp converts drill into bench unit.

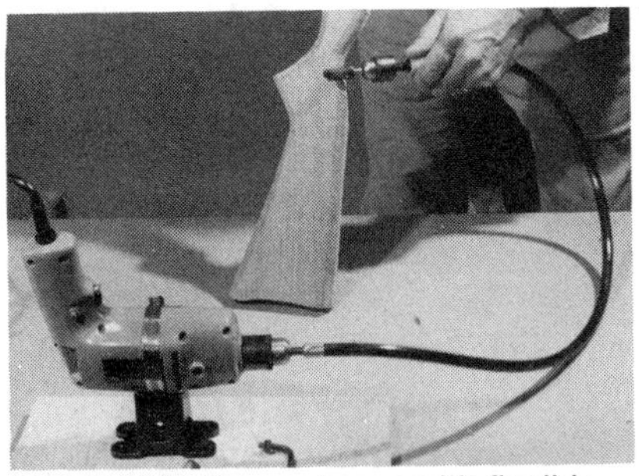

ROTARY RASP combines with flexible shaft to shape irregular surfaces.

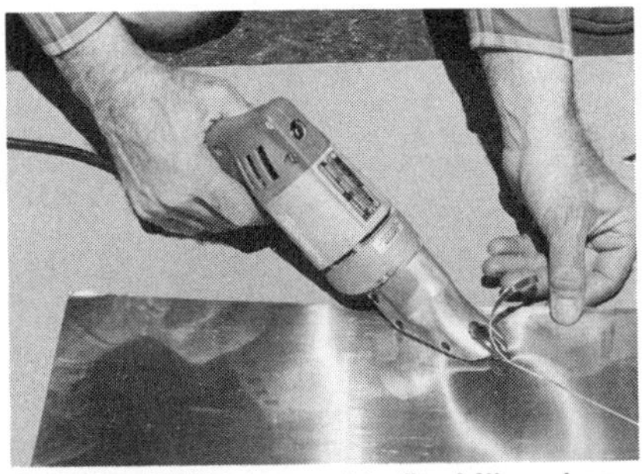

SHEAR HEAD assembly fits Milwaukee ¼-in. drill to cut sheet metal.

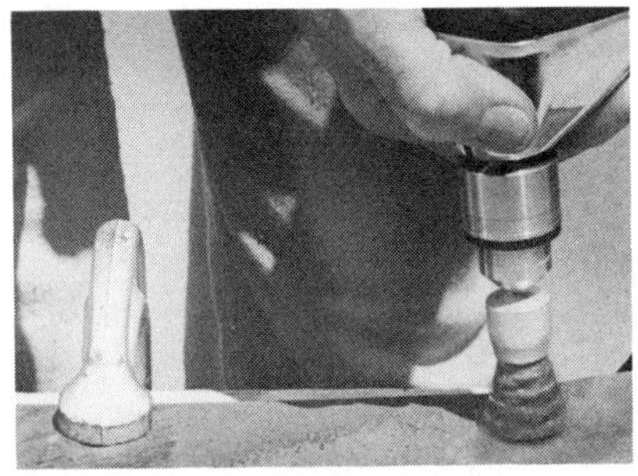

RUGGED, twisted-end cup brush quickly removes rust, scale and carbon.

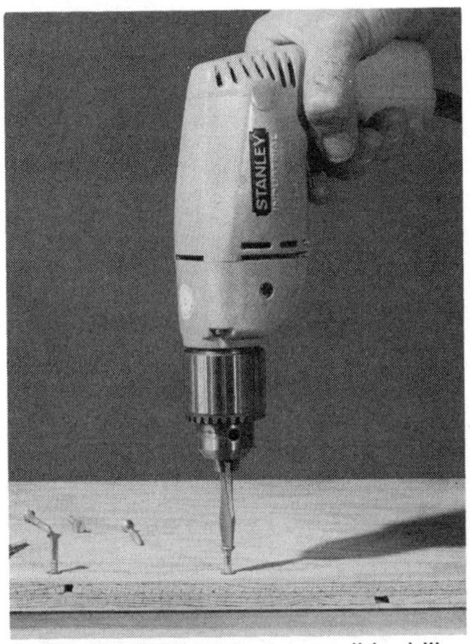

SCREWDRIVER bit in a reversible drill will drive, remove screws.

NAIL SPINNER sets finishing nails without predrilling, minimizes splits.

SWIVEL-JOINTED polishing pad and bonnet flexes to 30° angle.

DRILL PUMP drains plugged sinks. *Never use it on volatile liquids.*

Some operations such as light-duty drilling, sanding and polishing are better accomplished with drills having high rpm, in the range of 1200 to 2500. Drilling tough materials such as thick ferrous metals or masonry requires slower speeds that range between 300 to 500 rpm.

The variable-speed drill allows infinite rpm variation from 0 to maximum speed simply by a squeeze of the switch in the handle.

Practically all drills have locking buttons that lock the tool "on" for continuous use. A reversing switch is an additional feature which is handy for backing off screws.

Insulated tools protect against electrical shock while eliminating the need for grounding. A cordless electric model is particularly handy when working outdoors where electric outlets aren't available.

How to install a yard light

■ A YARD LIGHT does many things for a home. It bids welcome. It discourages prowlers. It adds nighttime beauty to the yard, and lights the way to your front door.

The biggest job in installing a yard light is digging the hole for the post and the trench for the cable. The required minimum depth is 18 in., and you'll find a narrow spade best for digging the trench.

Yard lights come with metal or wood posts, plain or fancy. The important thing when setting the post in concrete is to see that it's plumb before filling the hole. Here, in the case of a wooden post, a couple of C-clamps can be used to attach braces to it temporarily; with a metal post, notches in the braces will let you hook them over the top.

Use heavy-duty, flat, plastic-covered cable made for underground burial and run it up inside the yard-light post, leaving ample wire at the top for connecting it later to the socket. Buy three bags of dry-mix concrete to set the post, mix according to directions and fill the hole.

To connect the cable to an existing junction box in the basement, you have to pass it through a hole in the foundation wall or a hole in the joist header. The latter is an easier job if you have a poured foundation, but it means the cable must be partially exposed. In this case, the exposed part must pass through conduit before entering the house wall.

While they cost more, you can buy yard lights that turn themselves on and off at dusk and dawn by a built-in photoelectric control. This feature eliminates the need for a separate switch. However, the drawing on the opposite page shows how to install a separate switch at some convenient location in the house, and the wiring diagram below shows how you connect the wires of the cables to the black and white wires you'll find in the junction box when you remove its cover. Turn off the electricity when making the connections, and remember to connect black wires to black and white wires to white.

SEE ALSO

Electrical wiring . . . Extension-cord reels . . . Fluorescent lighting . . . House numbers . . . Patios . . . Testers, continuity . . . Wiring, electrical . . . Yard lighting

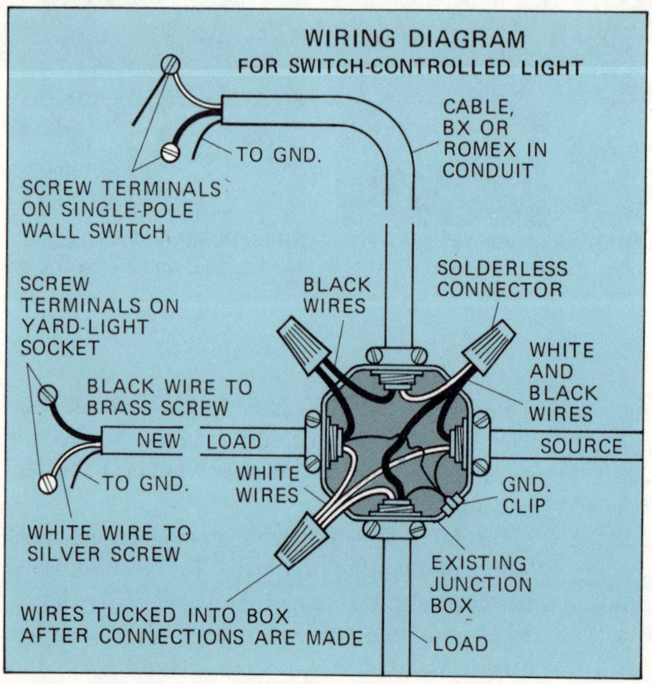

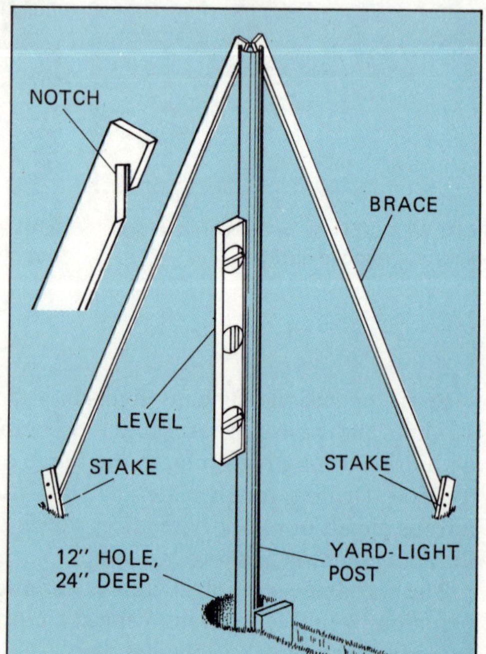

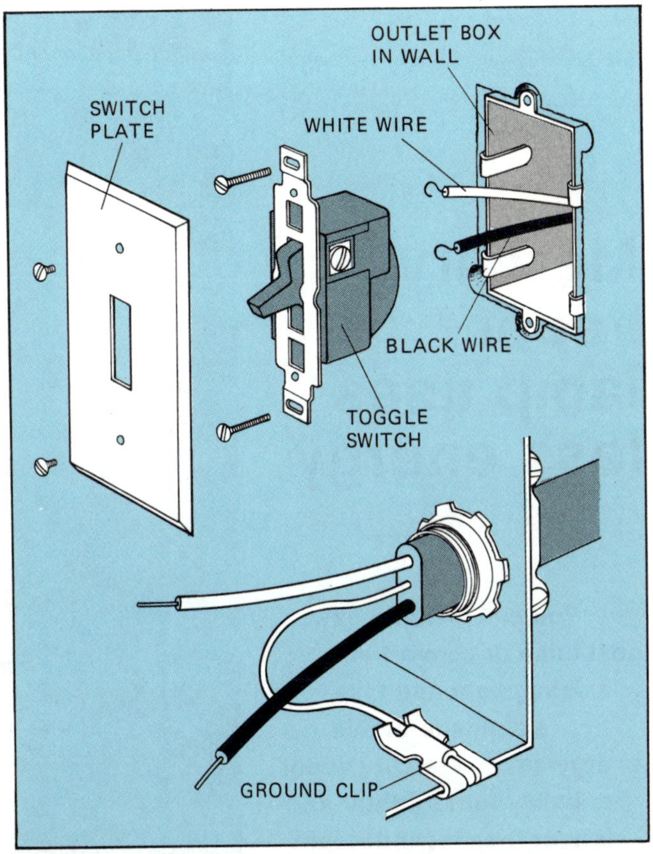
OUTLET BOX
IN WALL
SWITCH
PLATE
WHITE WIRE
BLACK WIRE
TOGGLE
SWITCH
GROUND CLIP

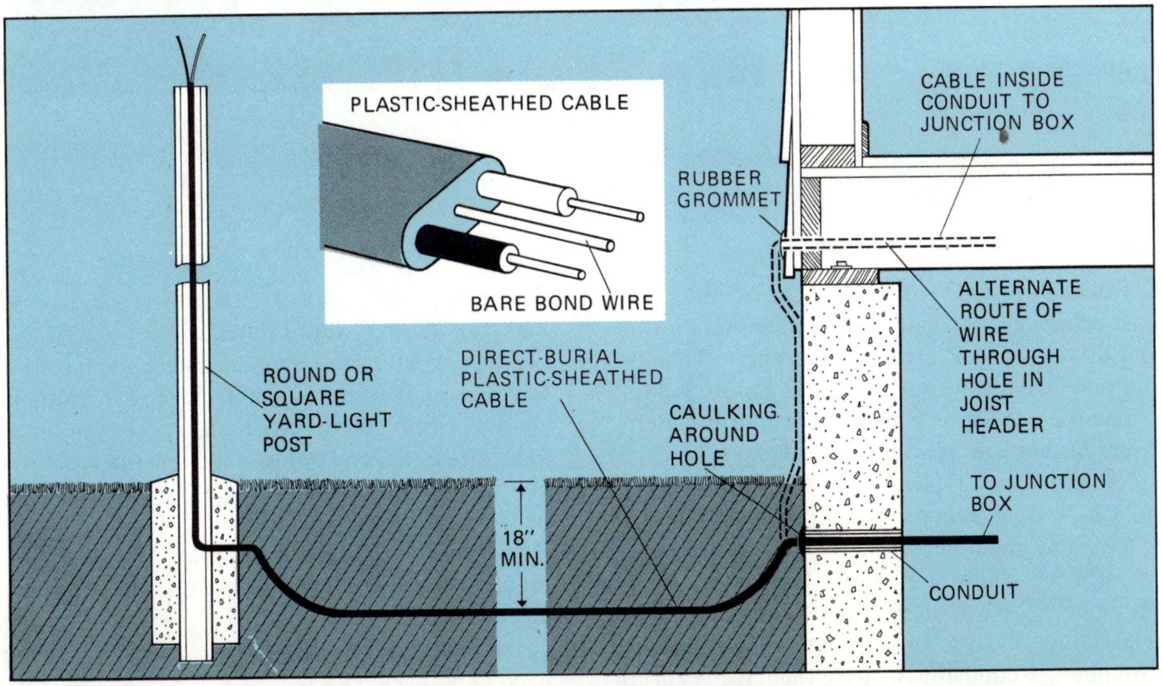
PLASTIC-SHEATHED CABLE
BARE BOND WIRE
CABLE INSIDE
CONDUIT TO
JUNCTION BOX
RUBBER
GROMMET
ALTERNATE
ROUTE OF
WIRE
THROUGH
HOLE IN
JOIST
HEADER
ROUND OR
SQUARE
YARD-LIGHT
POST
DIRECT-BURIAL
PLASTIC-SHEATHED
CABLE
CAULKING
AROUND
HOLE
TO JUNCTION
BOX
18"
MIN.
CONDUIT

Mercury vapor lamp uses less energy

You can install a new post lamp or convert an existing light and take advantage of this energy-saver. Mercury vapor bulbs burn brighter and longer than incandescent

By ROBERT W. TUREK

TODAY, ELECTRIC POST LAMPS offer the most economical and protective illumination for your driveway, walk, steps and entrances. Thanks to a new mercury vapor bulb, you can now illuminate the outside of your home with a brighter, longer-lasting light that uses less energy.

Compared to a typical 100-w. household-type bulb, a 50-w. mercury vapor bulb lasts 21 times as long and gives off almost twice as much light per watt. A 100-w. household bulb lasts about 750 hours (three months if lighted an average of eight hours a day), but the mercury bulb will burn about 16,000 hours (more than five years at the same daily rate). General Electric is one maker of mercury vapor bulbs.

The new elliptical mercury bulb operates on a 120-v. circuit. But since it requires a ballast, it cannot simply be screwed into a conventional light socket. Several outdoor lighting manufacturers, including Hacco, McGraw-Edison, Artolier and Montgomery Ward, have designed cast-aluminum postlight fixtures for the mercury vapor bulb. They offer excellent light distribution from an unbreakable lens.

Before installing a new lamp, check with your local building department to assure electrical code

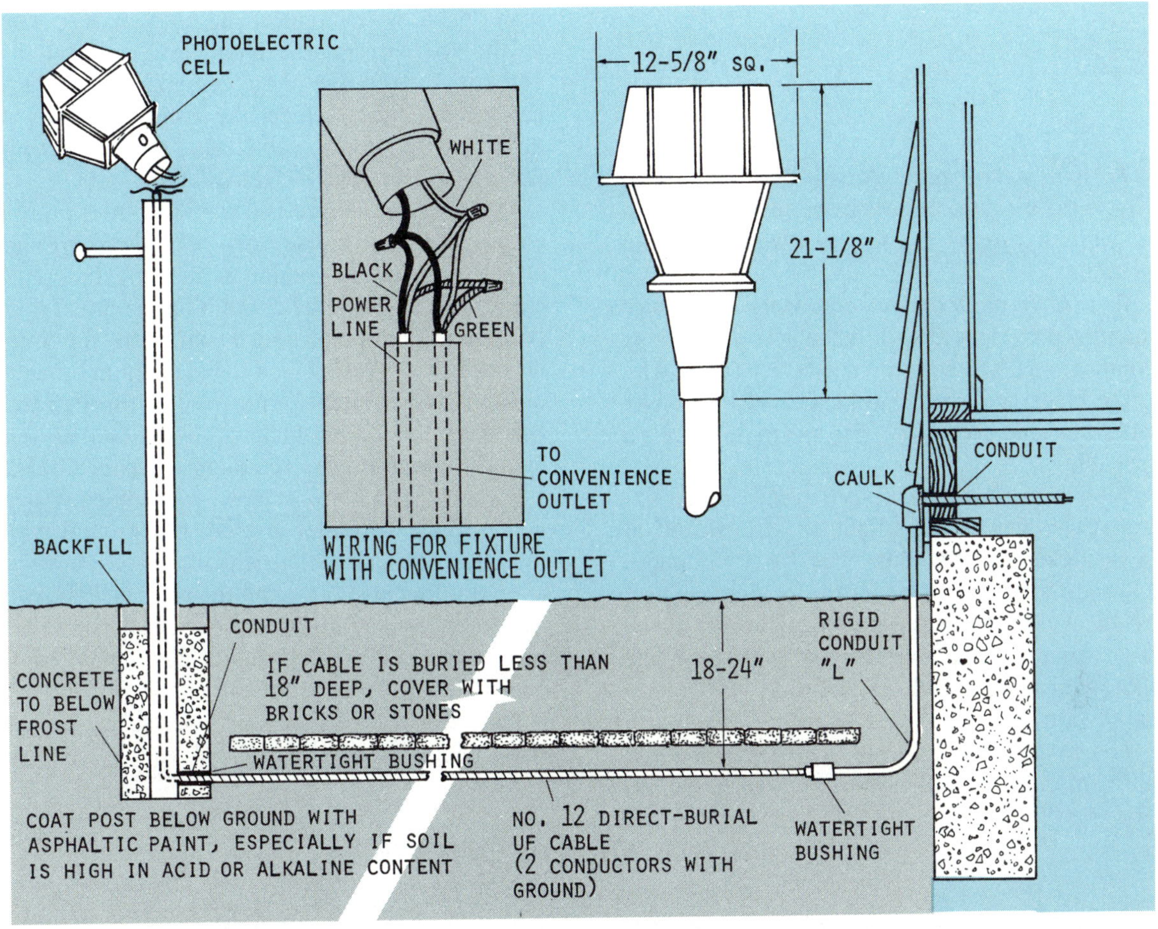

CONVERTING A standard electric post light can be as simple as removing the existing fixture head, and connecting the mercury vapor unit.

compliance. Then dig a post hole—lower than the area frost line—and a trench to the power source, following details in the diagram above. Once the cable is laid in the trench and wired through the post, place the post in the hole, plumb and secure it in both planes with rope and stakes (see page 2414). Usually a 45-lb. bag of concrete mix will fill the hole to about 6 in. below ground level. Backfill the hole and trench, and replace sod. Pull a plastic bag over the post top and seal it with tape to guard against moisture. Let concrete set 24 to 48 hours, then remove the bag and mount the fixture head by wiring as follows:

SEE ALSO

Electrical wiring . . . Extension-cord reels . . . Fluorescent lighting . . . House numbers . . . Patios . . . Testers, continuity . . . Wiring, electrical . . . Yard lighting

mercury vapor lamp, continued

To wire fixture only. Attach the black cable wire to the black fixture wire, white cable wire to the white fixture wire, and green wire to ground on cable.

To wire the outdoor, weatherproof convenience outlet to provide a plug-in receptacle at the post. Connect the black convenience-outlet (CO) wire to the black cable wire, white CO wire to white cable wire and green CO wire to ground wire on the cable.

To wire a photoelectric-cell collar to the fixture. (This device turns light on at dusk, off at dawn.) Connect the white wire from the photo cell and fixture to the white cable wire; connect the black wire from the photo cell to the black cable wire; then connect the red wire from the photo cell to the black fixture wire. Aim photo cell toward the north.

To wire a photoelectric cell, convenience outlet and fixture. Connect the white wires from the fixture, photo cell and convenience outlet (CO) to white cable wire; connect the black fixture wire to the red wire on the photo cell; connect the black wires from the photo cell and CO to black cable wire; then connect the green CO wire to ground wire on the cable. Use solderless connectors and wrap with electrical tape.

If the power source is a surface outlet on the exterior of your house, turn off the circuit and attach an L-shaped conduit to the outlet box. Pull cable wire through the conduit and connect it to corresponding color-coded wires in the outlet—white to white, black to black. If an outside outlet is not available, run conduit through the basement wall and make connections at the nearest junction box (see diagram, page 2413).

A metal fixture or post must be grounded. When no convenience outlet is used, run ground wire to fixture. With an outlet (which can also be wired at base of the post), ground the receptacle box to the ground post and fixture. A waterproof outlet box at the house entry should have an internal ground screw for ground-wire connection.

Converting a gas post light is easy, but the gas line should be capped by a professional gas-pipe installer.

INSTALLATION TOOLS AND MATERIALS

MATERIALS

1. No. 12 direct-burial type UF cable wire (2 conductors with ground)
2. Solderless connectors (6)
3. Plastic electrical tape
4. 45-lb. bag of dry concrete mix
5. Heavy-plastic bag (minimum 4-in. dia.)
6. Rope
7. Stakes (4)
8. L-shaped conduit
9. Conduit sleeves (2)
10. Watertight bushings (2)

TOOLS

1. Spade
2. Long-nose pliers
3. Wire stripper
4. Screwdriver

INSTALLATION OF LAMP POST

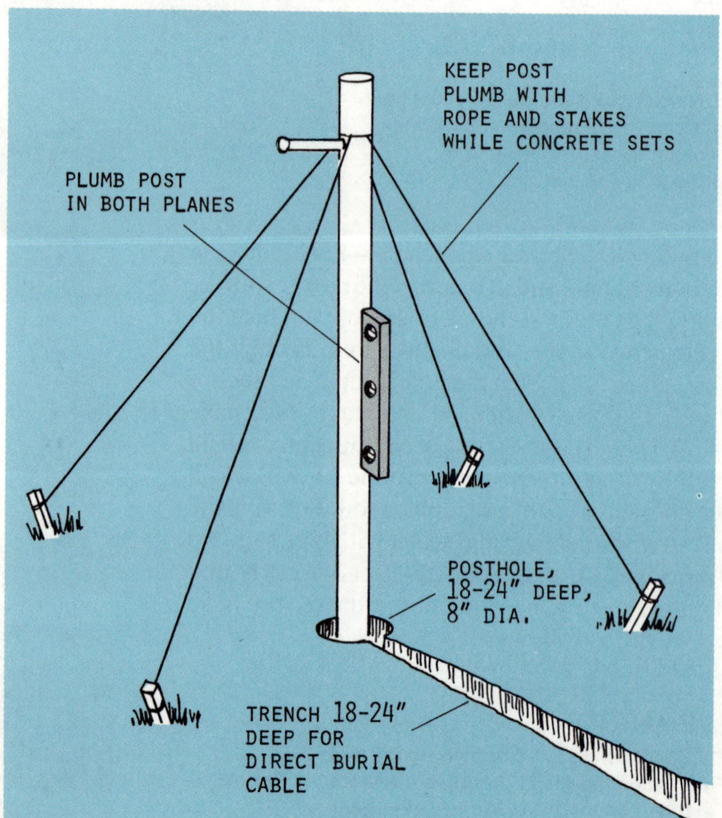

A shrubbery light for $3

By ARNOLD H. HUEHN

Add a little light to your yard with this clever inexpensive fixture made from a pie pan, a sign socket and a glass mayonnaise jar

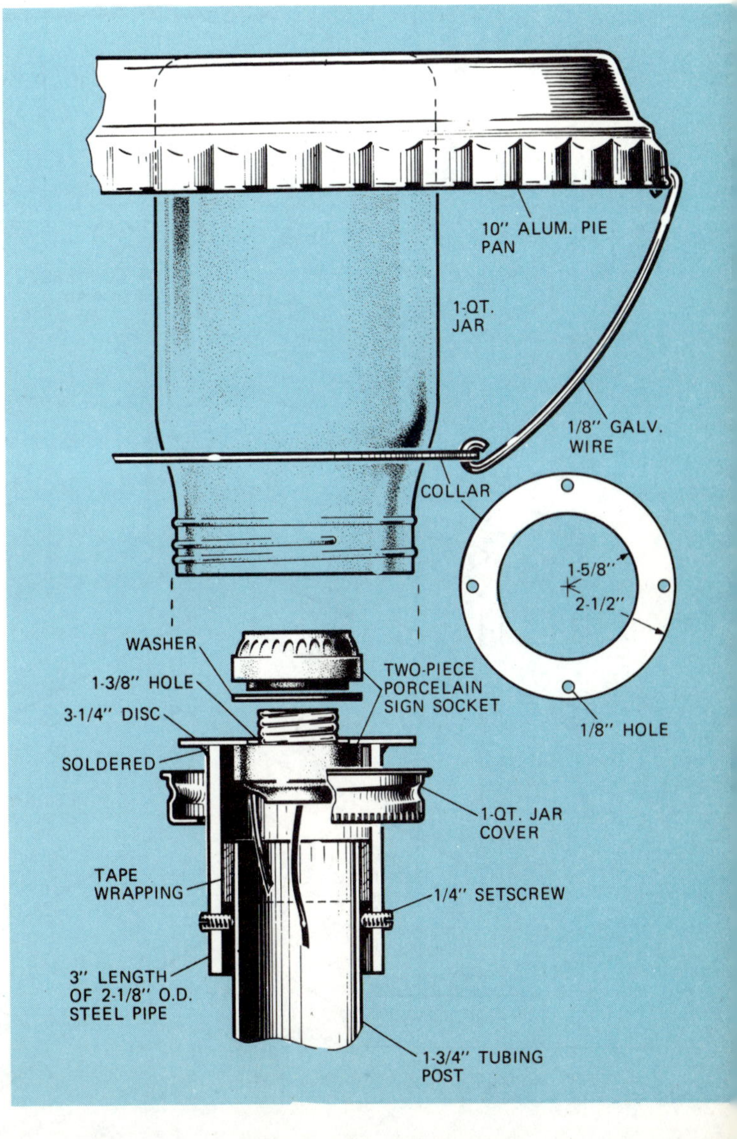

AN ALUMINUM pie pan and a quart mayonnaise jar make an attractive shrubbery light.

The pie pan top is held in place by four wire braces and a metal collar. Cut the collar from 16-ga. sheet aluminum with a circle cutter on a drill press. Make holes 90° apart in both the collar and pie pan for ⅛-in. aluminum wire.

Replace the vacuum-seal jar cover with a metal disc made from a round outlet-box cover with a knockout hole in the center. Enlarge the knockout to accept a standard porcelain sign socket and solder the disc to a short piece of galvanized pipe. The disc and jar cover provide a watertight seal. Three setscrews hold the light to its 1¾-in. o.d. post. Friction tape around the top of the 30-in.-long post builds up its o.d. so it fits snugly inside the larger pipe. Use a 40-w. bulb.

For a yard light, attach the light to a 5-ft. post. In all cases, set the post in concrete and bring up ample wire inside the pipe to connect the socket. Run heavy-duty, direct-burial cable underground and wire the light to an inside switch.

SEE ALSO

Electrical wiring . . . House numbers . . . Landscaping . . . Patios . . . Wiring, electrical . . . Yard lighting

Make your own potter's wheel

■ LIKE A FOREIGN LANGUAGE, such terms as "kicking," "wedging," "necking" and "throwing" are Greek to one who has yet to experience the fun of forming a hunk of clay into an attractive vase on a potter's wheel. But they soon become common parlance, and you'll know that necking in pottery means shaping the neck of a pot. I found that the best way to get started in pottery is to take lessons. The beginner can read how it's done and learn the fundamentals, but there's nothing like watching a skilled potter pull up a pot from a mass of spin-

BY SUSAN LANCASTER

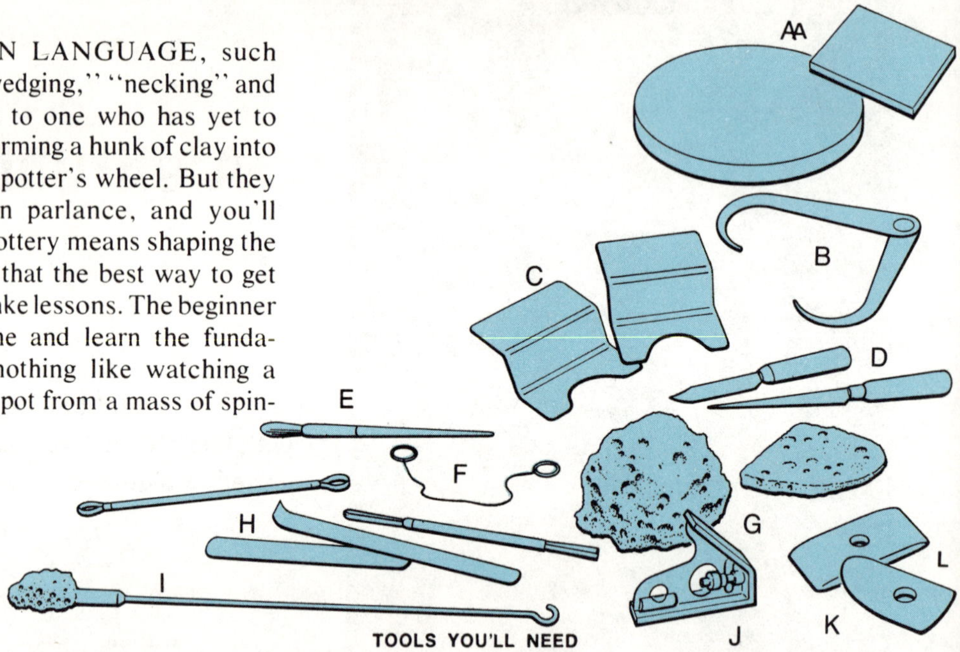

TOOLS YOU'LL NEED

A Plaster bats
B Calipers
C Lifters
D Paring/potter's knife
E Pointer
F Cutting wire
G Natural and elephant-ear sponges
H Foot rimmers
I Sponge on stick
J Level
K Wooden ribs

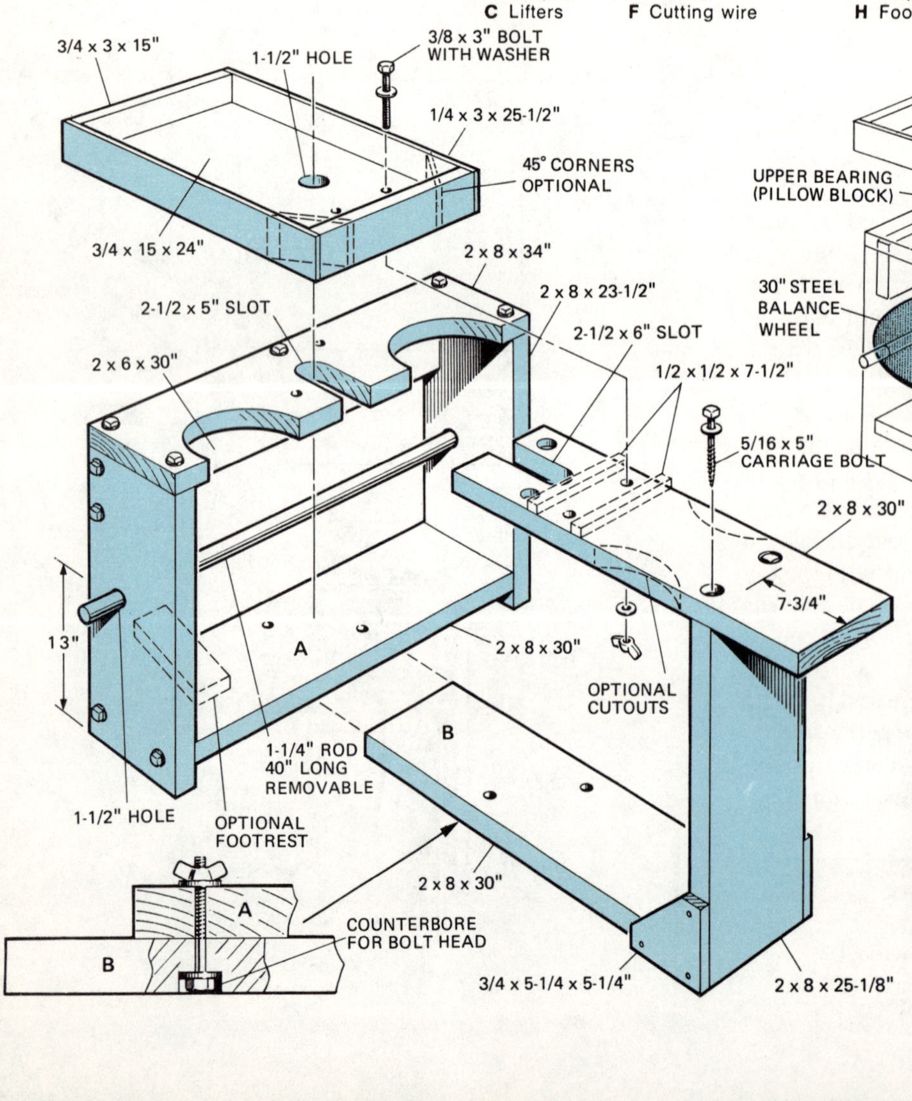

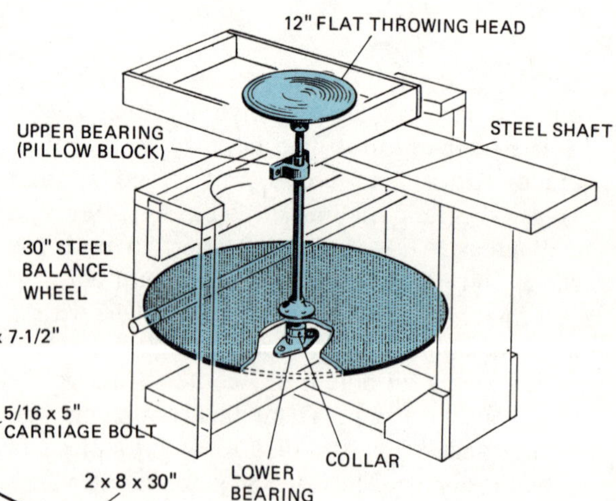

YOU CAN SAVE by making your own potter's wheel from a kit such as this one. It includes a 12-in. aluminum throwing head, shaft, and bearings and a 30-in., 100-lb. balance wheel, rubber-faced for foot traction. You provide the wood. Coordinating foot movements on the balance wheel control its starting, stopping, and speed for throwing. The kit sells for about $145 from American Art Clay Co., Inc., 4717 West 16th St., Indianapolis, IN 46222. Details at left show how to build the bench.

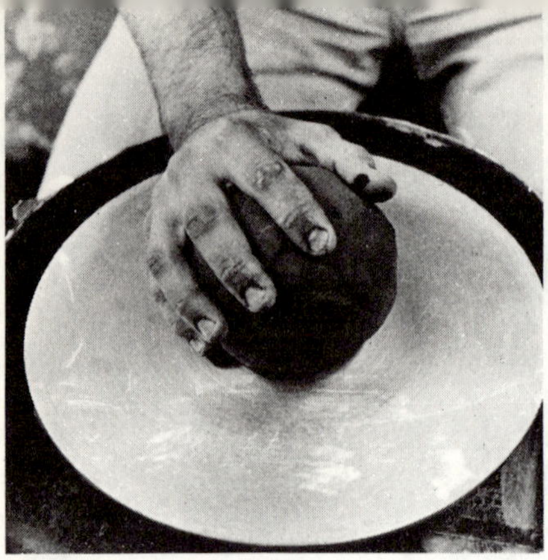

1. WEDGE clay to remove air bubbles and form two or three softball-size lumps. Then slam one lump on the center of the wheel head or on a moistened bat to make it stick firmly in place.

2. SET wheel in motion by kicking it forward with the right foot. When it spins remove the foot and begin working the clay ball with hands to the center of the wheel. Don't kick and shape at the same time.

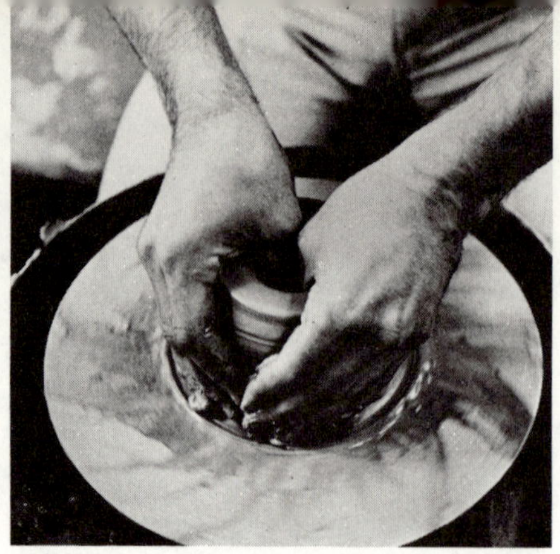

3. WHEN clay is centered, open it with the thumbs, working them down slowly to about ¼ in. from the base. Steady hand control is important; brace your right elbow against your side to help.

HOW TO WEDGE CLAY

Your clay is made workable by a process called wedging. Similar to kneading dough, wedging is done before the clay is placed on the potter's wheel, a necessary step to remove air bubbles and pockets from the clay.

First your clay lump is cut in half. Then one half of it is slammed down on top of the other, with cut side out. This step is repeated many times until the pockets of air are forced from the clay, and finally the well-wedged lump is shaped into a four-sided loaf by patting the ends with the hands.

Wedging the clay is a most important step, not only in removing air bubbles but in producing uniformity of texture in the clay.

7. AS NEEDED, trim the uneven top with a pin tool to keep the clay balanced so the cylinder stays centered. Trim enough from the top so no segment is carrying an extra mass that could disturb balance.

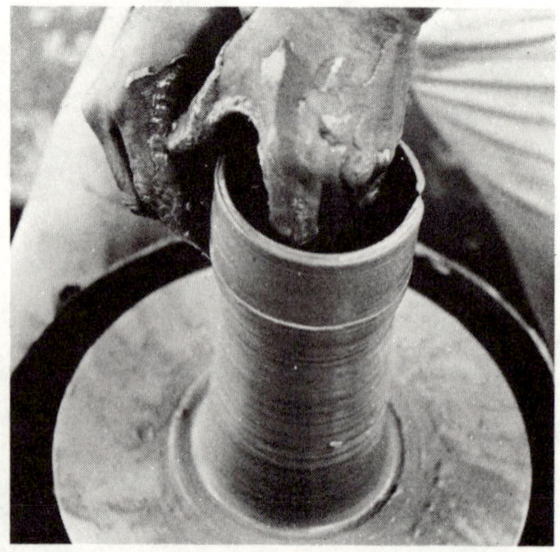

8. CONTINUING upward pulls produce a larger cylinder with a thinner wall. As the wall thins, slow the kick-wheel speed. If the work collapses, you'll have to remove the clay and start over.

ning clay on a potter's wheel to really see how it's done. Even then, the beginner is not going to "throw" a perfect pot the very first try. Like all hobbies, it takes practice.

After the pot has been shaped, trimmed and dried, finishing it requires materials and equipment difficult for the beginning potter to assemble on his own. This is another good reason for the novice to link up with a studio. The place where you take lessons will usually let you glaze and fire your pieces for a fee even after the course is over. First the dried piece, known as green ware, is fired in a kiln, either gas or electric, until the clay takes on the characteristics of an ordinary flowerpot. It is now known as bisque and is ready for glazing. Some studios use ready-mixed glazes and some mix their own and store them in big crocks in which the pots can be dipped. After the piece is glazed, it is fired again at a very high temperature. At the studio where I work, stoneware pottery is fired to 2350°F. in a gas kiln. This final firing produces a glasslike surface and makes the pot extremely durable.

The main costs of starting in pottery are the purchase of a wheel or a kit to build one and the initial lessons. Typically, lessons cost $5 to $7 for a three-hour session and are given once a week for 10 to 14 weeks. A separate charge for clay, glazes and firing is made on top of this. However, clay is cheap—about 12 cents a pound for stoneware clay—and the tools needed by a beginner are simple and often can be found in your own home.

I started with a knife and fork from my kitchen, and a sponge (used to wet the clay while throwing) from the cosmetics section of a drugstore. I cut off the corner of an old chamois to smooth the rim of the pot after throwing it, and I found a thin but strong piece of wire in the toolbox to cut the pot off the wheel head. You do have to buy trimming tools to finish the bottoms of your pieces after they become partially dry—"leather-hard" is the term potters use. These tools are available at most art supply stores.

4. START FORMING your cylinder by pulling the clay upward with your thumbs. Use little pressure with the hands. Each upward pull will gradually thin the clay wall and make the cylinder taller.

5. FOR BETTER control, join your hands whenever possible, locking the thumbs together or resting the left thumb on the right hand. Place and remove your hands slowly so you don't move the clay.

6. CYLINDERS tend to flare out at the top; they must be closed in by necking. Cup your hands around the cylinder center—a maneuver that makes the wall thicken and, gradually, rise straight.

9. USE A taut wire to cut work free of the wheel head after trimming excess clay from the base with a wooden tool. Put the wire under the base and pull. If the work is on a bat, just lift it from the wheel.

10. IF NO BAT was used and the work thrown on the wheel head itself, slide the work gently, after cutting it free, onto a board or plaster bat and let it dry until it's ready for glazing and firing.

RECOMMENDED BOOKS

There are many books that are helpful to the beginning potter. Here are two suggestions:

The Complete Book of Pottery Making by John B. Kenny, Chilton Book Co., Philadelphia, publisher; $4.95

Throwing on the Potter's Wheel by Thomas Sellers. Professional Publications, Columbus, Ohio, publisher; $4

For the more advanced potter:

Pottery, the Technique of Throwing by John Colbeck. Watson-Guptill, Inc., New York, N.Y., publisher; $10.

Clay and Glazes for the Potter by Daniel Rhodes. Chilton Book Co., Philadelphia, Pa., publisher; $12.50.

Step by Step Ceramics by Jolyon Hofsted. Golden Press, Inc., New York, N.Y.; $2.95.

Later on I made some plaster bats—solid, dish-shaped slabs that you attach to the wheel head when throwing a pot and remove to let the pot dry. The plaster for making bats can be purchased from a hardware store, and pieplates make good molds.

Firing charges can be rather high, especially if you make big pieces. The rate might be $1 a pound at a commercial art center, somewhat less at an adult education center. This fee covers the cost of both firings and the use of the glazes. When you are more experienced, you can cut these costs by purchasing your own kiln and mixing or buying your own glazes. Although some people feel the gas kiln produces a more beautiful and subtle glaze, many find the electric kiln, with its more evenly distributed heat, provides more predictable results. Electric kilns range in price from $250 to $500 and portable gas kilns from $200 to $600.

For the beginner, however, developing skill on the wheel will be the primary concern. The accompanying pictures demonstrate the steps in forming the basic cylinder from which most shapes are made. It is useful to have such pictures to refer back to again and again as you work. But pictures and books can only go so far and a complete beginner will find it hard to learn without some instruction from a teacher.

For instance, the very first step in making a pot—kneading, cutting and pounding the clay to eliminate air bubbles and produce a uniform texture—is hard to pick up on your own. "Wedging," as the process is called, is most easily understood by watching a demonstration. Later, when your pot disintegrates in a soggy pile on the wheel head for the fifth time in a row, perhaps the teacher can tell you the one small thing you were doing wrong so that it won't happen again. It will be a while before the pot you see in your mind will be the one you end up with. But in time it will come and you will get great satisfaction from turning out handsome and useful things on your potter's wheel.

Build a power hacksaw from washing-machine parts

By BRADFORD DITTMER

In this ingenious adaptation, the back-and-forth mechanism of a discarded impeller-type washing machine pushes a saw instead of an agitator

SEE ALSO

Cutoff machines . . . Cutters, sheet-metal . . . Metal casting . . . Metalworking . . . Motors, shop . . . Power-tool stands . . . Safety, workshop . . . Sheet metal . . . Torches

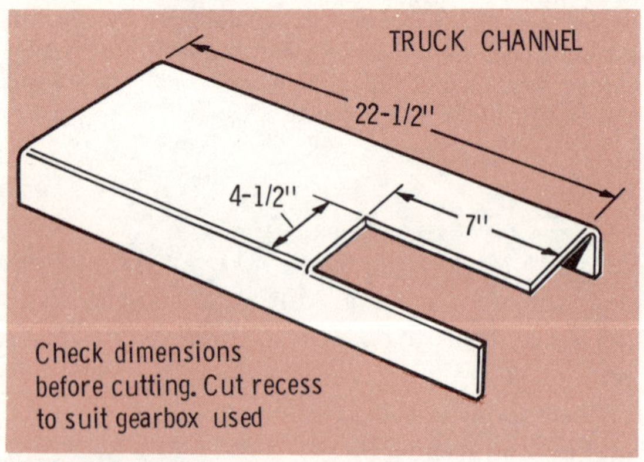

FOR ACCURACY, make a test stand using wood before cutting recess in the truck channel.

GEARBOX IS MOUNTED using ½-in. stock, washers and pins. First, test dimensions on wood base.

MOTOR IS MOUNTED on existing bolts on gearbox. Plate fastens to an angle to receive motor.

60-TOOTH GEAR is mounted on driveshaft against collar. Key parts line up on this gear's center line.

BRASS PLATE extended down one leg provides way to attach rack, takes springiness out of leg.

READY TO GO, saw includes counterweight added to outboard end of saw guide.

■ A WELCOME ADDITION to any metalworker's shop would be a power hacksaw, but few home shops boast of one because of the cost. Happily, you can treat yourself to this luxury by using the gearbox from a discarded washing machine (obtainable at a very modest price from your local appliance dealer; it's one less "trade-in" he has to haul to the junkyard).

Though any make of washer having a back-and-forth impeller movement can be used with the rack-and-gear method to drive the saw, I used a Sears Kenmore. The gearbox has built-in gear reduction, existing lugs for attaching a motor mount and saw guides, plus a 7-in. driving pulley. Half of the housing is gray iron casting, the remainder die-cast of a light-weight alloy.

Two changes were necessary: A hole had to be reamed in the large lug on the underside of the iron casting to accommodate the ½-in. rod on which the motor rides in the base, and the impeller shaft had to be shortened about 8 in.

perfect cutting speed

If you slip a 16-pitch, 60-tooth gear over this ¾-in. shaft and drive the 7-in. pulley with a ¼-hp, 1725-rpm motor rigged with a 2-in. pulley, you get just about perfect cutting speed—72 strokes per minute. Stroke length is about 6¼ in.

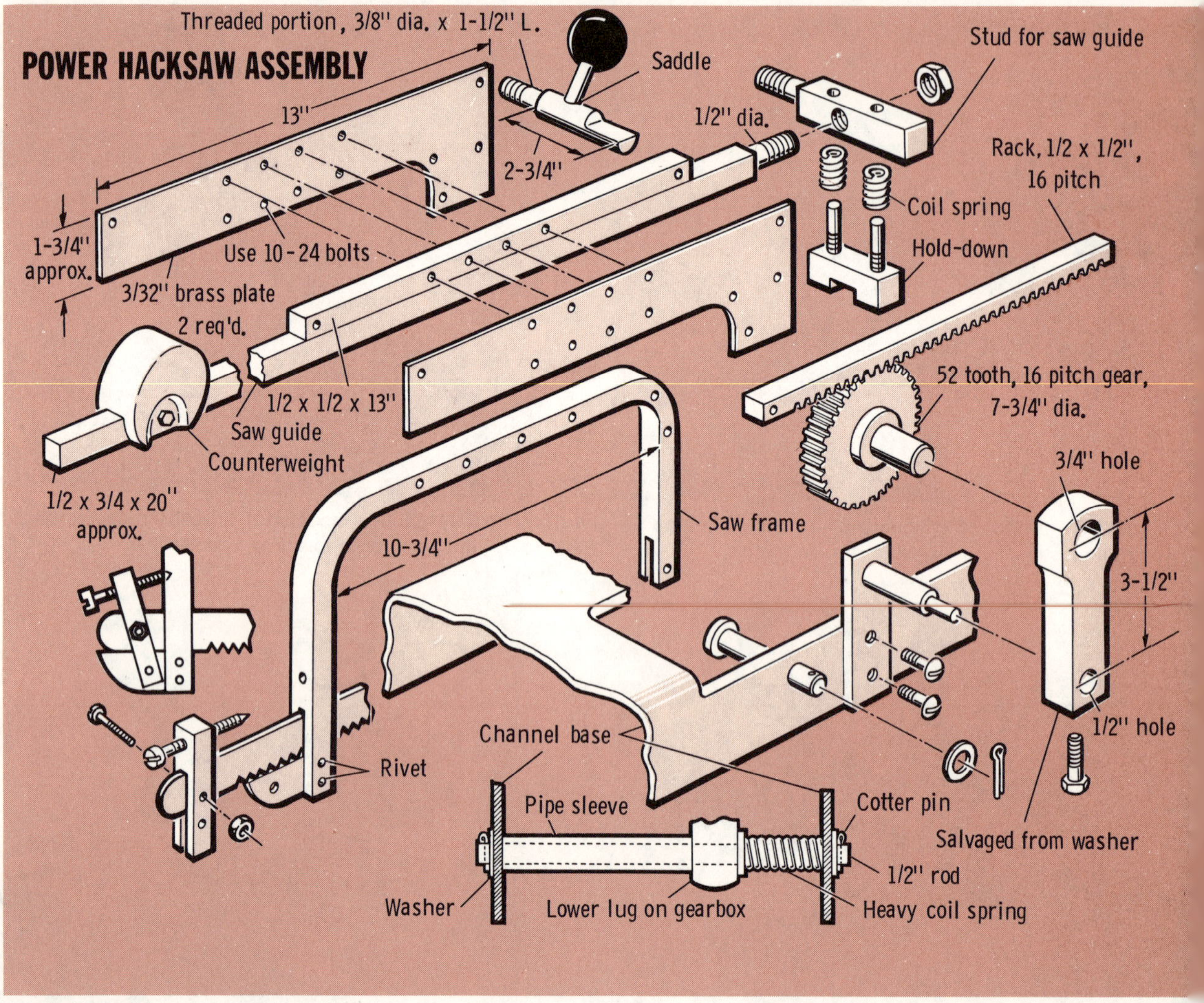

Of cold-rolled stock, the saw frame is made simply by heating and bending it, using a wood template. Slots to cradle the blade are hand-sawed with a hacksaw. They're cut to accommodate the 12-in. power-hacksaw blades that are sold by Sears.

Since the saw operates smoother if the flat surface contacting the saw guides is long, use a straightedge along the top of the frame after bending. Place the blade so it will operate as a drag saw.

trial-and-error base

Make a trial-and-error wood base for setting up the machine. Use about 30 in. of 2x8 stock and saw out the recess as shown. About 2½ in. back from the forward end of the recess and 1 in. down from the top surface, drill a ½-in. hole across the recess.

Next, mount the gearbox on a rod inserted across this recess. Block up the back of the box, set it in position, fit and assemble the rest of the fixtures. This done, you can then determine the measurements that you will need to build the permanent stand.

Place the gear on the driveshaft tight against the collar and fasten it with a taper pin. When assembled, all parts on the mechanism are lined up on this gear's center line.

The brass hold-down is notched to fit over the rack. Clamp it in place and drill a hole through both parts on each side of the rack with a No. 7 drill.

sliding fit

Next, tap ¼-20 threads and insert ¼-in. bolts in the holes and saw off the heads about 1¼ in. above the stock. If necessary, enlarge the holes in the stud to assure an easy sliding fit. The

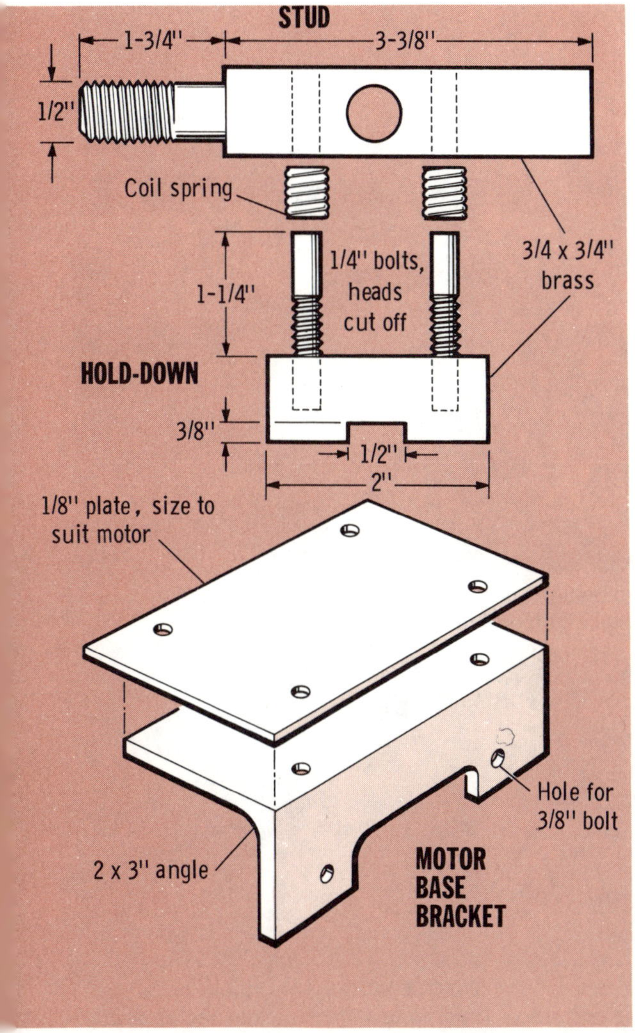

springs slipped over the studs should be of a suitable length to maintain a moderate down pressure on the rack.

To make the saddle, saw out a half-round section under the saw guide. This allows the saw to swing down far enough to finish the cut. Fit this part with a suitable handle for turning to up and down positions. Since the saw operates when the saddle is in any position, there is no need for an extra switch to stop the saw automatically after the cut.

The part salvaged from the washing machine (see drawing) is slipped over the small end over the ½-in. stud. The bronze, brushed end goes over the gear shaft to act as an outside bearing. Finally, add a ⅜-in. setscrew to hold it securely on the ½-in. stud.

Run the saw out to the end of the forward stroke. The face of the rear vise jaw should be set ½ in. ahead of the rear leg of the saw. The saw guide should be level when the blade is about ¾ in. above the floor of the vise. And, when the saw guide is level, the rack should be parallel.

When you have the rig checked out, use the measurements from your temporary setup to make the permanent one.

The base shown was made from 8-in. truck channel. (That explains those unused holes.) The legs are of light channel with the lower ends heated and bent to serve as feet.

setting the gearbox

To set the gearbox, drill holes for the ½-in. rod square with the sides of the channel and parallel to the top surface. Set the gearbox on the rod, block it in its final position and cut a pipe sleeve to fit over the rod between the lug and the far side of the channel. On the near side of the rod, place a stiff spring and use washers if necessary to hold the box in position.

Drill a ½-in. hole in a short piece of ¼ x 1¼-in. stock, and slip the hole over the ½-in. stud. Tip the gearbox to its vertical position, clamp the piece to the channel flange and drill for two ¼-in. bolts. If the spring on the rod is tight, your gearbox is set.

The motor-base bracket is cut from 1½ x 2½-in. angle to fit over two existing lugs on the back of the gearbox. Drill the bracket so it can be bolted onto the lugs with ⅜-in. bolts. Since the 2½-in. face is not wide enough to accommodate the motor base, use a plate—the size of the motor base—between the motor and the bracket. *Caution:* Be sure you set the motor so that the pulley is clear of the rack path on the back stroke.

construction tips

It's easier to assemble the saw sliding mechanism if you clamp the saw, saw guide and top slide together. The brass plates can then be clamped in place and holes bored for 10-24 bolts to hold the unit together. After removing the clamps, bore the remaining holes.

When using shims to insure a free-sliding fit, my experience has been that there is too much play when the shims are removed. Thus, I simply tightened the bolts to allow a free slide. It's not a must to use a 60-tooth, 16-pitch gear; a smaller gear—down to 50-tooth—can be used, but it will shorten the saw stroke.

Lengths of cold-rolled stock can be picked up at a local machine shop. If you have difficulty getting the gear and rack, write to Chicago Gear Works, 440 N. Oakley Blvd., Chicago, IL 60612.

Tune up your power tools

Periodic maintenance of all the power equipment in your workshop will assure well-functioning tools when you need them and help you get more mileage from each tool. Here's a look at both stationary and portable power tools

By GEORGE DANIELS

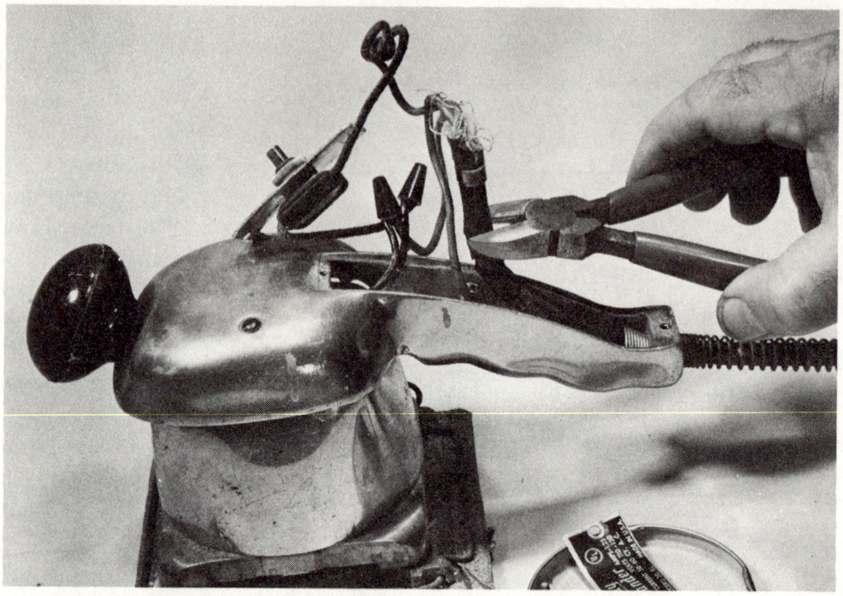

1 TO REPLACE a frayed cord that enters a tool through the handle, clip it off near end, but leave connections intact for future reference.

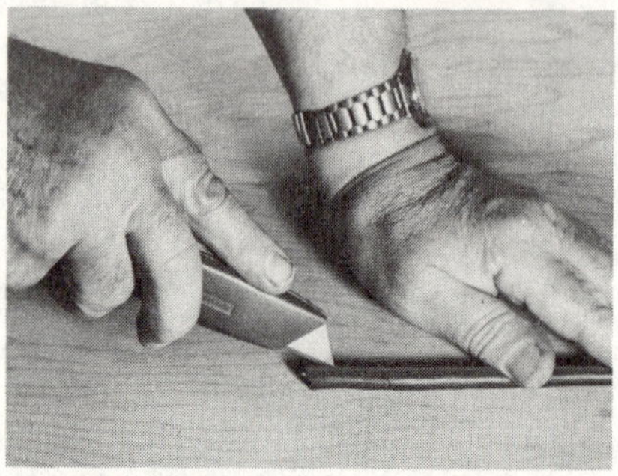

2 MAKE A SLIT in new cord's cover and bare enough wire to make connection. Trim off excess with scissors.

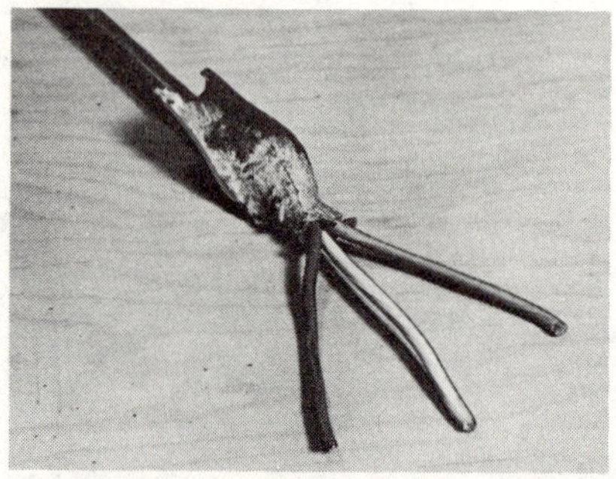

3 NOTE WIRE colors in new cord. Connect wires to motor leads and ground; use originals as guide.

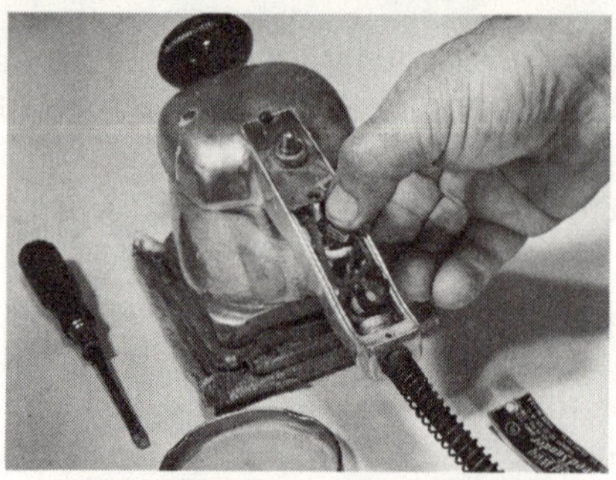

4 USE SCREW-ON connectors or pigtails and tape insulation when rewiring. Fold wires into handle.

5 USE THREE-PRONG plug with new three-wire cord to help assure grounding. Screw clamp grips the cord.

SEE ALSO

**Bandsaws . . . Bandsaws, sharpening . . .
Bandsaws, tables . . . Belt sanders . . .
Drill press techniques . . . Drills, portable . . .
Routers . . . Sabre saws . . . Table saws . . .
Wood lathe techniques . . . Wood lathes**

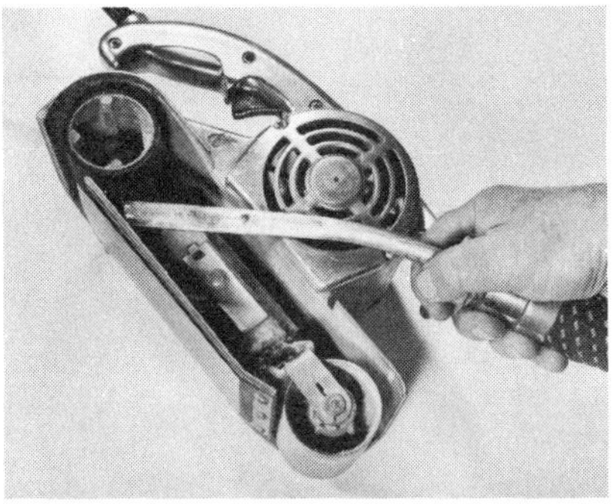

VACUUM-CLEANER snorkel made from soft copper tube flattened at end can clear dust from tight spots.

TO INSPECT toothed belt, put white card behind it and turn sprocket. Look for frayed edges and ripped teeth.

CLEAN slide ways and toolpost mount of compound rest with stiff brush. Lubricate ways whenever lathe is used.

BRUSHING with toothbrush cleans metal chips from feed-screw threads. Turn screw holding brush to threads.

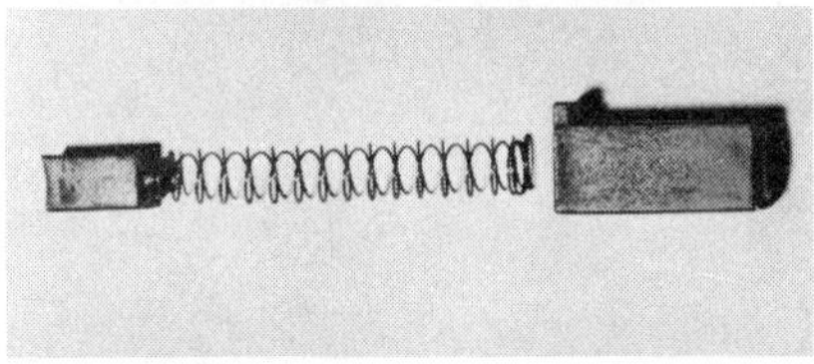

OLD TOWEL spread on bench when you open power tools keeps small parts from rolling away (above, right). Observe how parts go together and watch for springs that may pop out. Clean commutator (shown at card corner in photo above, left) with fine aluminum-oxide abrasive. Hold abrasive to commutator; turn fan; blow to clean off dirt particles. Ring connector fits top of holder to supply current (left).

■ THE BEST GUIDE to maintaining any power tool is the owner's manual. Keep yours filed in a safe place and, if you lose it, send to the manufacturer for another. Specify the age, model number and any other descriptive information you can find on the tool.

If your tool is an orphan for which needed replacement parts aren't available from the original source, look in a classified telephone directory for suppliers of the same type of item. You can often match bearings, motor brushes, drive belts and other parts.

lubrication rules of thumb

Locate all oil holes and occasionally feed them a few drops of light oil like 3-In-One or No. 20 engine oil. Self-lubricating graphited sleeve bearings need oil too, and many have oil holes. If not, put a few drops on the shaft at the end of the sleeve so it can work in; wipe off excess. Do not oil sealed-for-life, grease-packed ball bearings. The oil may leach out of the grease and wreck the bearing. Finally, don't overlubricate; oil may seep out and form a sticky mass of oil and dirt that gums up the works.

stationary power tools

■ **Table saws:** if you've neglected a table saw or any other tool with a cast-iron table, its ground surface may have rusted—especially in a garage workshop. Remove rust from the surface and grooves with a rust remover. Wear gloves and

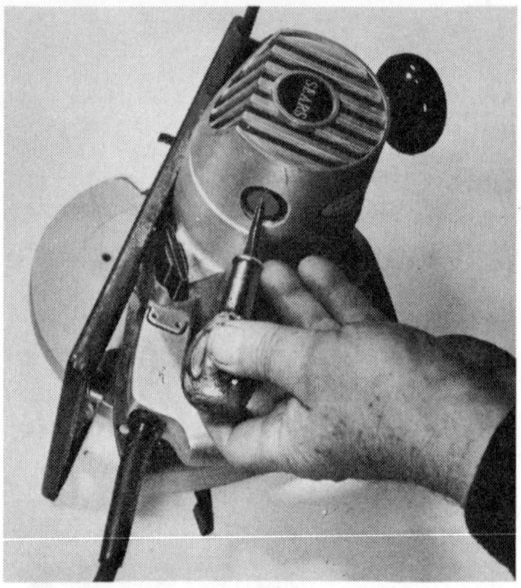

BRUSHES can be checked and changed in some tools like this Sears circular saw without opening motor housing.

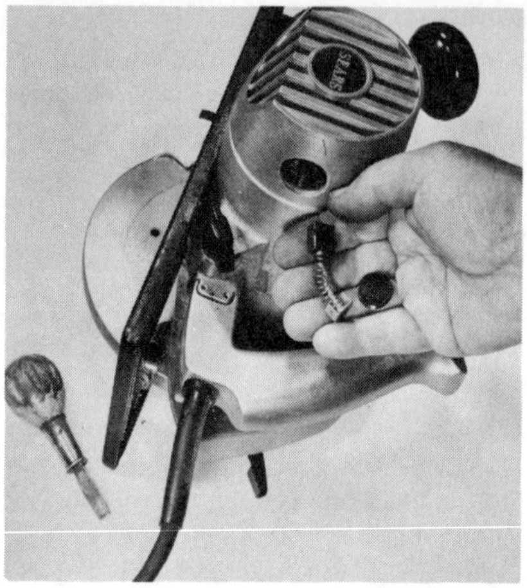

MARK BRUSH and spring clip with penciled X on one side so both can be replaced in original positions. Mark will shine on brush.

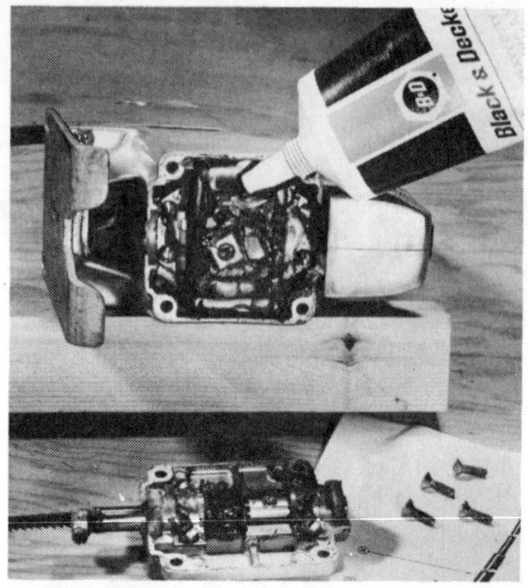

INTERVALS between regreasing gears of circular saws and sabre saws vary with model, but range from 100 to 200 hours of operation.

CLEAN SAWDUST from table saw with vacuum. Dirt can pack against stops and affect cutting accuracy.

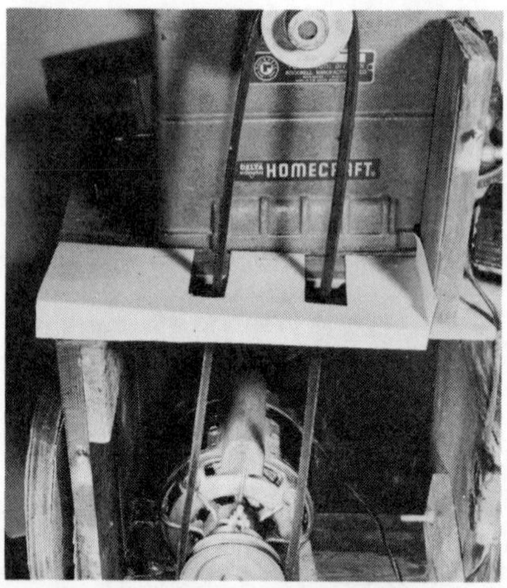

SWING COVER plate clear to get at wick-packed opening for lubrication of shaft bearing on some saw models (left). Saturate wick, but don't over-oil. Reduce dust in motor with cardboard panel cut to fit around belt (shown above) and second panel with vent holes to cover front (not shown in photo).

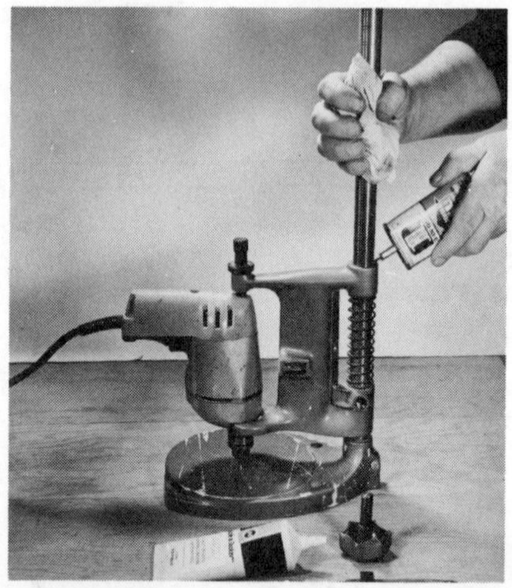

USE LIGHT oil to wipe protective film onto drill-press column; use gear grease on the feed-lever mechanism.

CLEAN RUST from tables and lathe ways with rust remover. Right side of this table has been restored.

USE TOOTHPICK to remove dust blockage from clogged oil holes. Work carefully so you don't push in dirt.

BANDSAW blade should be centered on tire, using wheel-tilting adjustment. Cover has been removed for photo.

goggles and follow the directions on the label. For added luster, rub the surface with 220-grit aluminum oxide paper. (In woodworking, rust removal is essential to keep rust from transferring to the work, which may cause finishing problems.) Protect the restored table with an oil film or rust-preventive lubricant.

To check your table saw's tilt control, first thoroughly vacuum-clean the unit. Set the control at zero, raise the blade to maximum height and place a try square on the table against the blade. If the blade isn't square with the table, adjust the stop under the table.

keep motor clean

Keep your saw's motor clean since sawdust can foul the centrifugal switch that changes over from starter winding to running winding. If it sticks in the starter position, it can burn out the winding. If it sticks in the running position, the motor won't start.

Check belt drive tension. You should be able to push the belt inward ½ in. on short spans and about 1 in. on longer ones. Minor slippage can be cured with a belt dressing like Woodhill Chemical's Belt Grip. An overtight belt doesn't last long and increases bearing wear.

sharp blade is a must

Be sure the blade is sharp. A dull one increases bearing and belt wear because of the heavier load and longer running time. It also increases the chance of the work being kicked back at you, so consider a sharp blade a primary safety factor in operating your saw.

■ **Radial-arm saw:** To cure out-of-square end cuts, use a try square to check squareness with the table. The means of adjustment varies, but is likely to be two bolts at the side of the bevel latch. Loosened, they permit tilting the motor until the blade is exactly flush with the square. Tightened, they hold it that way.

check with carpenter's square

Saw travel should also be squared with the guide fence. Make a trial cut through a wide board with a dressed edge against the fence and check it with a carpenter's square. If it's out of square, the saw track isn't perpendicular to the

WELL MAINTAINED 40-year-old lathe and motor are in fine shape. Weight of motor on hinged platform tensions belt to overhead jackshaft. Belt from jackshaft to lathe is tensioned by adjusting screw to reduce drive-belt load on the lathe's bearings.

HINGED jackshaft platform (far left) is adjusted by tightening or loosening nuts on either end of ½-in.-dia. threaded rod. Make a cover (near left) to protect oil holes close to sources of sawdust or metal particles. Snap-on sheet-metal cover (shown in hand) is used over lathe headstock bearing. Cover lathe bed ways when grinding.

fence. To realign, first loosen the track arm clamp handle and lay a steel square on the table with one edge against the fence. Then pull the saw carriage slowly across the table to see how much and which way the travel is untrue.

The adjustment is usually on the miter latch, often a hex nut and setscrew or cap nut. Try adjustments carefully. The hex nut may automatically swing the track arm left or right, depending on the way it's turned. When you're satisfied, tighten the setscrew or cap nut to hold the new setting. There are also other adjusting arrangements; read your manual carefully.

check for "heeling"

Saw "heeling" may occur even when the track arm is square with the fence. This means that the teeth at the back of the blade are not following the kerf made by the teeth at the front. You feel a drag when you make a cut. Check it by making a cut into a board, but without pulling it past the board. If the saw is heeling, you'll see tooth (heel) marks at one end. Viewed from the front, heel marks on the right mean the back of the blade should be shifted to the left. Marks on the left call for shifting the rear of the blade to the right.

To adjust for heeling, loosen yoke clamp handle and swivel adjustment bolts. The lock bolts are often under a cover plate near the swivel latch. Turn the yoke as required, tightening and testing, until the heel marks vanish. Then tighten the yoke clamp handle, followed by the bolts. On some saw models, heel-correcting adjustments are at the yoke's motor-pivot point.

■ **Drill press:** Since most drill-press motors in recent years have sealed bearings, only quill and feed lever mechanisms are likely to need oiling. If there's play in the quill from wear (not likely with average use), look for a wear adjustment bolt. Some drill presses have it. Check the drive belt for correct tension as described for table saws. The tension can be adjusted by moving the motor and retightening the mounting bolts.

■ **Bandsaw:** Check your saw adjustments starting with the blade by opening the upper wheel guard. If the blade is not centered on the wheel tire, use the tilting adjustment to tilt the wheel in or out until it is. Test by turning the wheel by hand with the drive pulley removed. Next adjust the blade tension. If your saw has no tension scale, adjust the tension handle at the top until the blade allows a side flex of ¼ in. on a 6-in. span between upper and lower guides. Set the upper guide far enough above the table to provide the span.

Prior to tensioning, be sure you have proper clearance between the blade and the guide pins in the upper and lower guide assemblies. For most blades, the distance between the guide pins and the blade is .002 to .003 in. Refer to your manual. You can get this clearance by placing pieces of medium-weight paper between the loosened pins and the sides of the blade, then tightening the pins in place against the paper. When the paper is pulled out, the proper clearance remains. Be sure upper and lower pins are in line so the blade isn't pushed out of vertical. Pins should be adjusted to come just behind the blade teeth. If they touch the teeth, they'll dull the blade. If they're too far back, they won't be able to guide the blade adequately.

set back support off blade

The blade support (ball-bearing wheel behind the blade) should be set 1/64 in. from the back edge of the blade. If it runs in constant contact with the blade, it may cause case hardening and eventual blade breakage. With proper clearance, it runs in contact only when work is pushed through the saw. Tires on bandsaw wheels last almost indefinitely as long as you keep them clean. If they're scored slightly from long use, dress them down a little with coarse sandpaper, but be careful not to remove too much surface from the tire.

■ **Lathe:** The wood lathe is equipped with heavy-duty headstock bearings because of the loads imposed. They may be roller, sleeve, or cone types requiring lubrication, or sealed "lifetime" ball types that require no additional lubrication.

lubricate lathe bed

The lathe bed ways (smooth-ground upper surfaces) and those of the compound rest (if the lathe has one) all require an oil coating for rust prevention and for lubrication since they are precision parts. Feed screws in the compound rest and tailstock also require oiling. For best maintenance and tension, see suggestions given earlier for belt-driven tools.

Check the bed with a level at both ends. If any twist in the bed is indicated, use shims under the mountings to correct it.

portable power tools

■ **Power drills:** Most power drills are easy to service. In "clamshell" form, the drill housing separates in two halves when assembly screws are removed. All internal parts are then exposed, including the grease in the gear case. The grease should be replaced after 100 to 200 hours of operation, or by a rule of thumb that calls for grease replacement after the second or third change of motor brushes. Scoop out most of the old grease with a screwdriver and wipe out the rest. The amount that comes out is a guide as to how much new grease you should put in, plus a little extra for the wiping cloth.

Use oil on the chuck shaft and in the rear motor bearing hole. The grease should be a tool type, formulated with enough viscosity not to work from the gear case into the motor. Black & Decker, Skil, Stanley and others offer such lubricants. They're sold in tubes and have a consistency like soft margarine. If the tool has a worm-gear drive, be sure the grease is suitable. Some companies make a special worm-gear grease. Don't use a free-flowing type like outboard motor lubricant.

replace motor brushes

On most tool motors, brushes should be replaced before they wear down to 3/16 in. in length. Any shorter, and the brushes may jam and break. They're easy to get at on most portable tools. In clamshell drills, they're in removable brush holders on opposite sides of the commutator. Change them in pairs, but take them out and replace them one at a time so the brush still in place serves as a guide for replacing the other. If you can't match a set of brushes for an orphan tool, you can flat-sand a larger size down to fit.

On some drills, brushes are accessible from the outside by removing plastic caps on each side of the motor housing. On others, you remove a few screws to take off the back of the handle or a section of it to expose the brushes.

■ **Sabre saw:** Sabre-saw brush replacements (usually from outside the housing) and lubrication are much the same as for drills.

removing the plunger

To get to the grease, remove the plunger housing at the front of the saw. This may also require removal of the tool handle. Before the plunger is moved out of position, note how the crank mechanism engages the plunger so you can fit the parts back together after the grease job. The typical amount of new grease you'll need is two tablespoons.

Don't force parts together when reassembling the saw. *If you do it correctly, no force is needed.* Use oil in the oil hole for the rear motor bearing. Also oil the felt seal (if present) at the bottom of the plunger housing.

■ **Portable circular saw:** Lubrication varies with the make and model, but most require occasional light oiling of the rear motor bearing through an oil hole.

remove blade first

To give your portable circular saw a grease job, first disconnect it from the power source and remove the blade. Next, unscrew the upper guard cover and disconnect the retracting spring of the lower (swinging) guard. Remove the dust cover that closes the side of the upper guard to expose the gear housing. Unscrew the gear housing cover screws and pry off gear housing cover to get at the old grease. Renew the grease following steps described for power drills. The typical amount in a 7-in. Stanley saw is ½ oz.

clean gear housing

You can thoroughly clean the gear housing with kerosene if you're careful not to let it enter the sleeve bearings. Then reassemble the saw by reversing the order of part removal.

Brushes on portable circular saws are usually accessible from outside the motor housing.

remove sawdust from vent holes

Clogged vent holes can cause overheating. Keep them free of sawdust accumulations.

■ **Router:** This is one of the simplest tools to maintain. Many have sealed ball bearings that require no further lubrication. If yours has oil holes, use a few drops of light oil in them at intervals. And check the collet that holds the bits just in case it is starting to show signs of wear. One important servicing measure: Use an air hose or pump to blow out any sawdust or chips that may have lodged in the motor.

■ **Sanders:** The attention a sander needs depends to some extent on when it was made. Many recent models require no lubrication as all bearings are sealed and permanently lubricated. Some older ones with self-lubricating bearings are much the same. The orbital model shown in the cord replacement photo has been regularly used for 25 years without lubrication. Your best bet, lacking the service manual, is to look for oil holes or fittings and oil them lightly. If brushings are visible and the tool has been in use for considerable time, light oiling is helpful.

It's wise to blow or vacuum sawdust accumulations out of the tool frequently. Check the brushes at intervals and replace them if necessary.

Stands for your power tools

By JACKSON HAND

There's valuable space going to waste under your power tools. Put it to work with these easy-to-build cabinets

SEE ALSO

Bandsaws . . . Bench saws . . . Drawers . . . Drill press techniques . . . Motors, shop . . . Plywood . . . Saws, bench . . . Table saws . . . Workbenches . . . Workshops

The four cabinet-style bases shown here have an expensive look, but actually were made at an average cost of about $30 each for plywood, nails, glue, paint and a set of husky casters.

Each of these tool stands was made of sheathing-grade plywood, which is a couple dollars cheaper per sheet than A-D plywood. The rough surface of the sheathing makes little difference, but if you like things a little smoother, use A-D plywood.

To capitalize on the 4 x 8-ft. sheet, dimensions are kept at 12, 16, 24 and 32 in. when possible. Actually these dimensions are minus half the width of a saw kerf so that a sheet will cut up, for instance, into three pieces a shy 16 in. wide.

Nails and glue are used throughout, except for fastening the drawer dividers and glides to the sidewalls of the drill-press unit. These are screwed and glued. Since there is a back (or a divider as in the case of the bandsaw base) to prevent the unit from racking, nail-and-glue assembly is sufficiently strong. Quarter-inch ply-

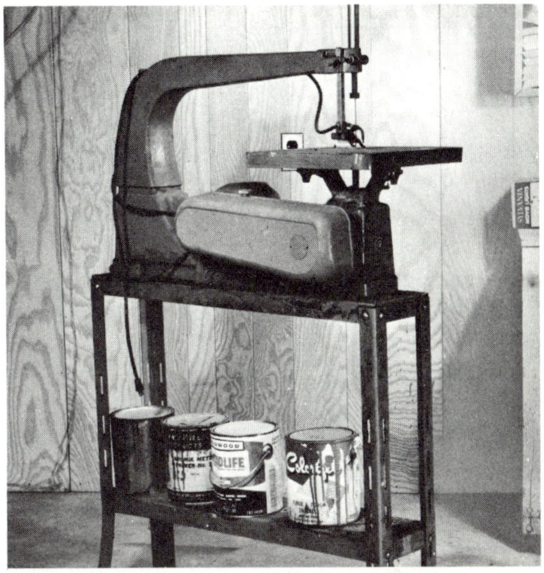

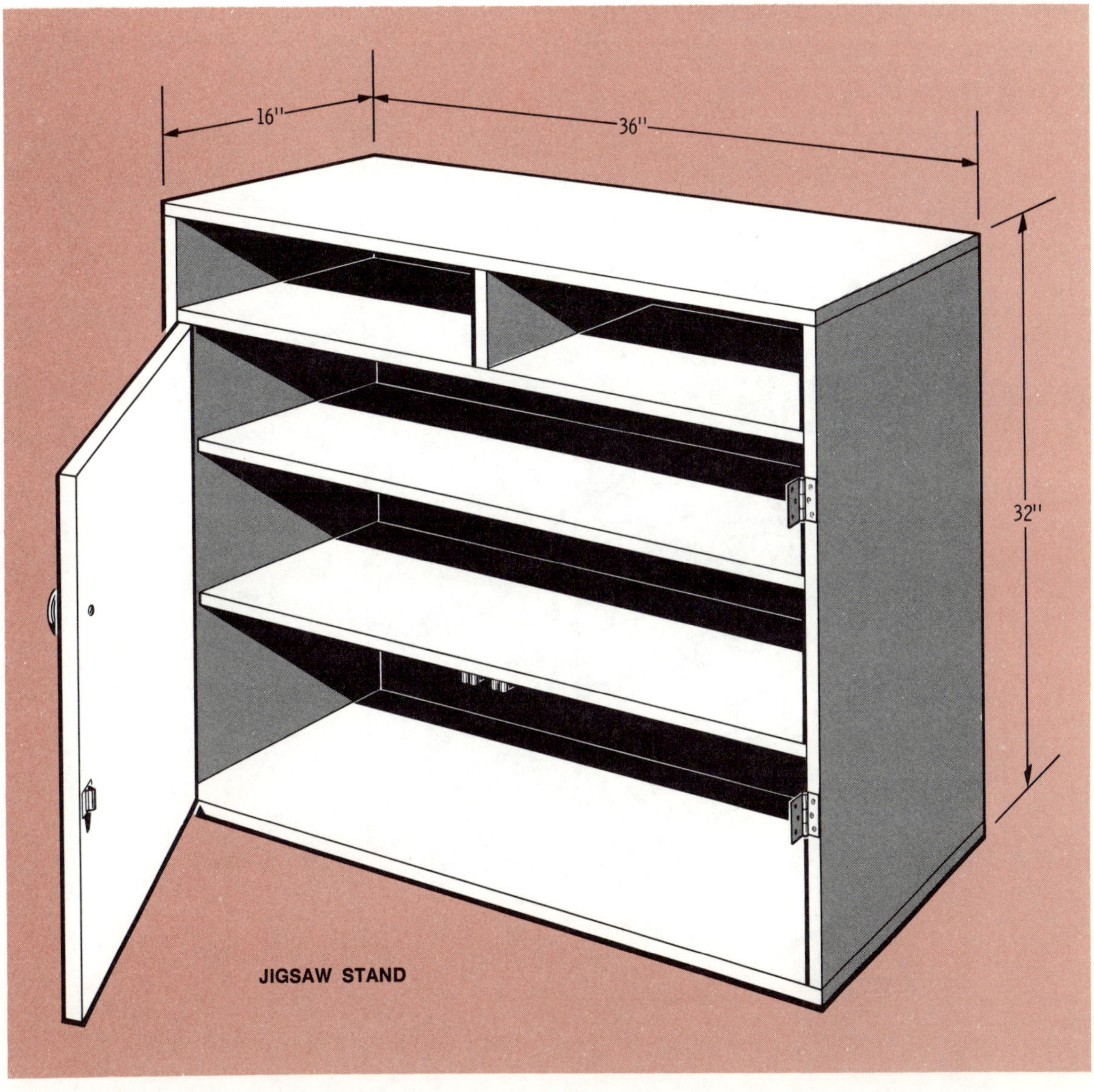

JIGSAW STAND

tool-cabinet designs, continued

wood or ⅛-in. hardboard work best for cabinet backs, drawer bottoms and dividers.

You'll thank yourself for going whole hog on the casters. If they are big enough (2-in. wheels) and well made, you'll roll tools around a concrete floor with ease. Cheap, small casters roll poorly and are blocked by the smallest sliver on the floor. For your guidance, the casters used on all the tools except the saw-jointer unit are Bassick No. 9706G-OC. The same casters were selected for the saw-jointer's cabinet-stand, but with a 2½-in. wheel.

The drill-press base is largely a "set" design for its use and its shape. You need a work surface beside a drill press for handy handling of the materials you use. The front-to-back depth (24 in.) makes it the best of the four stands for

HUSKY SWIVEL casters let stands roll easily over floor debris. Use sheet-metal screws to attach them.

DRILL-PRESS STAND

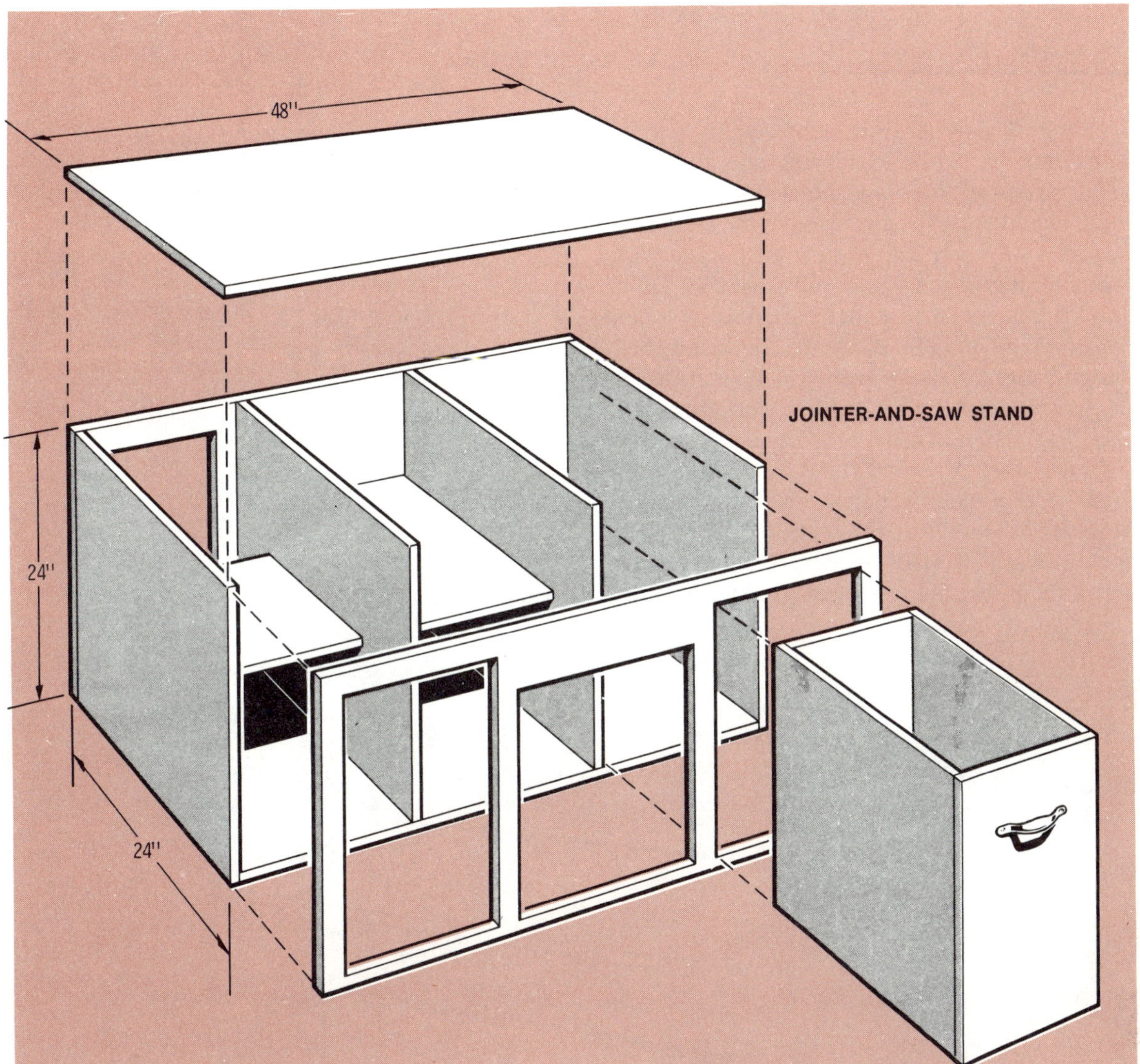

OPENINGS IN THE top of the stand to accommodate belts are cut to suit the tools. A sheet-metal chute is made to carry jointer shavings out an opening in the back.

YOUR SAW AND jointer should be side by side on a single stand. This one has storage, a sawdust bin, and a jointer chute.

JOINTER MOTOR on a hinged shelf adjusts the belt tension.

tool-cabinet designs, continued

drawers. The other three, however, can be adapted or intermixed to suit your requirements.

For instance, the open shelves of the jigsaw stand would be just as useful under the bandsaw. Or, let's say you don't want to bother with cabinet doors. Then you install plain shelf units in all the bases. As another variation, you can put doors on one side of the double-faced shelf design under the bandsaw to provide storage for things you want to shelter from workshop dust and dirt.

Got a lathe? A perfect stand for it would be a three-section modification of the jigsaw stand. Make it 5 ft. long (20 in. to a section) and the open shelves will be perfect for lathe tools. You can get at them, but they are protected from burial under lathe shavings.

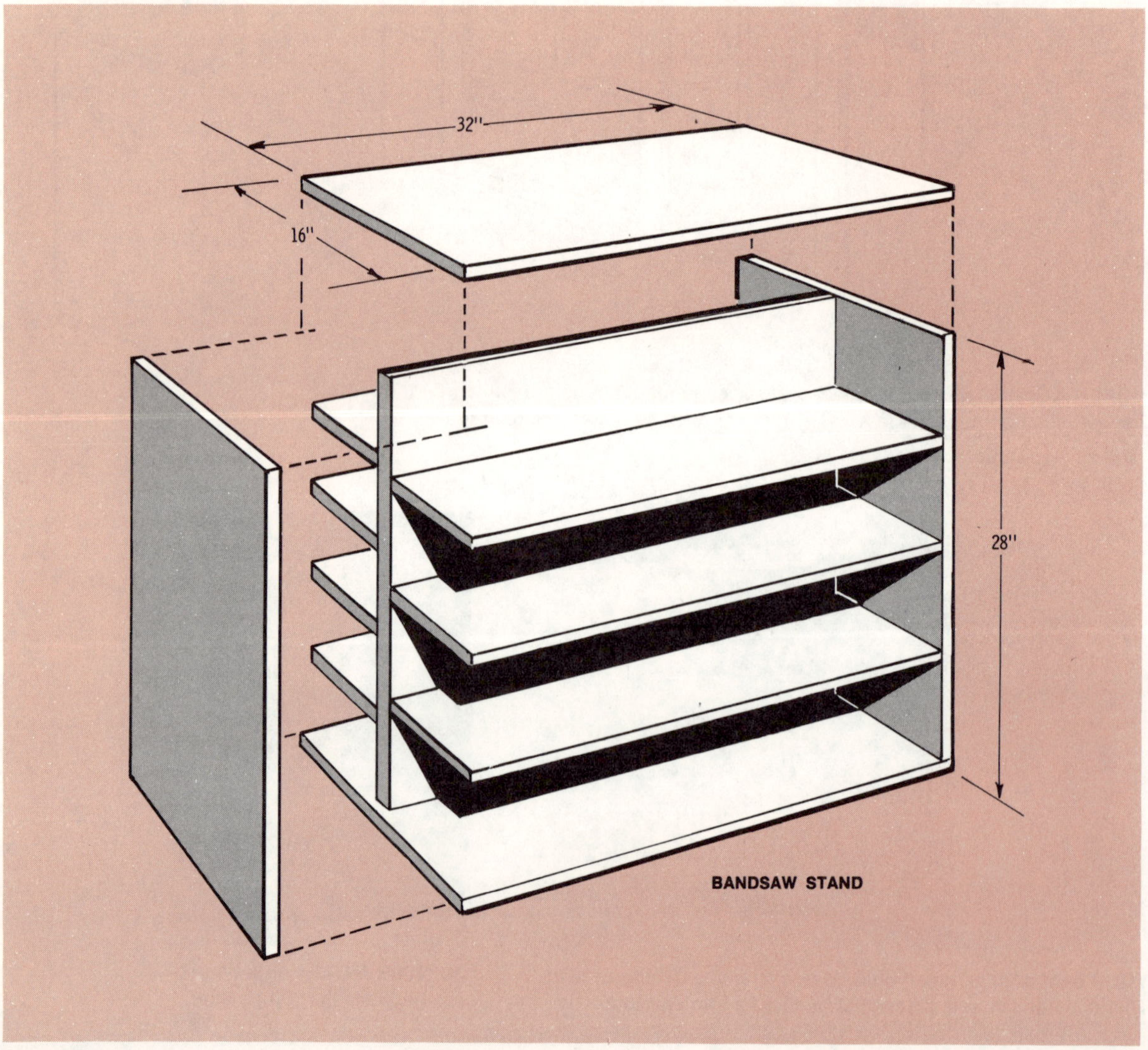

BANDSAW STAND

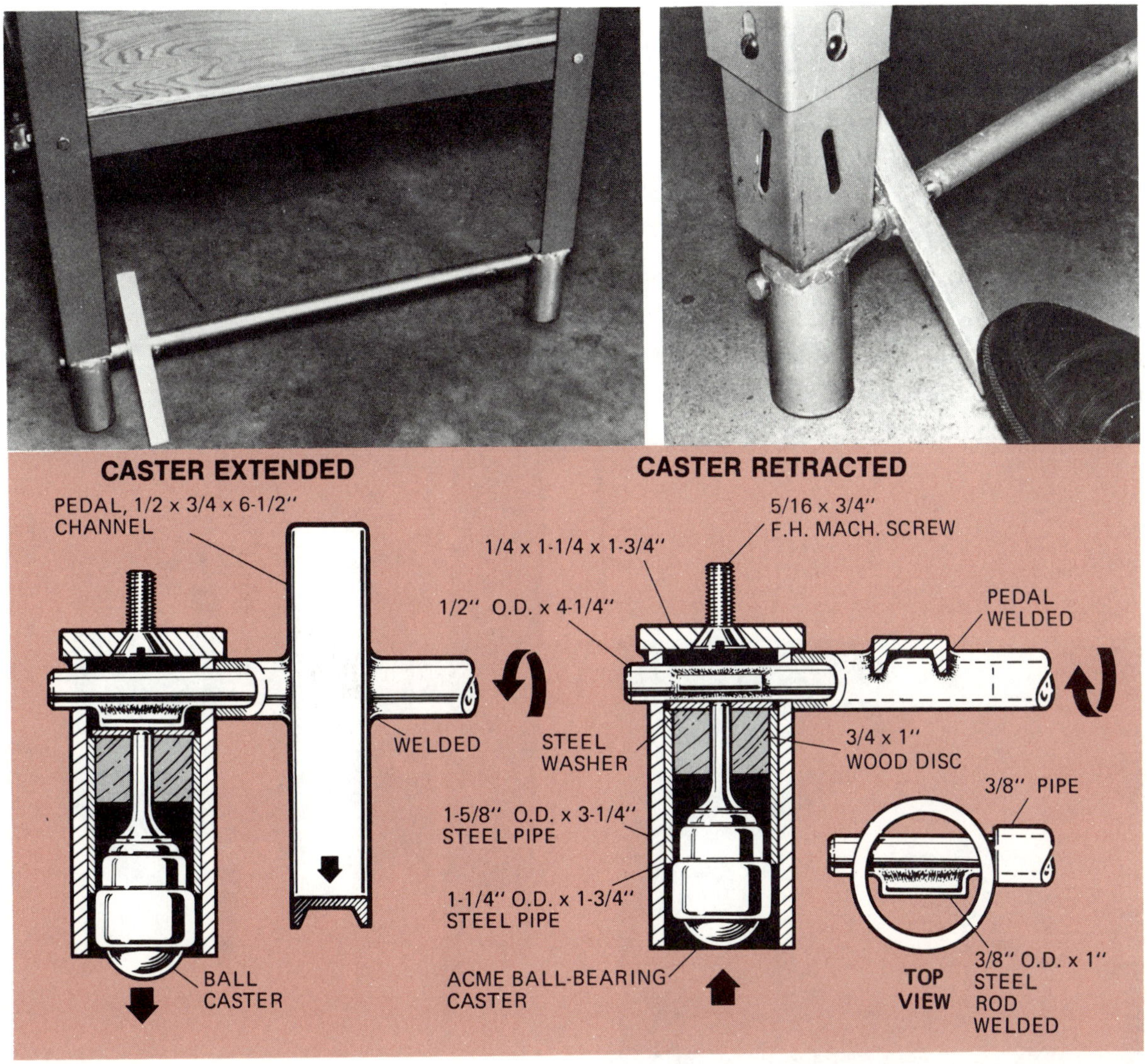

Retractable casters for your tool stands

By WILLIAM G. WAGGONER

■ TIRED OF PUSHING, shoving and groaning every time a piece of shop equipment needs moving across the room? Then picture yourself depressing a foot pedal and rolling the tool effortlessly. By making the retractable-type caster set shown in the drawings above, you can enjoy such shop convenience. When the lever is depressed, the ball casters are forced out of their sockets and locked in a ready-to-roll position. This retractable caster is easy to make—there is no machining called for, yet it's quick-acting and positive. And, as shown in the photos, one pedal activates the pair of casters. Basically, the idea is simply a fit of 1-in. pipe into 1¼-in. pipe, and the use of a 1-in.-dia. ball caster which seats neatly into the smaller pipe. The trade name of the caster used is Acme. While one set of casters is adequate for a radial or table saw it's best to have a caster on each leg of the stand to save your back.

SEE ALSO

Bandsaws . . . Bench saws . . . Drill press techniques . . . Motors, shop . . . Power hacksaws . . . Radial-arm saws . . . Shapers . . . Table saws . . . Workbenches . . . Workshops

Roll-away stand holds router and drill

By PAUL D. FIEBICH

Since it is on wheels, you can take this handy unit right to the job. In addition to holding a portable drill stand and router table, the cabinet features a sawdust chute and storage space

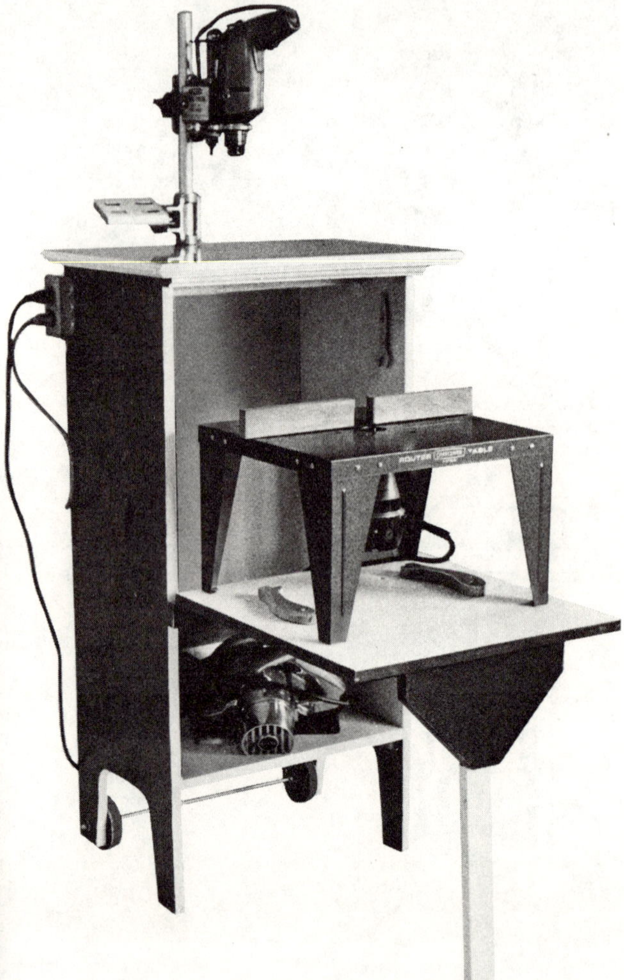

THE WHEELS on the rear legs of the unit let you roll this mini-workshop to the job or stow it away in a corner when you want it out of the way. It's just the thing for a handyman with limited space.

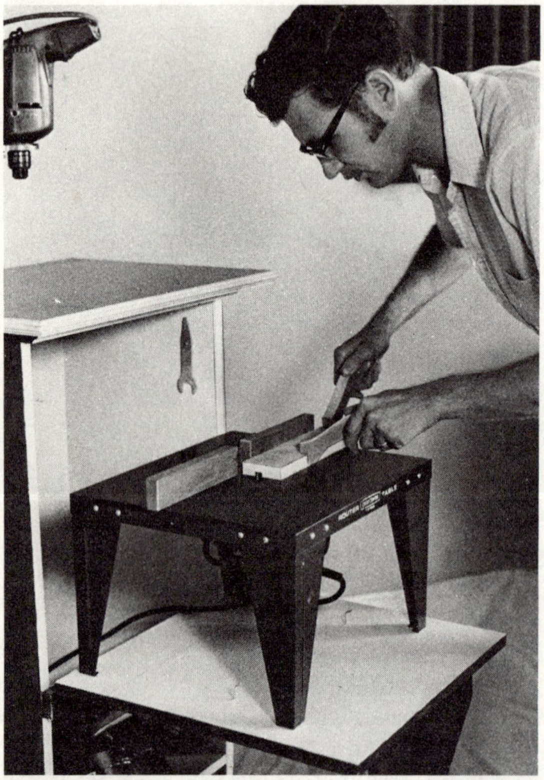

STEEL ROUTER table, bolted to a hinged shelf, converts router into a handy shaper. The table retracts and stores in the cabinet when you use drill.

SEE ALSO

Belt sanders . . . Circular saws, portable . . . Drills, portable . . . Pad sanders . . . Routers . . . Sanders, belt . . . Workbenches

■ DESIGNED SO YOU can wheel it about like a hand truck, this compact tool cabinet provides a dandy place to mount a portable-drill stand and a portable router table. What's more, there is an open shelf below where you can store a sabre saw, circular saw and finishing sander. For the man whose "workshop" consists mainly of portable electric tools, you won't find a handier setup anywhere.

Bolted to a shelf, the router table retracts into the cabinet when the shelf and supporting leg are swung upward, and a built-in sheet-metal chute funnels wood chips from the router to a catch

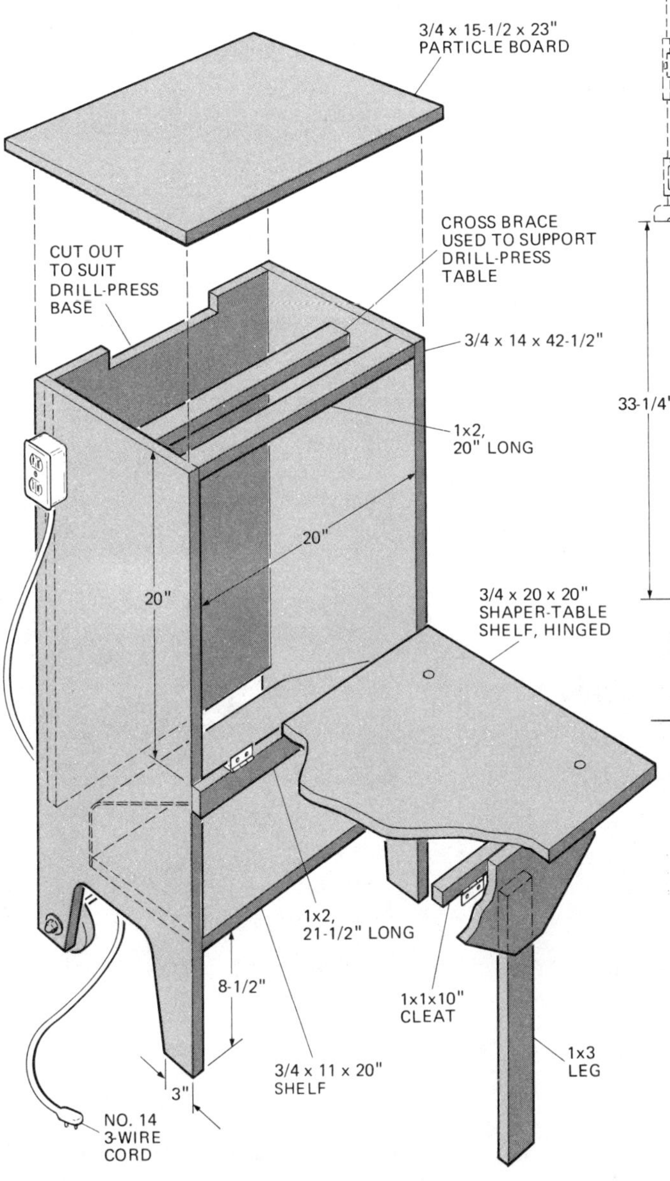

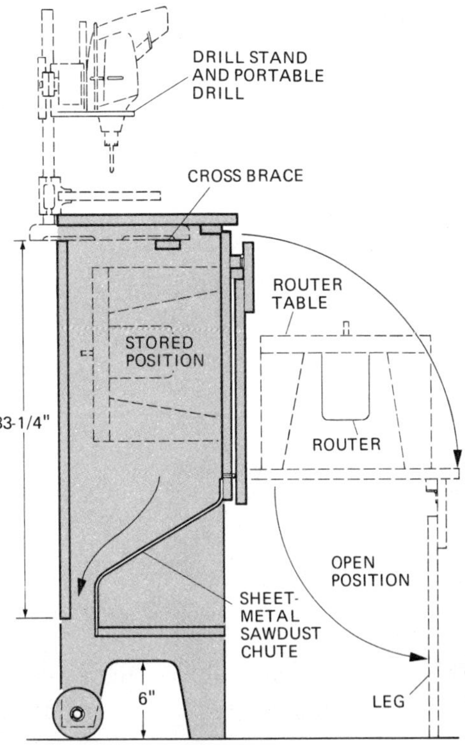

SIDE VIEW
(SIDE REMOVED)

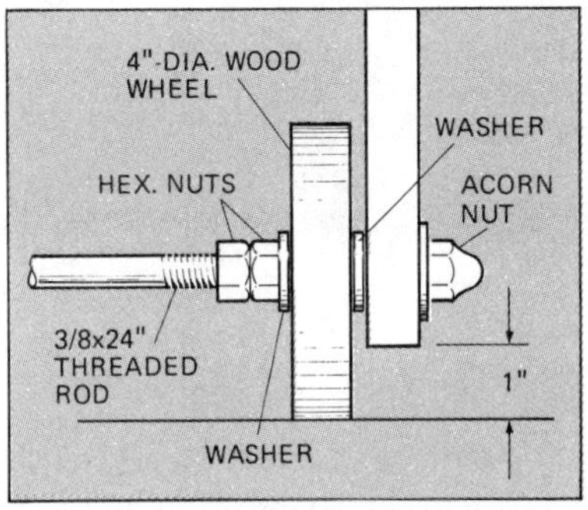

box at the rear. With the base of the drill stand anchored below the cabinet's top, the latter offers a king-size drill-press "table."

I designed the cabinet for my Shopmate drill, Sears drill stand and Sears router table, although it can be made to suit other makes of tools. While I used ¾-in.-thick particle board, the cabinet can be made of fir plywood. Both ends of the cabinet are alike and are nailed to a 20x34¼-in. back, an 11x20-in. bottom shelf and a 1x2 top rail 20 in. long. A second cross rail 20 in. down from the top supports the sheet-metal chute at the front. The 4-in. wheels and supporting ⅜-in. axle must be in place, of course, as side members are glued and nailed.

The supporting leg for the router-table shelf is hinged to a 1x1 cleat glued and screwed to the front face of the shelf, then the shelf itself is hinged to the top edge of the 1x2 cross rail.

The side-view drawing shows how the base of the drill-press stand rests in a notch cut in the back panel and is bolted to a cross brace installed between the end members of the cabinet. A surface-mounted duplex receptacle on one side of the cabinet fitted with a 6-ft. cord provides a plug.

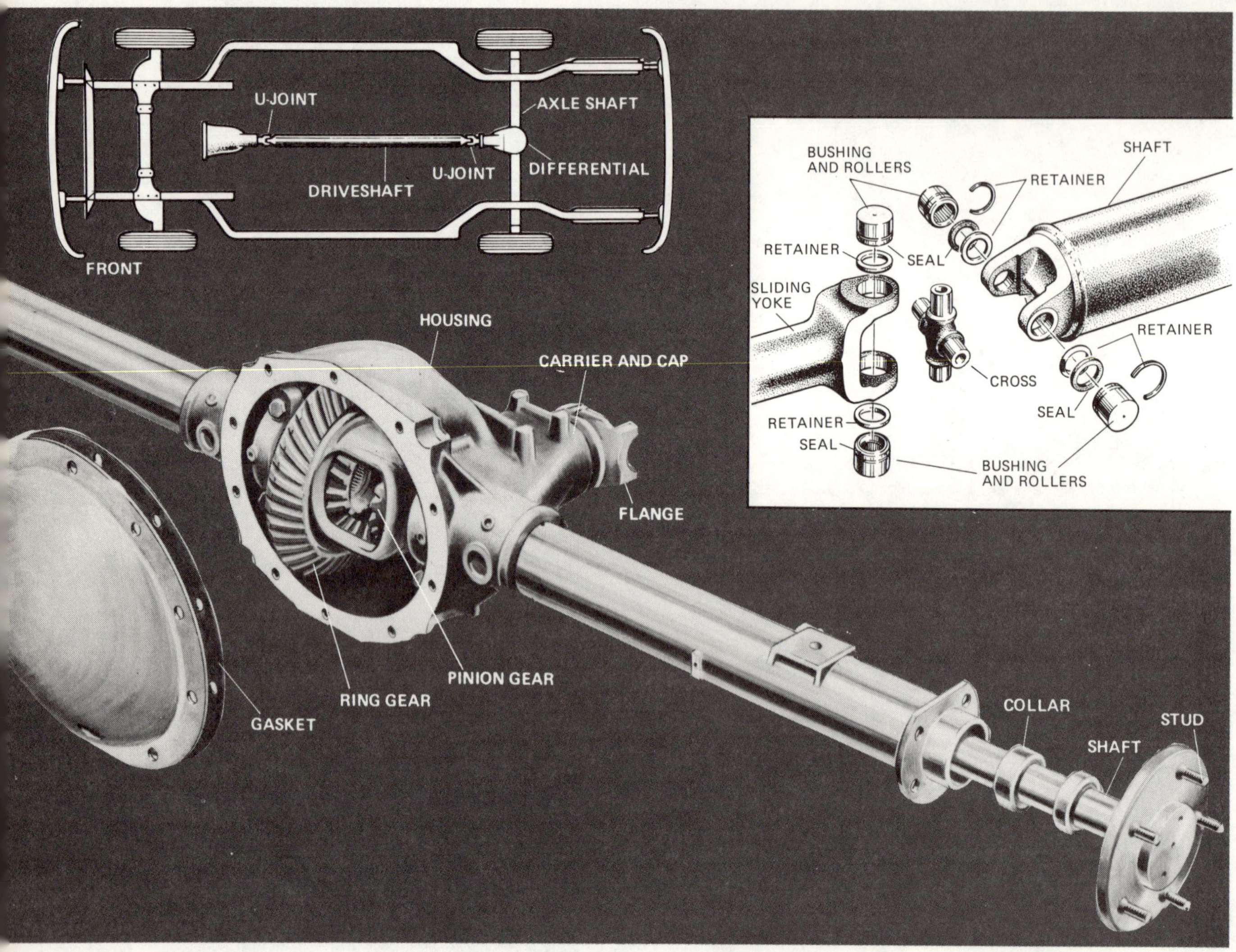

How to diagnose power-train noise

■ THE POWER TRAIN of cars with rear-wheel drive consists of an engine, clutch and manual transmission, or automatic transmission, propeller shaft, universal joints, and rear-drive train composed of a differential, axle shafts and axle-shaft bearings. In a discussion of power-train noise, front suspension and tire/wheel assemblies, although not parts of the power train, have to be considered when discussing noise problems.

The power train of cars with front-wheel drive consists of an engine and a front transaxle made up of a clutch and manual transmission, or an automatic transmission, front differential driveshafts and shaft bearings. There are no propeller shaft, universal joints or rear-drive train. However, tire/wheel assemblies, although not parts of the power train, have to be considered when discussing noise problems.

There are thousands of individual parts contained in the power trains of a rear-wheel or front-wheel-drive vehicle. Most parts emit noise when they fail. However, trying to put a finger on the problem area is frequently difficult because power-train noise is elusive.

For example, noise that seems to be coming from the rear-drive train of a rear-wheel-drive automobile may, in fact, be coming from the propeller shaft, transmission, tires or even the engine. Making snap judgments can lead to unnecessary, expensive repairs. Finding the source is the most important step in correcting a noise condition.

Troubleshooting power train noise is a Saturday mechanic's job and procedures outlined here are intended to help. However, repairs are another matter.

In some instances, you should be able to make repairs yourself, as you

SEE ALSO
Engines, auto . . . Lubrication, auto . . . Motor oil . . . Noises, auto . . . Noises, auto engine . . . Transmissions, auto . . . Tune-up, auto

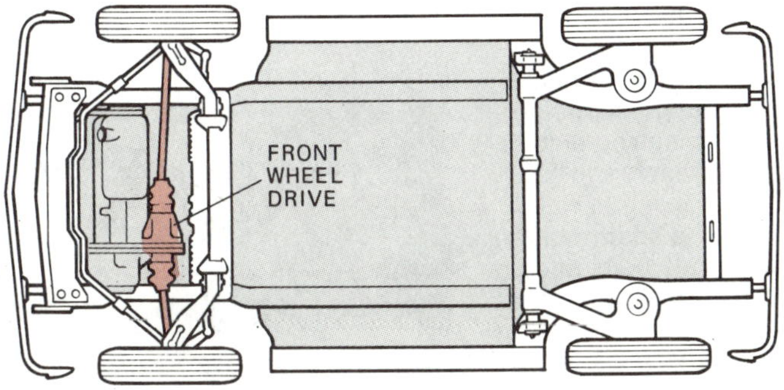

FRONT-WHEEL-drive cars lack drive-shaft; all power train components are up front.

will see by reviewing the repair information. In other cases, repairs cannot be made without doing a major overhaul.

Troubleshooting rear-drive train noise

The majority of noise complaints deal with suspected rear-drive train noise in rear-wheel-drive cars. The following procedure will help determine if the noise you hear is coming from the rear or elsewhere:

1. Remove the rear axle (differential) filler hole plug. If the plug is recessed, use a special wrench available from a parts and accessories dealer.

2. Check the differential lubricant level by inserting your pinkie. Lube should be no more than ½-inch below the filler hole. Add lubricant, if necessary.

Use only lubricant recommended by the manufacturer (consult the maintenance guide in the service manual). Recommendations differ according to climate (lighter-weight lubricants for colder climates) and the type of differential. Antispin (positraction) rear axles require an additive or special lubricant. A suction-type lubricating gun can be obtained to fill and drain differentials.

3. Find a smooth tar or asphalt road, and drive the car for 20 minutes to warm up the differential. Then start from a stop, increasing speed gradually. Note the speedometer or tachometer reading at which noise is loudest.

4. Analyze the noise.

■ Differential gear noise is most pronounced when the car is accelerating, cruising or coasting 30–40 mph and 50–60 mph. If noise isn't heard at these speeds, dismiss malfunctioning rear-axle gears as the source.

Differentials make some noise, which automotive engineers call the "commercially acceptable noise level." This light sound—more like a tone than a noise—is normal. It occurs within a narrow band between 40 and 60 mph. If the tone is there, it's going to stay there.

■ Rear-axle shaft bearing noise is a growl or grating sound. However, a bad front-wheel bearing sounds the same.

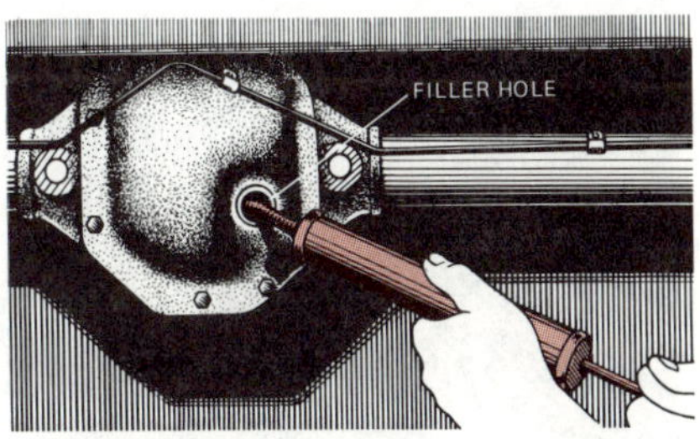

SUCTION-TYPE lubricating gun is used to fill and drain differentials.

To pinpoint the source of a bad bearing, accelerate the car to 60 mph, turn off the ignition and shift the transmission to neutral. Swerve the car from side to side, so the load on the rear switches from one wheel to the other. If the growling or grating noise becomes amplified, a bad rear-axle shaft bearing exists.

Confirm the existence of front-wheel bearing noise by jacking up the front wheels. Spin each wheel and listen for noise. Shake the wheels. A loose wheel indicates a loose (noisy) front-wheel bearing.

5. With the car standing still, and the transmission in neutral, increase engine speed until it reaches the range at which the noise was loudest during the road test. If you hear noise, look to the engine or exhaust system as the source.

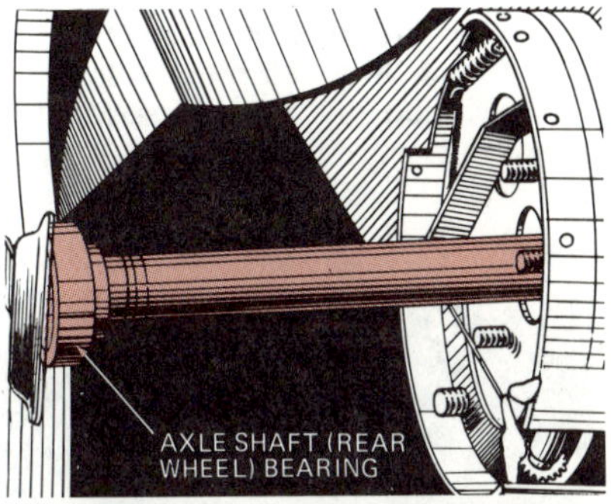

TO REPLACE an axle-shaft bearing, unhook and slide shaft from differential.

6. To check the clutch, keep the transmission in neutral, run engine speed up to the noise range as you engage and disengage the clutch. If you hear noise, a bad clutch part probably exists.

7. To check on the transmission as a cause of noise, disconnect the propeller shaft from the transmission output shaft and increase engine speed to the noise range, with the transmission in high gear. Noise? Look in the transmission.

8. Noise made by tires can be distinguished from rear-axle noise by driving the car on a different road surface. If the pitch changes, tires are the noisemakers. If the pitch stays the same, suspect the rear axle. You can also check tires by temporarily increasing tire pressure to 50 pounds. Noise made by tires will be noticeably altered, but rear-axle noise will continue as before.

Rear-drive train repair

If lubricant level is low because of a leak around the differential cover, do not drive the car until repairs are made. Low lubricant is the main cause of differential failure.

To repair a leaking case caused by a bad gasket, do this:

1. Disconnect the propeller shaft from the differential universal-joint flange (see below, *Replacing A Universal Joint*).

2. Remove the differential cover bolts. Place a pan under the differential to catch lubricant and snap the cover loose.

3. Clean the flanges of the differential case and cover. Remove all pieces of old gasket material and sealer. When flanges are clean, wipe them dry.

4. Apply gasket sealer to the flange of the differential case and press on the gasket. Then apply sealer to the face of the gasket. Install the cover and torque bolts to the specification in the service manual, which is probably 25–30 foot-pounds.

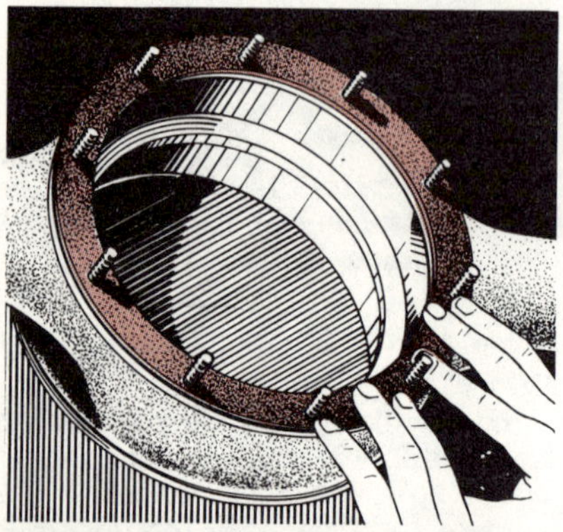

APPLY sealer and press new gasket firmly into place; install cover.

Rear-axle overhaul and replacement of axle bearings are jobs most people leave to a mechanic. However, before having a mechanic replace ring and pinion gears, be certain rear axle noise isn't being made by a worn drive pinion bearing. Replacing the ring and pinion costs about $150 more than replacing a drive pinion bearing.

If the mechanic replaces the ring and pinion, he should adjust ring-to-pinion backlash. Excessive, or insufficient backlash causes early failure. Generally, a ring-to-pinion backlash adjustment of .005 to .009 inch is called for. Backlash is adjusted by adding or subtracting shims, or by adjusting nuts.

Propeller shaft, U-joints

A bad propeller shaft won't make noise, but causes vehicle vibration. Universal joints that are about to fail emit a clunking noise, which is apparent at low speeds.

To verify that a universal joint is going bad, drive the car between 5 and 10 mph with the transmission in high gear. If clunking is pronounced, put the car on a lift and grasp the propeller shaft near each universal joint. Try rocking the shaft back and forth. It should not move.

If there is play in the shaft, tighten the universal joint flange bolts and do another road test. If noise isn't caused by loose flange bolts, replace the universal joint. Driving a car with a bad universal joint will eventually cause the propeller shaft to break loose, possibly causing loss of control.

Replacing a universal joint

1. Raise the car.

2. Use a file to scribe a mark across the rear universal joint flange and the differential companion flange. This is done to assure correct propeller shaft alignment when the shaft is reinstalled.

UP FRONT, draw propeller shaft to rear, away from transmission shaft.

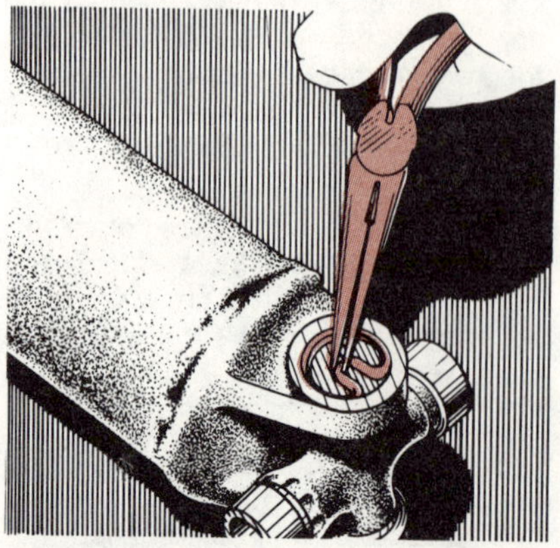

PULL bearing cap snap-ring retainers, if present, to release hold on U-joint.

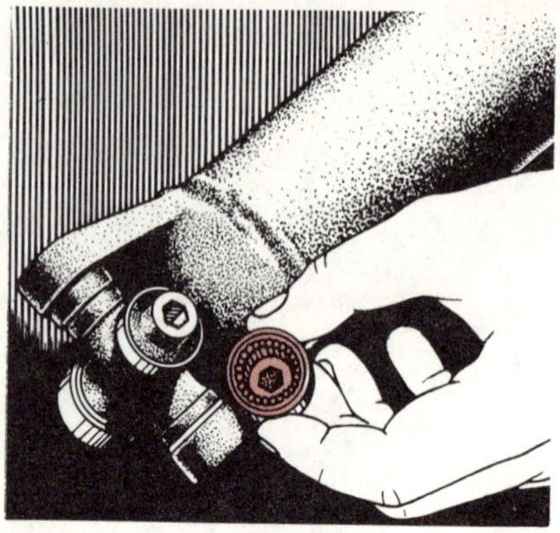

INSIDES of caps have bearings that are weak link of U-joint assemblies.

3. Remove the propeller shaft by removing the rear universal joint flange bolts and sliding the shaft off the transmission output shaft.

4. Place the propeller shaft on a workbench with the end possessing the suspected defective universal joint mounted in a vise. Do not tighten the vice forcefully, since you may damage the shaft. Use it to hold the shaft steady. Place the other end of the shaft on supports to keep the shaft level.

5. If the universal joint bearing cap has a snap-ring retainer, pull the retainer out with a pair of long-nose pliers. Tap around the outside of the bearing cap with a hammer until the cap pops loose. Slide the universal joint from the propeller shaft yoke.

If the universal joint bearing cap does not have a snap-ring connector, get a piece of pipe large enough to encircle the cap. Place the pipe over the cap and hit the end of the pipe with a hammer. This breaks the bearing cap retainer loose, forcing the retainer and cap from the propeller shaft yoke. Rotate the propeller shaft and remove the other cap, using the same method. When the two bearing caps have been removed, slide the universal joint cross assembly from the propeller shaft yoke.

6. Install the new universal joint by sliding the cross assembly into the propeller shaft yoke. Press on the bearing caps. Then, seat the caps securely by tapping them in place with a soft-faced hammer.

7. Install the propeller shaft, seeing that the reference mark on the universal joint flange lines up with the reference mark on the differential companion flange. Install and tighten the universal joint flange bolts as tightly as possible.

Noisy automatic transmission

Noise from an automatic transmission usually indicates the need for repair. However, as with differential gear noise, automatic transmissions emit a "commercially acceptable noise level." This noise is a low-key whine that increases in intensity as the car accelerates in first gear. Once the transmission shifts to a higher gear, the pitch of the whine drops.

Noise other than a low-pitch whine is not normal. This includes a click, knock, scrape or shrill whine. The noise may be coming from the vacuum modulator or torque converter.

A word about modulators

If a vacuum modulator valve is present in your transmission, it is screwed into the transmission housing and connected to the carburetor by a vacuum tube. Most automatic transmissions use a vacuum modulator valve.

A modulator valve that fails causes the transmission to shift harshly or erratically and may produce noise. Since a modulator valve is relatively inexpensive, replace it at the first sign or transmission trouble. If you are lucky, no further repair will be necessary.

To replace the modulator valve, raise the car, remove the vacuum tube and unscrew the modulator valve and spring-and-pin assembly. Retain the spring-and-pin assembly to use with the new modulator valve. When the new valve has been installed, check the automatic transmission fluid level, since some fluid may have been lost when you removed the old valve.

Torque converters

A loose or cracked torque converter can make a knocking, clicking or scraping noise. Isolate noise to the converter by raising the car, placing the transmission in gear and having someone accelerate the engine to simulate the speed at which noise occurs. Place your ear at the torque converter and then at the transmission to pinpoint the source.

If it is the torque converter, remove the converter cover. Make sure converter plate bolts are tight. Rotate the converter plate and look for cracks in the plate. Replace a cracked one.

Noise inside the transmission indicates the unit will have to be overhauled.

Clutch noise

The purpose of a clutch is to disconnect the engine from the transmission as gears are being shifted, and to permit the engine to start and run. If an engine remained coupled to the transmission, it wouldn't attain starting speed because of resistance imposed by the transmission. A running engine in a stationary car must remain detached from the transmission, or the resistance imposed on the engine by the transmission will cause the engine to stall.

When the clutch is engaged and the car is put in motion, the clutch employs friction to drive the engine and transmission as a unit. A pressure plate and a clutch disc are the two main parts of a clutch assembly. The pressure plate is attached to the engine flywheel, while the clutch disc is located between the flywheel and pressure plate. The clutch disc drives the clutch shaft, also called the throwout bearing shaft. It couples the clutch and transmission.

The clutch disc is the key element. It possesses a layer of friction material on both sides. When the clutch is engaged, heavy torsion springs force the clutch disc, flywheel and pressure plate firmly together. The three parts act as one as they rotate. Engine torque is thus able to be transmitted from the flywheel, through the clutch, to the transmission.

When the clutch is disengaged (clutch pedal depressed), a part called the clutch fork applies pressure to a clutch release bearing, (also called the throwout bearing). This bearing rotates against, and puts pressure on, the clutch release levers. The clutch release levers, in turn, compress clutch springs. This action forces the pressure plate to the rear, disengaging the pressure plate from the flywheel. The two then rotate independently, as the clutch disc and clutch shaft become stationary.

There are several different kinds of clutches, but all work pretty much the same. A major difference is whether they are dry or wet.

Dry clutches, which have graphite coatings that act as a lubricant, are used in cars and light trucks. Some dry clutches, especially those in imported vehicles, employ a hydraulic assist that acts similarly to the booster of a power braking system.

One type of hydraulic assist forces fluid from a master cylinder into the clutch housing. The oil presses against a piston, which applies pressure to a series of discs that are connected to the clutch disc. The disc turns and power is transmitted to the transmission.

Heavier vehicles generally use a wet clutch, which should not be confused with clutches employing hydraulic assist. Wet clutches supply oil to the clutch for lubrication.

Clutch problems

Noise coming from the clutch usually warns of a broken or rough-running component, such as a pitted or chewed up throwout bearing, broken clutch lever or fork, broken torsion spring, cracked or loose clutch disc. To resolve clutch noise, and the problem it suggests, the assembly must be overhauled or replaced.

Most clutch problems involve a clutch that slips or drags. A clutch that slips is characterized by car speed that doesn't keep pace with engine speed. The car lacks power, especially when going uphill.

To determine if a clutch is slipping, park the car on level ground and let the engine idle. Set the parking brake, depress the clutch pedal and shift the transmission into first gear. Press down on the accelerator pedal gradually while you slowly release the clutch pedal. The engine should stall. If the engine doesn't stall, the clutch is slipping. A slipping clutch is caused by lack of clutch pedal free-play, worn clutch disc face, oil- or grease-contaminated clutch disc face, weak clutch springs, or pressure plate or flywheel runout. Runout refers to a nonconcentric condition.

Clutch pedal free-play adjustment is the only service a clutch requires. Free play refers to the amount of movement in the clutch pedal before the clutch disc engages.

Wear of the clutch disc is normal. As a clutch disc wears, the amount of free play is reduced. If specified free play isn't maintained, wear will be hastened.

Free play should be adjusted periodically, as specified by the maker. The adjustment differs from car to car, so see your service manual.

A dragging clutch makes noise. To determine if a clutch is dragging, keep the clutch pedal pressed to the floor and press the accelerator pedal halfway. Shift into gear. If there is a grinding noise, the clutch is dragging.

Clutch drag is caused by excessive free play, weak or worn torsion springs, bad throwout bearing or a warped clutch disc.

Noisy manual transmissions

A noisy manual transmission often signifies a problem requiring major overhaul. A gear or bearing may be broken, or the main shaft spline could be worn.

Manual transmission noise could also mean that there isn't enough lubricant in the gearbox. Many owners don't pay attention to the lubrication requirements of a manual transmission. This is a mistake. A manual transmission should be kept filled with lubricant of the correct viscosity to avert damage.

Consult the lubrication guide for your car to determine the recommended lubricant. Remove the filler plug of the transmission case. If lubricant level is below the bottom of the filler hole, add sufficient lubricant to bring the level to the bottom of the hole.

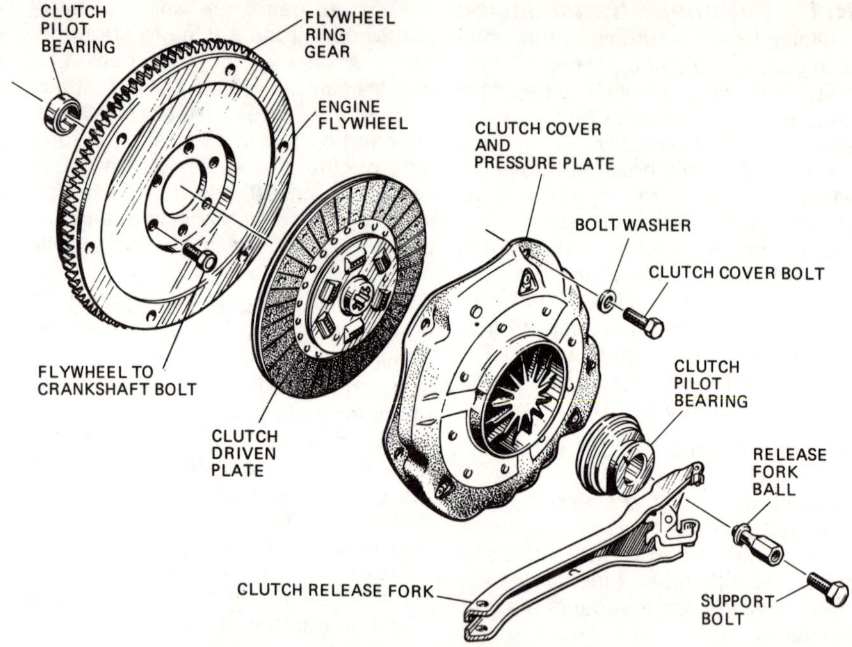

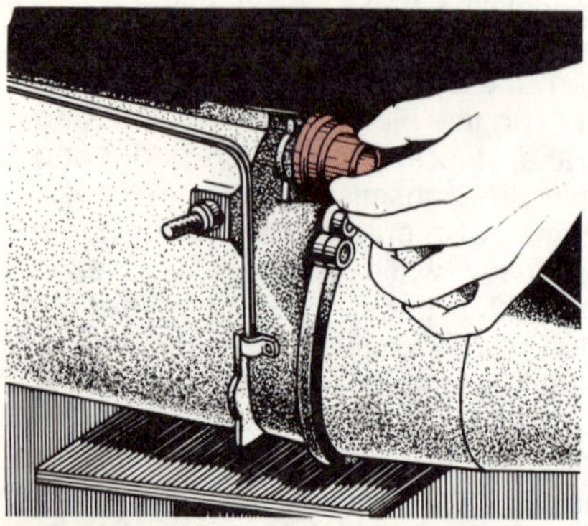

TRANSMISSION vacuum modulator valve is often cause of many shifting problems.

Engine noise

Engine noise can be a click, rap, thump, whine, rattle, slap, chuck or thud. Noise can be loud, faint, sharp, dull, intermittent or constant. It can occur when the engine is cold, warm, under load, on acceleration, or deceleration, at idle or when cruising.

The best way to analyze engine noise is by frequency. There are four categories.

1. Noise that occurs once every revolution.
2. Noise every cycle (two revolutions).
3. Noise that occurs intermittently, without apparent relation to engine revolutions.
4. Noise that occurs continuously.

Use a neon sparkplug tester to establish the frequency of engine noise. Be sure engine oil level is at the FULL mark on the dipstick. Warm the engine to operating temperature and connect the neon tester to one of the sparkplugs. With the engine idling, notice whether engine noise occurs once or twice for each flash of the tester or if there is no relationship.

If noise occurs twice for each flash (once every revolution), it is caused by some part driven by or driving the crankshaft, including pistons, piston rings, piston pins, crankpins and main journals.

If noise occurs once for each flash (once each cycle), it results from a part driven by the camshaft. In this category are valves, valve-related components (springs or stems), fuel pump, distributor or camshaft gear.

If the noise has no relationship to the flashing of the neon spark-plug tester, it is being caused by some component which has no relationship to the rotation of the crankshaft or camshaft. Included in this category are parts attached to the engine, such as the alternator, starter and distributor. You have a better chance of isolating noise to one of these components by using an engine stethoscope or a length of garden hose. Place the stethoscope or hose on the suspected parts and place the other end at your ear. Loud noise indicates the defective component.

Continuous noise is either a whine or rubbing sound that is caused by a rotating part. A constant whine is usually produced by a defective timing gear, oil pump drive or distributor drive. The flywheel may cause a rubbing sound.

To further isolate engine noise, short out each cylinder. With the engine idling, use a pair of insulated sparkplug cable pliers to pull the cable from each plug, in turn. If the noise stops, the problem is located in that cylinder.

Front-wheel-drive noise

The presence of noise in the front axle of front-wheel-drive vehicles is normally confirmed by the presence of an instability and/or steering-wheel shimmy condition. Noises are usually grinding or grating sounds, which distinguish them from engine noise.

The most common causes of noise in the front axle assembly are:

- Worn, loose or seized driveshaft ball joint.
- Worn, loose or seized wheel bearing.
- Too much play in the driveshaft and differential side gear serrations.
- Too much play in the driveshaft and hub serrations.

Noise and accompanying instability and/or steering-wheel shimmy normally mean the front axle has to be overhauled. However, before doing this make sure your mechanic determines that the noise is not the result of a front suspension problem. Lubricate the chassis. If this doesn't get rid of noise, check the strut suspension components (coil springs and bushings) for damage.

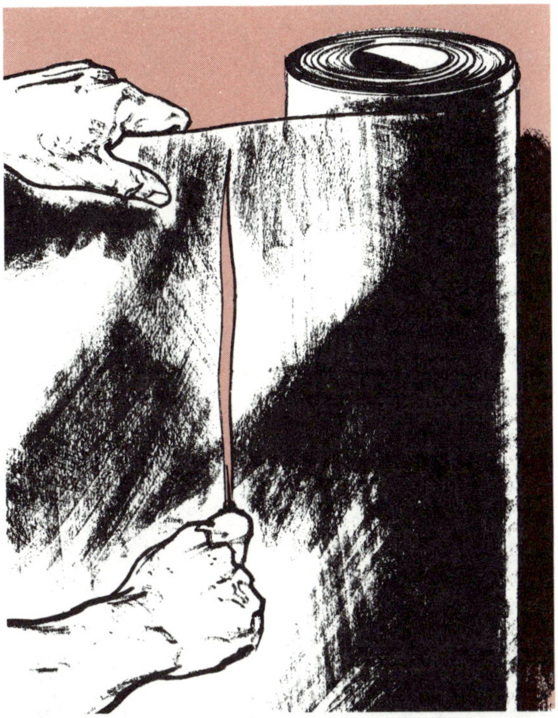

PLAY IT SMART the next time you cut a piece from a roll of paper by starting the cut a couple of inches down from the top. The uncut portion will support the piece as it's cut so it won't droop and tear.

PLASTIC SOAKER HOSE is a better protector than regular garden hose when bracing young trees with guy wires. Being green, it blends better with the tree, and being flat, it "molds" around the trunk.

A FOLDING SHELF on a stepladder can be locked in its open position by adding a screen-door hook and eye to each side. You'll find they prevent the shelf from tipping and stabilize the ladder itself.

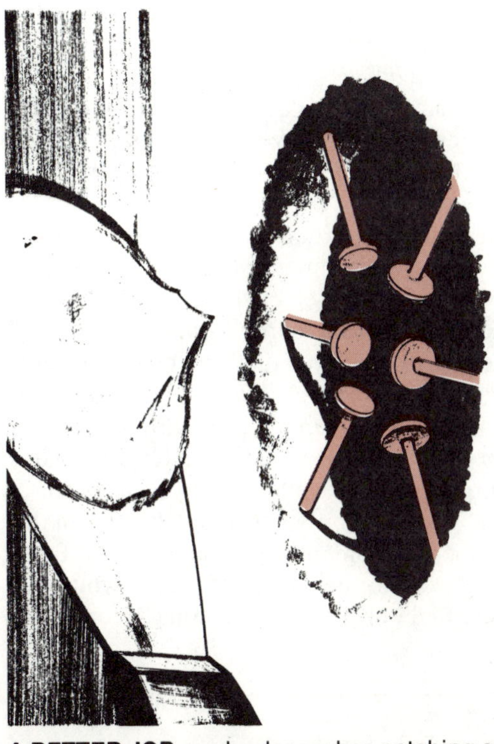

A BETTER JOB can be done when patching a hole with spackling compound if you first ring the hole with nails as shown. Radiating like spokes of a wheel, the nails will help anchor the plaster patch.

How to cure muddy photo prints

By IVAN BERGER

■ PRINTS FROM other photographers pour across my desk each month—and surprisingly many of them, even when the contributors are professionals, are muddy, murky, dull and lifeless. There are mere grays where there should be blacks, and the whites appear to be seen in dim light through a dirty window. Yet the causes and cures of muddiness are easy to understand. I should know—in the years since I started printing (when I was 11), I've had to find out every cure in the book, because I've made most of the blunders.

The first step, of course, is to look closely at your prints. I'm convinced that the reason so many people try to sell or show off muddy work is because they're so carried away by the image of the picture itself that they can't take an objective look at how horribly that image is displayed. So take that look: A good print virtually always has at least one spot of pure, rich black, and one of pure, sparkling white to set off its range of middle tones. If you've deliberately broken this rule, fine—presumably you had a reason. But if your prints accidentally lack true whites or blacks, find out what you're doing wrong.

SEE ALSO

Cameras . . . Darkrooms . . . Developing, photo . . . Dryers, photo . . . Filters, photo . . . Photography . . . Used cameras

First, look at your negatives. If they don't cover the full range of tones, from a few, almost black spots of highlight to a few spots of shadow that are almost clear with a wide range of gray tones in between, you'll have trouble getting a good print.

When you take the picture, make sure you expose correctly, then follow the manufacturer's developing times and temperatures *exactly*. Adjust the exposure index setting of your light meter, setting the meter to a slightly higher than normal film speed if your films are

1

4

2

5

3

GOOD PRINT (far left), has a wide tonal range, from white to black and all gray tones between. Muddy prints above are caused by: (1) overexposure, underdevelopment; (2) too-low paper contrast; (3) thin negative over-exposed in printing for deeper blacks; (4) thin negative underexposed for cleaner whites; (5) thin negative "saved" as far as possible by contrasty No. 4 paper—but still a bit flat and muddy because of deficiencies in the negative.

consistently overexposed or setting it a bit lower if you normally underexpose negatives.

But most muddy prints are made from negatives that could yield better prints with better work. One of the easiest temptations to bad workmanship is to overexpose and underdevelop the print. In our impatience to see the picture, it's easy to blast a print with so much light that an image will pop into view as soon as the developer hits the paper, or to pull a print out of the developer when it begins to "look all right" under the safelight, even if the entire recommended developing time (usually about a minute) hasn't yet gone by. Unfortunately, that doesn't give the developer time to work evenly and thoroughly on the whole print. As a result, the prints are muddy and often mottled with poor highlight detail.

A second temptation—letting underexposed prints linger in the developer in hopes that they'll somehow improve—will only give you fog, stain, a lack of highlight detail, or all three at once. Never try to make up in development for a gross exposure error. If you have to change development times more than 20 or 30 seconds from the recommended time, remake the print with another exposure (stabilization printing, which gives you no leeway to fool around with processing time, is a great teacher of exposure discipline).

IMPROPER INSPECTION—raising the print from the tray—lets developer run off or oxidize, causing blotchy, uneven development, contrast loss and stains. The proper technique is to hold the print just below the developer surface.

use the correct exposure

And make sure you have *exactly* the right exposure—often an exposure difference of only 10 or 20 percent can turn a merely adequate print into a good one, or vice versa. Your goal is a print that not only contains a full range of tones, but has all the shadow and highlight details that were in the negative. Correct paper contrast will help with this.

Overdevelopment or underdevelopment can still occur when you follow the paper manufacturer's developing-time recommendations, if your developer is at the wrong temperature or concentration. Underdevelopment (and, frequently, stains) will also occur if you try to process too many prints in a tray of developer or let it get contaminated by stop bath or fixer (refill it with fresh developer when its level drops visibly; discard the whole tray at the first sign of discoloration or sludge).

Proper agitation and inspection make a difference, too. Swishing the paper around in the developer with print tongs (preferably rubber-tipped, to prevent print scratching) or by rocking

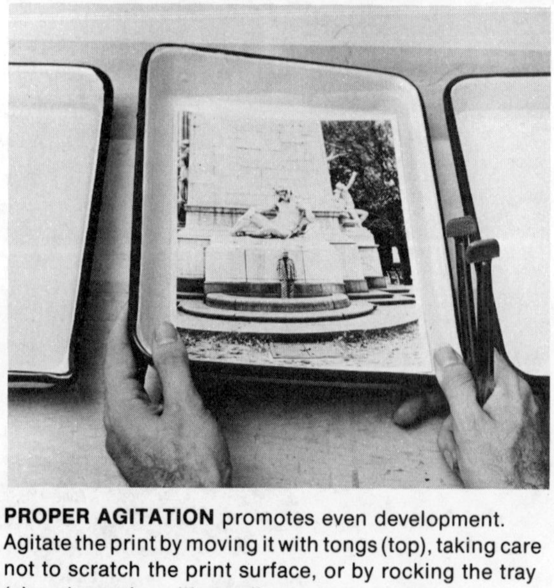

PROPER AGITATION promotes even development. Agitate the print by moving it with tongs (top), taking care not to scratch the print surface, or by rocking the tray (above)—easier with smaller trays, many of which are designed to rock easily, even on flat surfaces.

the tray will ensure that development starts and continues evenly; agitation in the stop bath means that it will stop evenly, too. And agitation in the fixing bath for just the right amount of time will ensure prints that (if properly washed) will last for years. Agitation is the right way to handle a print—but hauling it out of the developer for inspection is the wrong way; developer drains off in spots, oxidizes in others, and that's another cause of uneven development. The best way to inspect a print is in a good white light, after it's been developed and fixed, but learn, too, to compensate for the slight differences in tonality between a processed, wet print and a dry one—what you see in the fixing bath is not quite what you'll get.

If you don't work in your darkroom very often, your chemicals and paper may hang around for months before they're finally used up, and can go stale in the meantime. To prevent this, buy small quantities of paper (even though it costs less per sheet in larger packages), and refrigerate it between darkroom sessions (let it get back to room temperature before you use it).

mix just what you'll use

Your chemicals, especially developers, should be mixed up only in batches just big enough to fill the biggest tank or tray you use. Keep records of how much you use each chemical, discarding it when it's been used to its rated capacity; the lives of many film developers can be extended, though, by adding a "replenisher" after each use. Stale paper can sometimes be salvaged by adding Kodak Anti-Fog to your developer, but fresh paper will do an even better job.

Stale materials may cause stains, veiled highlights that never show pure whites, or fog that covers the whole paper, including borders. It usually prevents both proper blacks and whites from forming; in fact, the inability to get a proper black, no matter how much you expose the paper, is usually a sign of staleness.

But the inability to get a proper white is more often an effect of light fog. Fog that covers the whole paper visibly is usually caused by light leaks. Darkrooms that look dark when you first turn off the light may not be. A few small light leaks can sometimes be tolerated for printing (but never for film loading) provided none of them admits enough light to illuminate the darkroom (if you can see where you're going in the "dark," it's too light) and none shines directly on the paper. Check for enlarger light leaks, too.

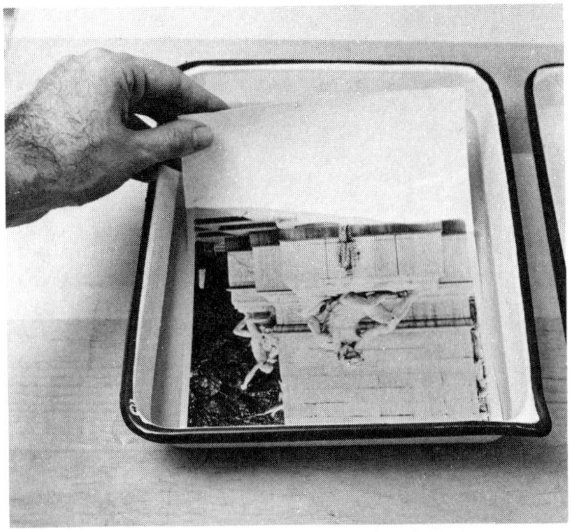

PRINTS THAT "POP UP" almost as you put them into the developer are overexposed; shortening developing time this way seems like a great time-saver, but the developing is uneven and blotchy with poor contrast.

Fog that just veils the highlights is harder to spot. Usually it comes from safelights. The easiest test is to unpack and expose a sheet of paper in complete darkness, then partially cover it with a box and turn the safelights on again. After five minutes, move the box to uncover half of the remaining area; then develop. If you can see a shadow line across the print, you have a fogging problem. Such fog can also come from light that bounces from a white easel back up to the paper emulsion.

Muddy prints are low in contrast, but not all poor contrast is due to the mud-producing errors noted above. Low-contrast subjects (often the result of shooting on a cloudy day) can explain a few "flat" prints; under or overexposed negatives that lack full tonal range will explain even more. These errors can be partially corrected (see Fig. 4) by printing on a "harder," or higher-contrast paper, such as Nos. 4, 5 or Agfa Brovira 6, just as soft papers (No. 1) can help with negatives too high in contrast. If you don't want to stock several paper grades for fear the less-used grades will go stale, use a variable contrast paper (though you'll still need graded papers for contrasts above No. 4 or so). Dust or dirt on your enlarging lens will also cut contrast, as will a cheap, low-grade lens (the difference between enlarger lenses, I've found, is less in detail resolution than in contrast). Condenser enlargers will also give a bit more contrast than diffusion-type ones.

Privacy screens get admiring glances

By ROBERT W. HOFFNER

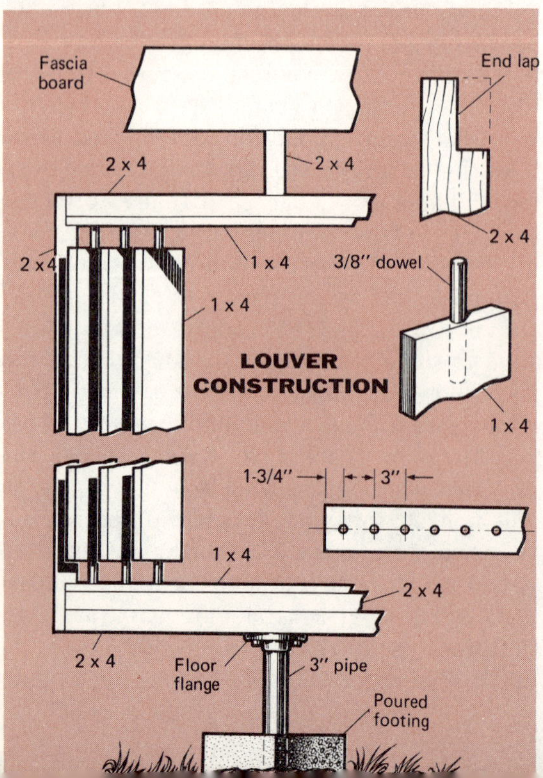

■ THERE WERE several reasons why my wife and I decided to add a fence to our home. For one thing, the bedroom on the southwest corner was unbearably hot every summer and, for another, we wanted privacy when entertaining on the patio. The screen we selected (above) satisfied both requisites with a bonus to boot: It features movable louvers that let cool breezes in or shut them out, as we choose.

Redwood was our choice for the project. It's good looking when installed, it weathers attractively and, most important, it is long lasting. The frame is constructed of 2 x 4s with the top and bottom rails doubled up for strength. The louvers are of nominal 1 x 4 stock with a ⅜-in. hole drilled to approximately a 1-in. depth on both ends to receive the dowels upon which they pivot.

Make certain that you extend your footings (for the posts) below the frost line in your area; a frost upheaval could twist the framing and make the louvers inoperable. The louvers can be fastened in the rear for easier operation.

By ADAM F. WOJNOWSKI

SIMPLICITY OF design gives this screen its look of elegance. It is simply squared 2x4 boxes connected with stringers 6 in. long.

■ BUILT ALMOST ENTIRELY of scrap, this handsome fence (shown above) satisfies a champagne taste on a beer budget. By sizing the grille-like squares to suit the cutoffs I had on hand, the only items I had to buy were four 10-ft. 2 x 4s, nails, and the white paint I used to finish it.

I built the fence in two 8-ft. sections on the patio floor. Then as each section was completed, it was raised and fastened to the supporting posts with galvanized 10d common nails. These should be toenailed as shown in the drawing.

Before starting construction, you'll be wise to make a scale drawing of the area to be screened. Though the fence shown consists of 12-in.-sq. blocks and 6-in. stringers, the overall length of your fence could cause a change in these figures. Thus the dimensions shown in the drawing at the right should be considered merely as a starting point when you lay out your own design. By altering the dimensions to increase or decrease the size and number of the boxes, you can let in more or less light as you wish.

All of the hardware used should be of the non-rusting type. Then, whether you decide to paint or stain the wood, the handsome appearance of your fence will not be marred by weathering.

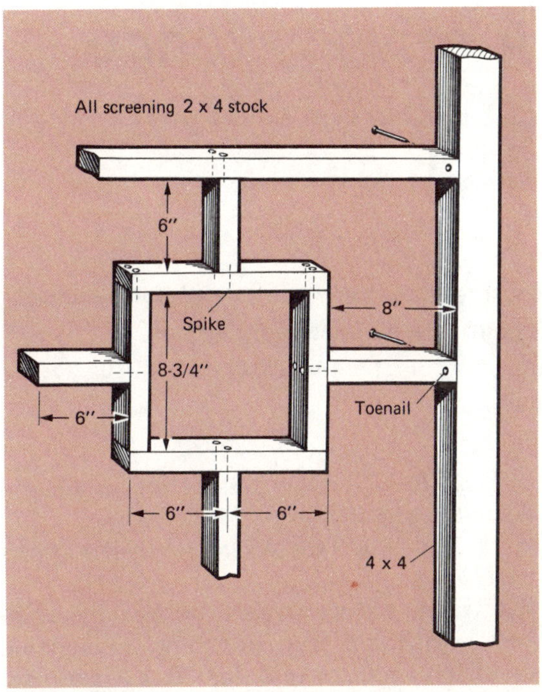

SEE ALSO

Barbecues . . . Benches, deck . . . Decks . . . Fences . . . Garden shelters . . . Gazebos . . . Patios . . . Picnic tables . . . Planters

DECORATIVE DESIGN assures privacy for neighbors on both sides of the fence. The louvers, which are set at angles to the posts, allow plenty of air flow across the property.

A privacy fence attractive from both sides

Good fences make good neighbors—especially if you build one as handsome as this. It's built from treated lumber to last for years

■ THERE ARE TWO reasons for installing a fence along your property line:

■ Security—you want to keep youngsters or pets either in or out.

■ Privacy—you don't want to be ogled by neighbors when sunbathing, swimming, entertaining or fiddling about the yard. Also, lack of adequate

SEE ALSO

Circular saw blades . . . Circular saws, portable . . . Paneling, plywood . . . Power-tool stands

SHORT LENGTH of fence (above) at right angle to the long run ties into a 4x4 in the latter. The back view (below) shows that the look is good no matter which side the fence is viewed from.

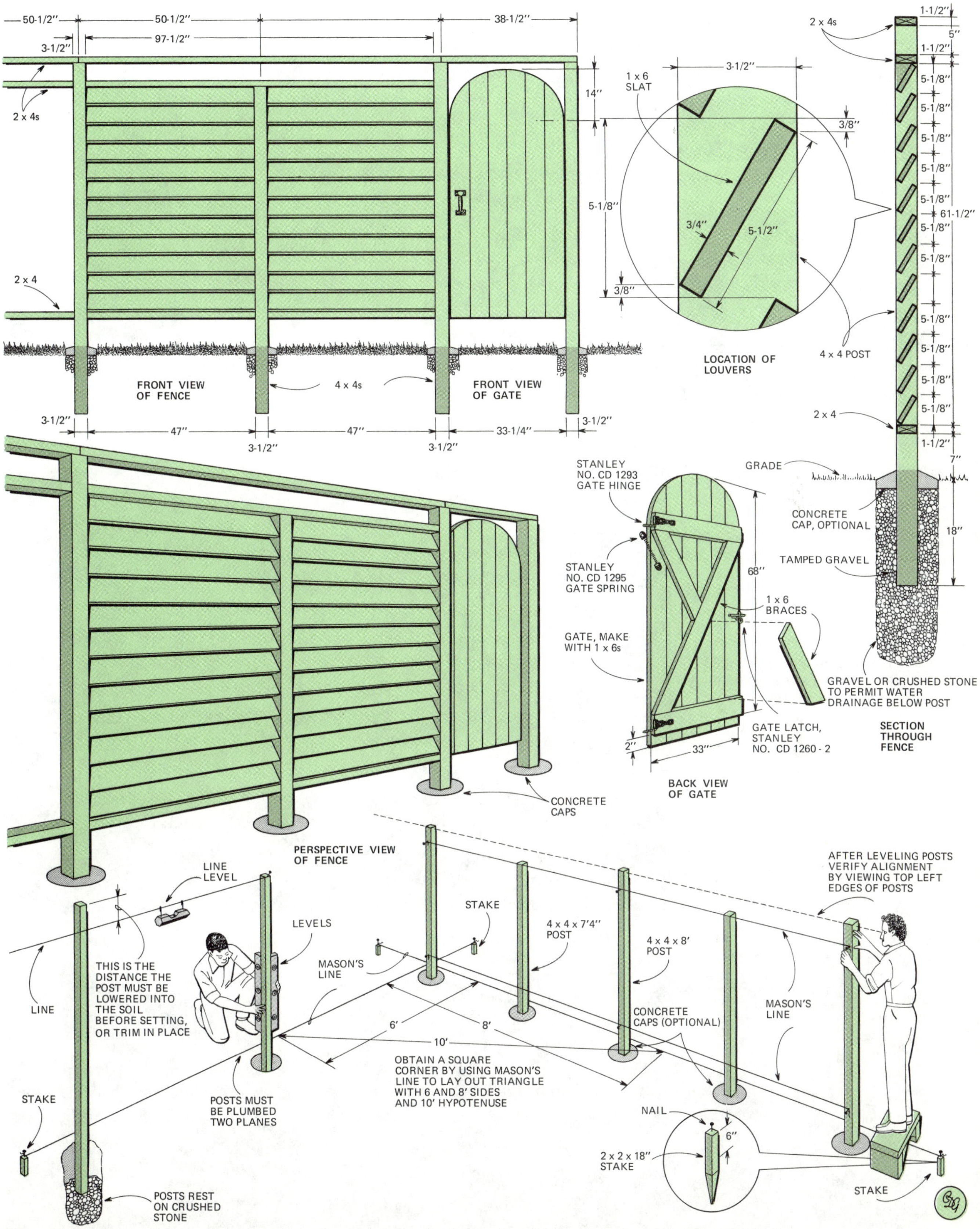
50-1/2"
50-1/2"
38-1/2"
3-1/2"
97-1/2"
2 x 4s
14"
5-1/8"
2 x 4
FRONT VIEW OF FENCE
4 x 4s
FRONT VIEW OF GATE
3-1/2"
47"
47"
33-1/4"
3-1/2"
3-1/2"
3-1/2"
1 x 6 SLAT
3-1/2"
3/8"
3/4"
5-1/2"
3/8"
LOCATION OF LOUVERS
2 x 4s
1-1/2"
5"
1-1/2"
5-1/8"
61-1/2"
4 x 4 POST
2 x 4
1-1/2"
7"
GRADE
CONCRETE CAP, OPTIONAL
18"
TAMPED GRAVEL
GRAVEL OR CRUSHED STONE TO PERMIT WATER DRAINAGE BELOW POST
SECTION THROUGH FENCE
STANLEY NO. CD 1293 GATE HINGE
STANLEY NO. CD 1295 GATE SPRING
GATE, MAKE WITH 1 x 6s
68"
1 x 6 BRACES
2"
33"
GATE LATCH, STANLEY NO. CD 1260 - 2
BACK VIEW OF GATE
CONCRETE CAPS
PERSPECTIVE VIEW OF FENCE
LINE LEVEL
LEVELS
LINE
THIS IS THE DISTANCE THE POST MUST BE LOWERED INTO THE SOIL BEFORE SETTING, OR TRIM IN PLACE
STAKE
MASON'S LINE
4 x 4 x 7'4" POST
4 x 4 x 8' POST
6'
8'
10'
CONCRETE CAPS (OPTIONAL)
OBTAIN A SQUARE CORNER BY USING MASON'S LINE TO LAY OUT TRIANGLE WITH 6 AND 8' SIDES AND 10' HYPOTENUSE
POSTS MUST BE PLUMBED TWO PLANES
STAKE
POSTS REST ON CRUSHED STONE
AFTER LEVELING POSTS VERIFY ALIGNMENT BY VIEWING TOP LEFT EDGES OF POSTS
MASON'S LINE
NAIL
6"
2 x 2 x 18" STAKE
STAKE

FENCE route is marked using stakes and mason's line.

STAKES are driven at each point where an intermediate post will go.

CLAMSHELL digger gives neat holes for rigid post installation.

EACH scoop removes a good amount of soil. Keep it for backfilling.

ON FENCE shown, holes were dug to about an 18-in. depth.

BEFORE planting the intermediate posts, you must determine fence height. This is best done by using a line and level.

IT'S EASY to set a post if you have someone to steady it while you backfill.

USE a spirit level—in both vertical planes—to plumb the posts.

POSTS can be cut before planting and set to touch elevation line.

IN SOME CASES, you will find it easier to install a post in the ground, then mark it and cut it off in place (far left). Horizontal rails (near left) are fastened to the posts using 10d common nails toenailed at the joint.

BEFORE measuring the length of the second rail, install the top rail to the taller posts. The added rigidity will make the job easier and ensure a more accurate fit at the ends.

SECOND RAIL is toenailed to posts at both ends, and spiked to the center post.

SHORT LENGTH of fence with gate is secured with nails toed into building.

LOUVER installation starts at bottom; a square aids placement of next board.

BOARD'S EDGES are lined up with the pencil mark on post edges as shown.

CUT 1x6s slightly full to gain a force fit; tap board into place.

NAILS are toed through louver face; dull points to prevent splitting.

fencing can often lead to time-consuming conversations at inopportune moments.

If you want a fence for security reasons, chances are you will opt for one of the maximum-security types with links of steel draped between metal poles. These are generally installed by professionals, and in most cases, the owner is more concerned about strength than looks.

But if need for privacy is your motivation, you're sure to like the look of the fence shown on these pages. Designed to be attractive to residents on both sides, our fence is built of pressure-treated Koppers Outdoor Wood (Wolmanized).

The fence shown replaced one of a similar de-

MAKING A GATE

GATE is assembled by butting 1x6s; brace nails are driven at an angle.

X-BRACE adds strength and rustic look. Boards can be butted or lap-jointed.

AFTER constructing the gate, use a sabre saw to cut the top to shape.

If your fence requires a gate, you must set a 4x4 post on both sides of the opening. After plumbing and setting the first post, cut two lengths of scrap wood to equal the desired door opening. Use these as a jig when digging for and setting the second post. The gate shown was created by butting 1x6 boards edge-to-edge and holding them in that position with horizontal cross braces. An X-brace was also added, to assure a rigid gate. Drive 4d common nails at an angle for maximum holding power. The hardware used is shown on the drawing; all parts are available at well-stocked hardware stores (or can be ordered). Gate spring makes certain the door stays closed.

sign which was installed only 11 years ago. Though the cedar posts at that time were soaked in creosote, decay and rot actually started within five years. This time around I selected Outdoor Wood because of its resistance to termites and to decay due to moisture. Happily, the salt treatment does not alter the wood's characteristics. The chemicals do leave a greenish cast, which is replaced by silver-gray patina as wood weathers.

installation is simple

Though many people who I have talked with thought otherwise, there really is no mystery to installing a fence. Start by studying the drawings of our version so you understand clearly just how it goes together. Then take measurements so you can work up a materials list. The fence shown consists of 4x4 posts (in two lengths), 2x4 rails at three elevations, and 1x6 lumber for the louvers. Use only galvanized nails (or mechanical fasteners, if preferred) for all connections. Conventional steel nails will rust and produce ugly stains; rusting also diminishes a nail's holding ability. Use at least 10d common nails to fasten rails to posts, and 8d finishing nails—toed through louver board edges—into the posts.

Begin by checking with your local building department to make certain your fence will comply with local fence codes. Be advised that a noncomplying fence could be ordered removed upon receipt of a complaint; that can be a costly oversight. Codes generally spell out height and types of fences permitted as well as distance required from property lines.

If the fence is being put up on a lot line, it's also a good idea to discuss it with the neighbor who shares the line. A short discussion of your attempts to beautify your yard can go a long way toward preventing hurt feelings. Besides, you may find a construction assistant this way.

laying out the fence

Use pointed stakes and a mason's line to lay out the fence run. Dig holes for, and install, the end posts first. Use a taut mason's line stretched between tops of both posts to determine elevation for all intermediate posts. Notice that in the design shown, the post heights alternate every other post. The posts can be cut to length before they are planted by measuring from hole bottom to line. My preference is to install posts and cut them in place. This way, slight height adjustments can be made for ground contour.

The 2x4 rails on the fence are installed by toenailing at boths ends. For added rigidity—on the 2x4 rail that is second from the top—do some spike-nailing at its center in short, intermediate 4x4 post.

Tips: Because of the salts impregnated in pressure-treated lumber, toenailing near an end can cause splitting. To avoid such splits, predrill pilot holes or blunt nail points slightly before driving.

finishing

You can leave your fence as is and let it change color as it weathers (my choice), or you can apply a quality outdoor wood stain. If you decide to use a stain, check for areas that may need sanding. Use a 100-grit abrasive paper to stand off any edge splinters and the like. Dust and apply stain according to directions.

Wind-damaged door

My wood combination door was flipped open by the wind and split along the hinged side. New doors are expensive. Is it possible to repair it?—E. Corbell, Memphis.

If the split or splintering is clean and can be tightly fitted back into place, a sound repair is possible. Spread waterproof glue uniformly along the length of the split, then apply a few C-clamps to bring the split together tightly. Where the split extends to the bottom of the door, you will need to use bar clamps. You can reinforce the glued joint further with corrugated fasteners spaced 12 in. apart.

Brass or plating?

How do I tell for sure if metal is genuine brass or some other metal brass-plated?—Jay Holden, San Francisco.

A magnet will show if a ferrous metal, such as steel, has been brass-plated. If the metal under the plating is steel, the magnet will be strongly attracted to it. But if the metal is all brass, which is a nonferrous metal, the magnet will not be attracted. However, there are other nonferrous metals that are sometimes plated with brass, and these pieces would not affect the magnet either.

Painting fiberboard walls

I have fiberboard walls – that's what I hear they are called—on a back porch. The paint appears to be that which was applied originally, but now the walls are in need of repainting. Should I use a latex or an oil paint?—Jim Winston, Topeka, Kans.

From your description I suppose that these walls have been made with tongue-and-groove "planks," that were either prepainted or factory painted. I would prefer to use a latex paint after applying a primer of the type intended for such paint.

Crawl space ventilation

My home is on a slope with two of four 8x10-in. vents in window wells 20 in. below grade. There's a 27-in. insulated crawl space with a plastic-covered dirt floor. Do I have enough ventilation? And should the vents be open or closed in winter?—Edward D. Mattox, Lewisburg, W.Va.

If I understand your description correctly, you should have adequate vent area. The vents should ordinarily be left open during the winter months.

"Sweating" floor tiles

I recently tiled a half bath in my basement. Now the tiles have loosened and the cement is soft and oozy underneath. The top surface of the tiles seems to be damp, almost wet at times. I used asphalt tiles and was careful to spread the cement uniformly. What's wrong and what can I do now?—T.F., Ore.

Did you use the recommended waterproof adhesive, which is also resistant to the alkali in the concrete floor? If not, then you're not going to like what I'm about to suggest: Remove the tiles, clean the tiles *and* the floor and re-lay them as before, using the *proper cement recommended for application below grade.* It's a messy and rather tedious job but there are solvents available that will ease the chore somewhat. This, it seems to me, is the only sure way to correct the trouble.

Mitered joints move

In my three-year-old home the door and window trim (casing) is mitered at the upper corners. These joints open during the heating season and close in the summer. I'm going to paint the trim. Is there a way to stop this opening and closing?—Milton Greer, Aiken, S.C.

A permanent remedy is doubly difficult as this is caused by slight shrinkage and expansion of the trim wood, and perhaps of the frames. You might pry off one trim member, coat the joining miter surfaces with white glue or epoxy adhesive and then renail the member, without nails in the miters, as these could crack the casing next heating season. Any ordinary crack filler would probably be squeezed out and form a bead or ridge at the joints. Trim pieces must be removed with care to prevent damage, and the glued joints sanded after nailing and refinished to match.

Stubborn screens

Screens in my combination windows either stick or raise and lower with great difficulty. How can I make them easier to operate?—Mrs. Jack Thomas, Kansas City, Mo.

There is a silicone lubricant you can get in aerosol containers from your paint or hardware dealer that generally eases these parts and makes them slide with little effort—provided the channels have not been kinked, bent or otherwise damaged. It's a good idea to clean the channels first with a mild soapy solution, using a brush to remove the dirt and grime that collect in them in time. Then spray each channel and slide the screens up and down several times to distribute the lubricant uniformly.

Roll-away projector stand

By HOWARD R. CLARK

This wheeled cart stores everything you need for putting on shows and also doubles as a mobile food server. You can build it in either a modern or traditional style

SETTING UP for a slide or movie show can be a bothersome chore if you have to drag the projector out of a closetful of clutter, find a table to put it on, then go searching for those stray film reels or slide trays. This mobile projection stand solves the problem by keeping everything at your fingertips. You just roll it out, set the projector on top, and you're ready.

The wheeled cart is roomy enough to store both a slide and movie projector, plenty of trays or reels, extra editing equipment and even a tape recorder for adding sound to your presentations. The top surface puts the projector at a height of about 32 inches—a convenient working level that lets you operate it comfortably from a sitting position.

The slickest feature of all is a built-in, slope-front control panel that slides out like a drawer from one end. The panel contains three switched power outlets and a back-lighted slide viewer for checking and editing your transparencies. The outlets enable you to plug in not only the projector but additional equipment like a tape recorder and a floor or table lamp. With a lamp plugged in, you can control room illumination yourself without having to ask someone else to turn the lights on and off every few minutes.

SEE ALSO

Mobile furniture . . . Photo hints . . . Photography . . . Slides, photo . . . Theaters, home

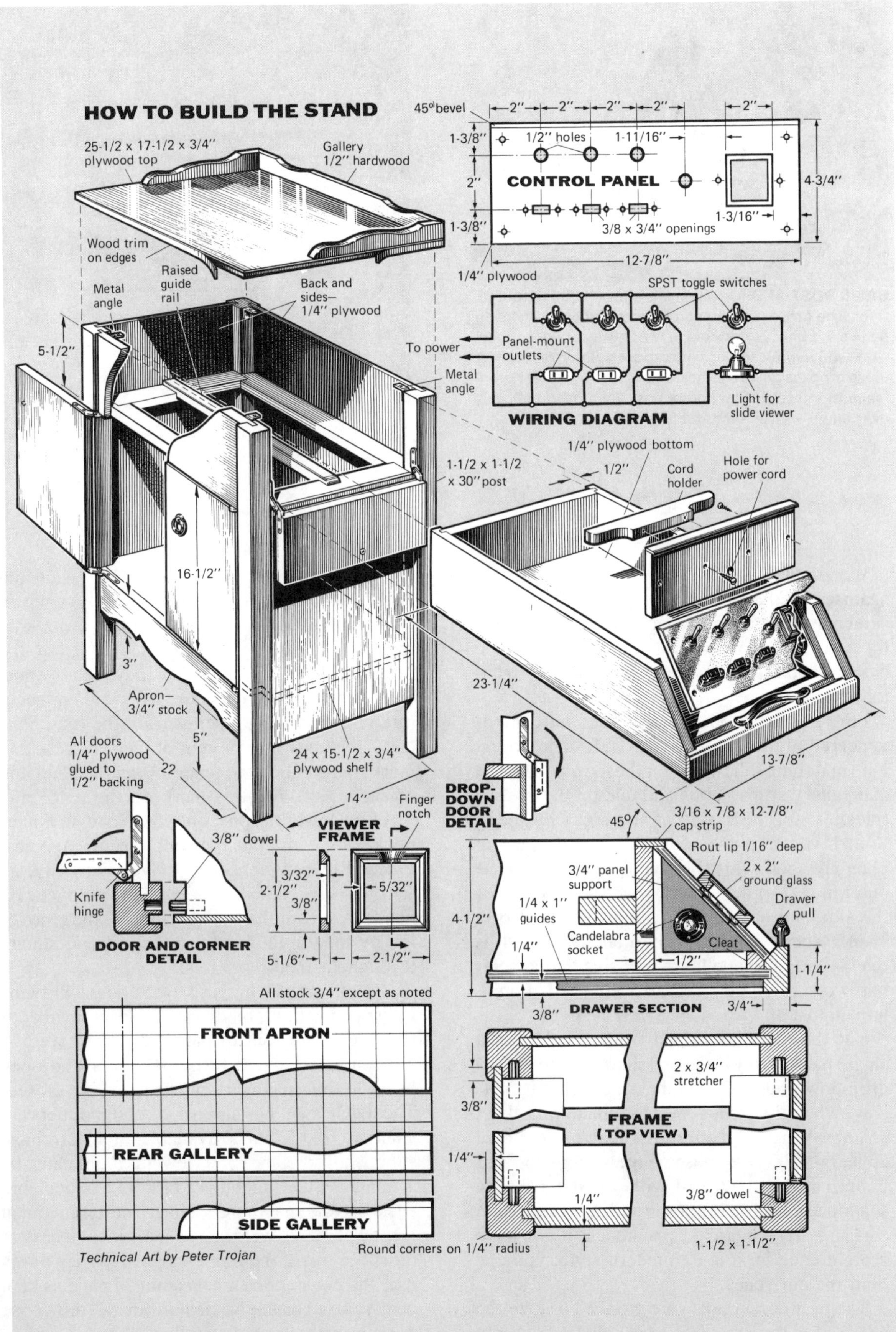

Technical Art by Peter Trojan

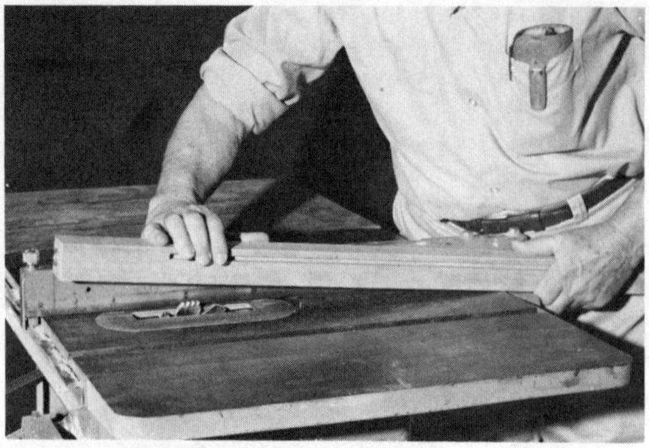

BASIC POST-AND-RAIL frame is shown in the photo at right. The grooves in the corner posts for back and side panels are blind, extending only part way down so they won't show where the legs are exposed. Setup for cutting these grooves on a dado head is shown above. Mark the fence to indicate blind end of post, then drop the post over blade at this point and feed it forward.

When not in use, the cart rolls out of the way against a wall and can double as a dining room sideboard, mobile snack bar or roll-around stand for a portable TV set. Decorative clear-plastic casters make good wheels since they're trim-looking.

For a rich appearance, use hardwood-veneered plywood for the top, sides and doors, with matching solid stock for the leg posts, apron and gallery strips. You can build up the ¾-inch thickness for the top, front and doors by gluing ¼-inch veneer plywood to a ½-inch backing of plain plywood. This trick will let you cut all the outer faces from the same ¼-inch sheet used for the side and back panels, saving the cost of a ¾-inch sheet. Birch is a good choice since it is readily available and less expensive than fancier hardwood plywoods, yet can be finished to simulate almost any wood tone you desire.

Cut the main doors and front panel from a single piece of plywood and do the same for the drop-down side door and the panel below it. This way, when the pieces are assembled, you'll get an unbroken flow of grain for a neat, professional appearance. The exposed edges of the top and doors can be concealed with wood tape. The scalloped edges on the apron and gallery give the cart an Early American appearance. If you have a preference for a more modern style, you can omit the curlycues.

The four corner posts are grooved to take the edges of the side and back panels for a sturdy construction. The grooves are ¼ inch wide and ⅜ inch deep and can be cut on a table saw with a dado head set to a ¼-inch width. Note that they're blind, stopping five inches from the lower ends of the posts so they won't show where the legs are exposed. To cut them accurately, measure five inches from the rim of the dado blade toward the rear of the saw table and mark this point on the fence. Align the blind end of each post with this mark on the fence and carefully lower the post onto the blade, making a pocket cut. Continue the cut by feeding the post forward to complete the groove. This way, all four posts will come out identically grooved. By hand, chisel out the rounded ends of the grooves left by the curved blade so the cuts are square throughout their length.

Use offset knife hinges so the doors will swing fully open without binding. The drop-down door that hides the control panel must be carefully positioned so it clears the drawer in the open position, but makes a snug fit when it's closed. The toggle switches and panel-mount outlets are standard radio parts available at electronics-supply houses. The slide viewer is illuminated by a small 7½-watt nightlight bulb in a candelabra socket. Note that there's a finger notch cut out at the top of the viewer frame. This makes it easy to lift slides out of the frame's recess. When not in use, the power cord for the control panel is kept neatly coiled around a cleat inside the drawer so it's out of the way.

Pick the right propeller

By JIM MARTENHOFF

YOUR PROPELLER is a pump. It moves a cone-shaped column of water, producing thrust. The water is cone-shaped because it expands as it moves away from the boat. Its diameter depends upon the diameter of the propeller. Speed of movement is determined by the speed of the propeller and its pitch.

The faster you can move that discharge cone, the faster your boat is going to go. There are, of course, a variety of factors limiting perfect performance. You can have too much pitch, for example, and turn the propeller too fast, losing bite and overspeeding your engine.

Propeller experts delve into a multitude of details when computing probable speed performance. They twiddle their slide rules and ulti-

SEE ALSO
Boating, safety . . . Canoes . . . Outboard motors

TIME A RUN over a measured course, compare the true speed to the theoretical and determine prop efficiency.

mately come up with a set of figures, but the average small-boat skipper can do the same with a lot less work. All you have to know is a simple rule of thumb and how to use it. You can stand on a dock, look at a man's boat, and tell at a glance what speed he probably makes. All you need is gear ratio and pitch.

Pitch is the big secret. This is the distance a propeller would move through the water in one revolution—like a woodscrew moving through wood—if it didn't slip. Propellers always slip, and the slippage is worked out as a percentage.

Diameter of a propeller, and its pitch, are usually stamped on the prop hub in that order. A propeller marked 16x18, for example, is one with a diameter of 16 inches and a pitch of 18. They are interrelated. If you increase the diameter of a prop to make a larger discharge cone of water, you may have to reduce the pitch.

pitch ratio

Your engine can only do so much work; diameter and pitch must share the mechanical muscle. Engineers think of the relationship as pitch ratio. This is pitch divided by diameter. That 16x18 wheel has a ratio of a bit over 1.1, and if it were an 18x16 the ratio would be under 0.9.

This is useful background, but it has already been done for you on a correctly propped craft. High-performance hulls usually call for a pitch ratio of as much as 1.5, while heavy cruisers might go down to 1.0 or 0.8. Yet you can stump

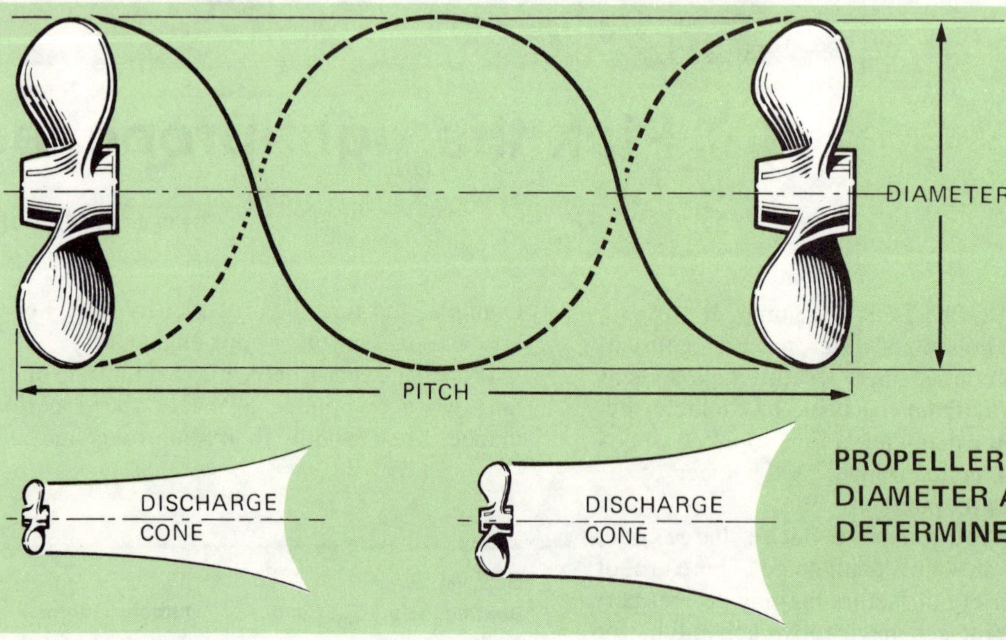

PROPELLER PITCH, DIAMETER AND RPM DETERMINE SPEED

the experts by overloading your boat or distributing weight unevenly to upset its trim. Hence the need for this know-how. If you loaded your fishing boat with a huge, heavy ice chest and other gear so that performance fell off, a little prop judgment might solve your problem.

Forget everything but pitch. Use this figure to figure your possible speed. This is the speed you would make if there were no prop slippage. Clock your boat over a measured distance and compare true speed to theoretical. The difference is "apparent slip," as the engineers put it. Slip is not an ideal way to determine efficient performance, but it's handiest if used with understanding.

You figure theoretical speed by multiplying propeller pitch in inches by shaft rpm. Note this is shaft turns, not necessarily what your tach reads. If you have a 2:1 gear reduction between engine and prop, your shaft turns at half the speed of the engine. The 5000 rpm on the tach means only 2500 shaft rpm. Engineers multiply pitch by shaft rpm, then divide by 1056 to find theoretical speed in statute miles per hour, or divide by 1216 to find knots.

This is a lot of work, so here's a trick so simple that you can often figure theoretical speed mentally, knock off expected slippage, and get true speed frequently within a mile or so of the actual figure. It never ceases to surprise friends when you can stand at a dock, listen to pitch, gear ratio and rpm figures, and then announce probable speed.

figuring speed

Here is how it works: Theoretical speed, in statute miles per hour, for each 1000 shaft turns, equals pitch minus one. That 18-inch prop we've been talking about will deliver a theoretical speed of 17 statute miles per hour for each 1000 shaft revolutions. This thumb-rule goes off only with low pitch props of 12 inches or less, or with more than 20 inches, so it fits the average small boat well.

Let's work an example. You have a 21-inch-pitch prop on a big outboard with a 2:1 gear reduction. The tach at top speed shows 5000 so the prop is turning 2500 rpm. With the minus-one rule, the 21-inch prop makes 20 mph per 1000 turns, that's 40 mph at 2000 plus another 10 mph for the last 500. Theoretical top speed is 50 statute mph, and timing shows true speed to be 37.5 mph. The lost 12.5 mph is 25-percent slip, acceptable for an outboard. For a stern drive you might expect about 20, inboards may run 15, and very good installations and race boats can be 10 percent or less. Heavy cruisers and houseboats may go as high as 35 percent, and hull designs will influence slip figures.

High slippage figures may indicate a propeller problem, and trying other props so that peak rpm is correct is one good way to look for increased efficiency. And efficiency is what you're after when you look for the correct prop.

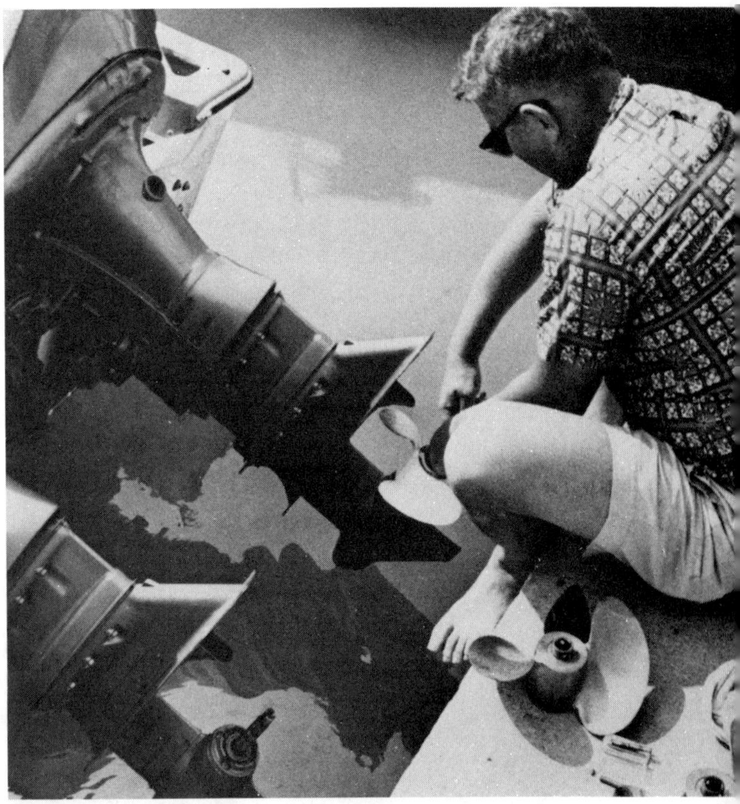

SOME PROP SLIPPAGE can be corrected sometimes by testing various props and timing performance.

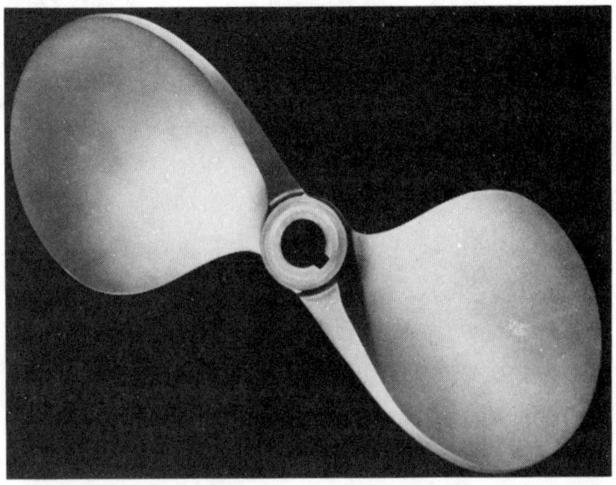

RACING PROPS, like this new titanium model from Nicson Engineering, may top 90 percent performance.

A pull-toy circus train

This colorful little circus train, built from scraps, will be the pride and joy of any young ringmaster

By ELMA and WILLARD WALTNER

SEE ALSO
Gifts, Christmas . . . Miniature houses . . . Playgrounds . . . Toys . . . Weekend projects

■ CHUGGING ALONG at the end of a string, this colorful little circus train will bring shrieks of delight from any two or three-year-old. All you'll need to buy to make the train are a few screws, screw eyes, L-hooks, a couple dowels and some *nontoxic* paint. The wood should be available in your workshop scrap box.

If you make it five cars long, the train will carry the 10 animals, each car holding two. If you own a lathe, you can quickly turn such parts as the engine's smokestack and boiler, as well as the wheels. However, if you don't have a lathe, the smokestack can be turned with your electric drill. Drill a wood block lengthwise, slip it over a bolt, tighten with a nut and chuck the end of the bolt in the drill. Cradle the drill in a vise and rig up a second block as a rest for your chisel. You

continued

can "turn" the wheels without a lathe by using a hole cutter in your drill or drill press.

Use glue and small finishing nails to assemble the cars and sand the edges smooth. In the case of the cage car, the two holes for the ½-in. "gate bars" go all the way through the roof and are $\frac{5}{16}$ in. for a loose fit. The ends of the gate bars are pointed so they seat automatically in the holes, and ½-in. lengths of small dowel are inserted crosswise to prevent the bars from being pulled all the way out. The holes for the three center dowels, which provide stalls, are drilled in the base only. All other matching holes are spaced and drilled the same in both base and roof.

To simplify things, it's best to paint the roof and base before gluing the dowels in place. The dowels are left unpainted. Round the outer edges of the wheels with sandpaper, paint the designs on them and attach them to the wagons with roundhead wood screws so they will turn freely. The photo will serve as a guide when you paint the wagons and add the fancy designs on their roofs, sides and wheels in bright colors.

An L-hook is turned into one end of each car and a screw eye in the other; screw eyes are used at each end of the engine. The engine cab is sawed from either a solid or glued-up block.

The animals are sawed from 1 or 1⅛-in. pine with either a bandsaw or jigsaw, and ⅛-in. holes are drilled for tasseled and braided tails of yarn. For safety's sake, it's important that you use nontoxic paint and anchor the yarn tails firmly in their holes.

ENGINE

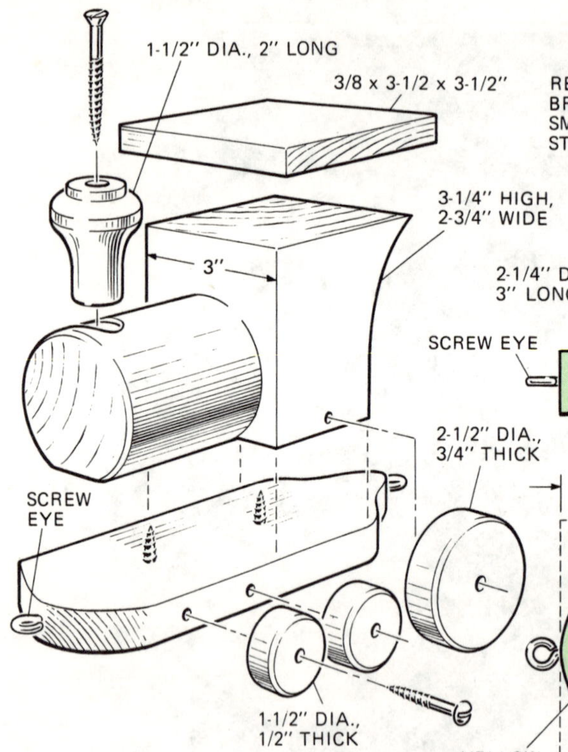

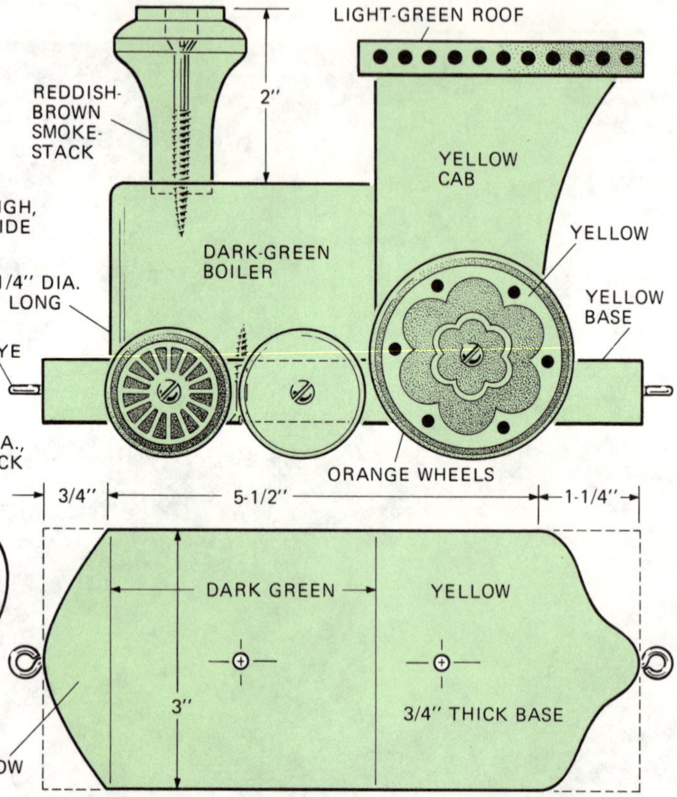

CAGE CAR

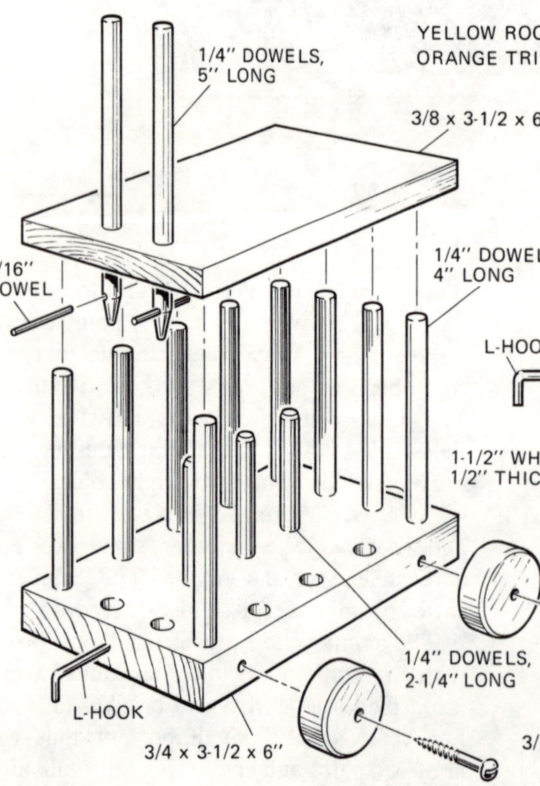

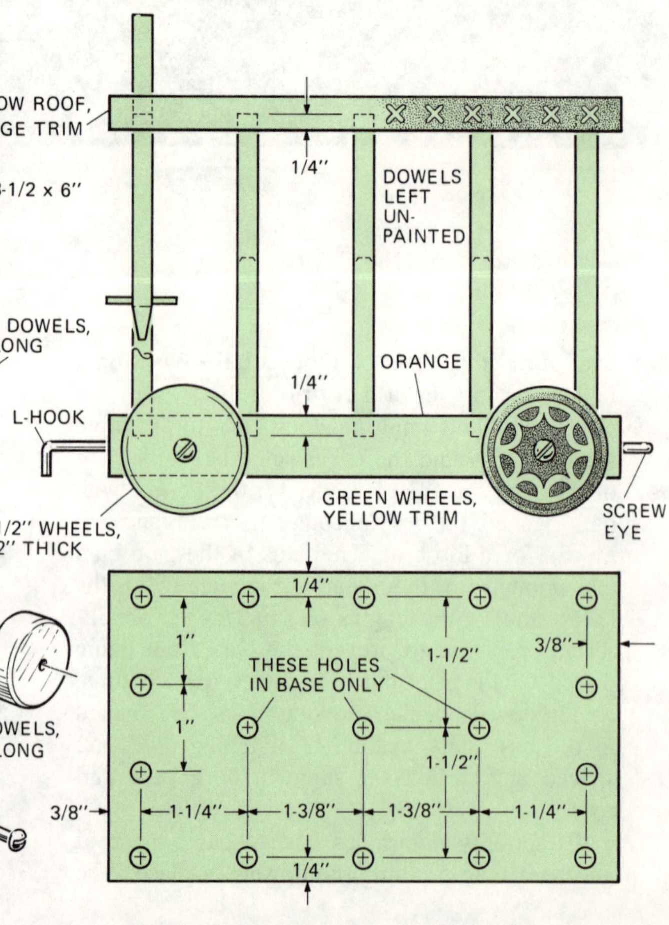

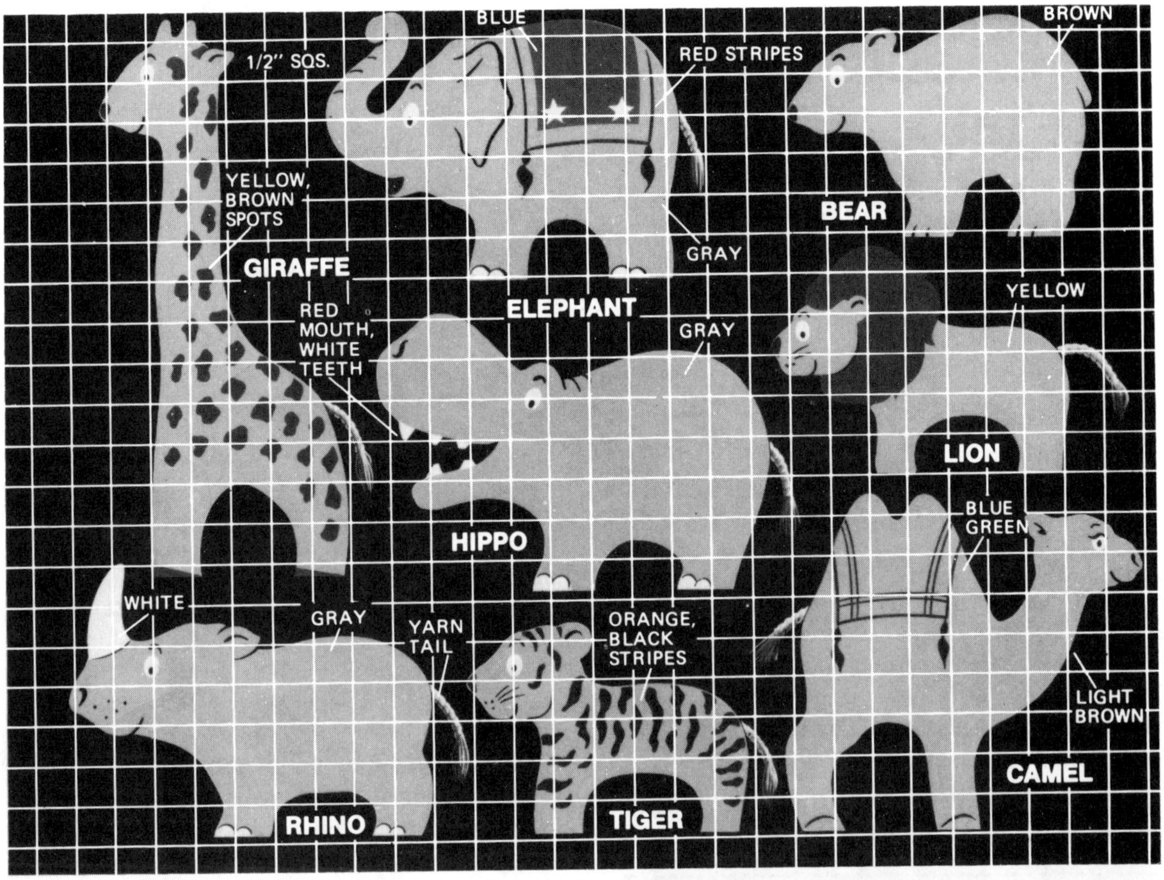

GIRAFFE CAR

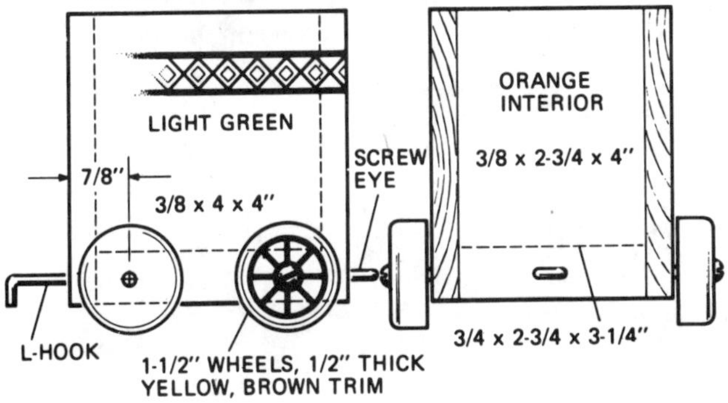

BOXCAR

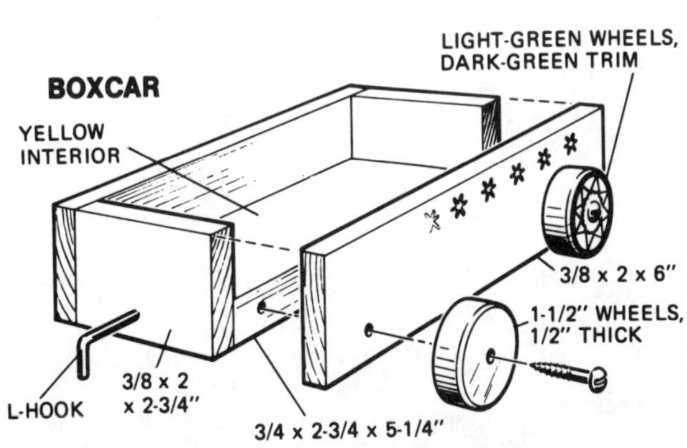

Ducks and dachshunds that talk

By ELMA WALTNER

■ TODDLERS LIKE TOYS they can pull all around the house. If they also make a noise, so much the better. Here are a couple of animal pull toys you can make in your shop that are sure to please any toddler. Mom Duck and her kids waddle along quacking merrily and Danny Dachshund makes himself heard and waddles his hind quarters as he is pulled. Off-center wheels provide the waddle, and compression-spring necks make the heads bob. Both the ducks and the dog have the same voices. It is produced by pieces of clock spring being snapped against sounding boxes by hardwood ratchets.

SEE ALSO

Dump trucks, toy . . . Gifts, Christmas . . . Playhouses . . . Toys

The series of photos on the opposite page show all of the steps necessary in making the ducks. Notice in each case that the voice-box holes are bored before the blocks are slotted and sawed out. Postcard stock is just right for the cardboard sounding-box discs. A dab of glue is used to hold the ratchet (clacker) on the axle and

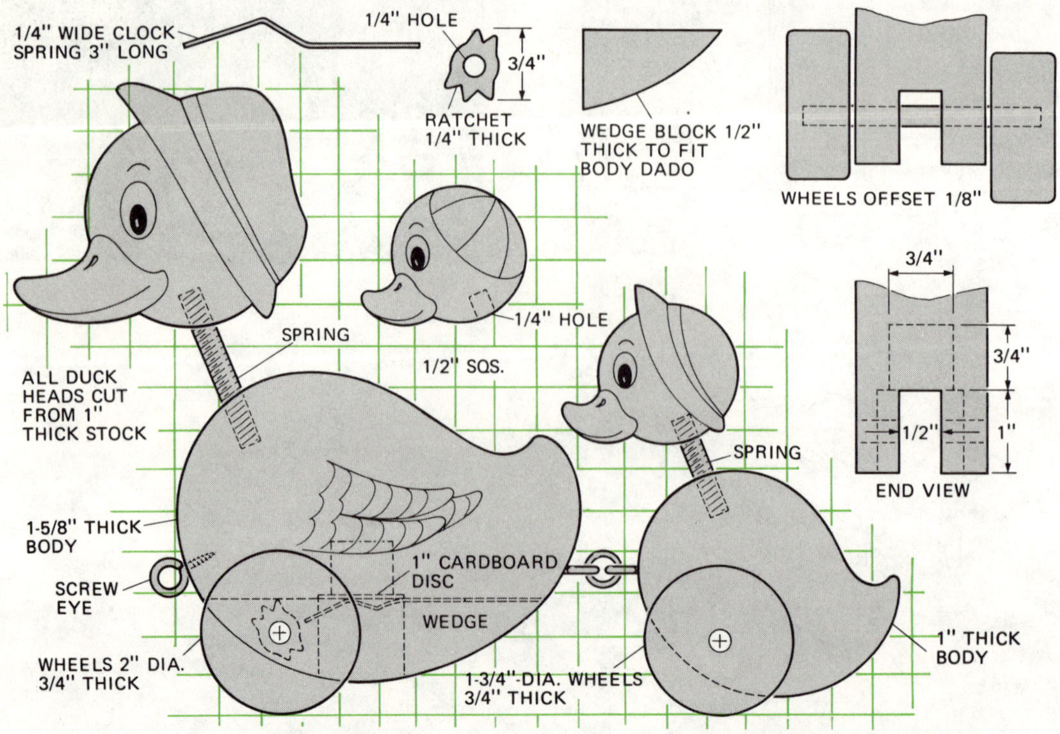

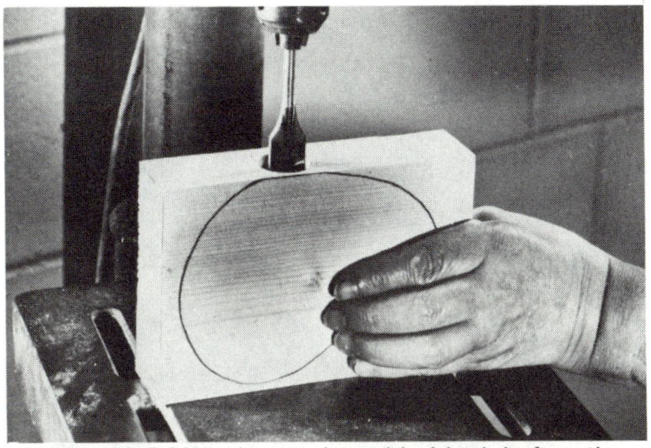

SOUNDING-BOX holes are bored in block before the body is cut out. Drill 1-in. hole first, then ¾ in.

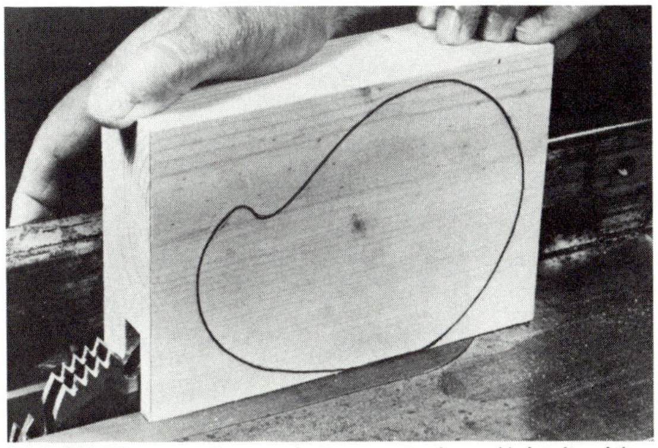

BLOCK IS passed over dado saw to form ½-inch-wide slot in bottom edge, drilled for axles then sawed.

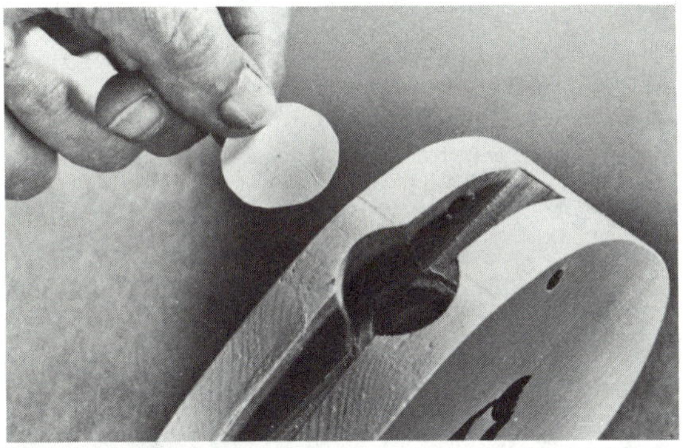

THIN CARDBOARD disc is glued to ledge formed by large hole to cover the ¾-in. sounding-box hole.

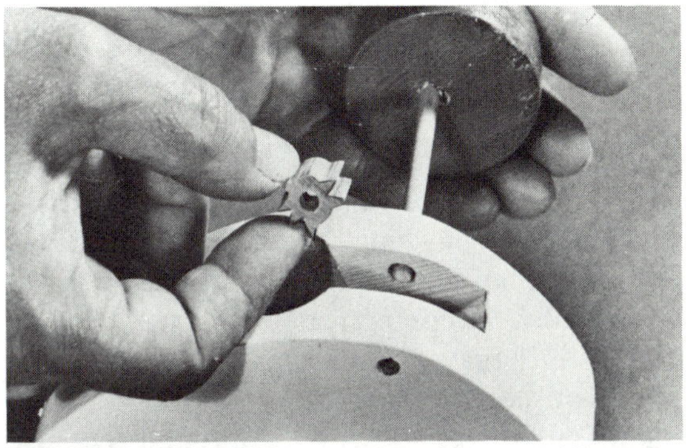

RATCHET IS SLIPPED over axle as it's passed through slot. Glue on each side holds ratchet on axle.

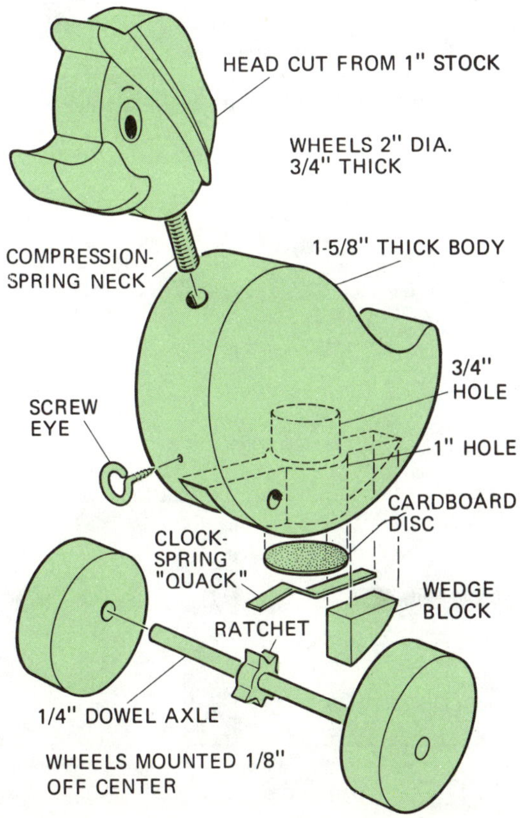

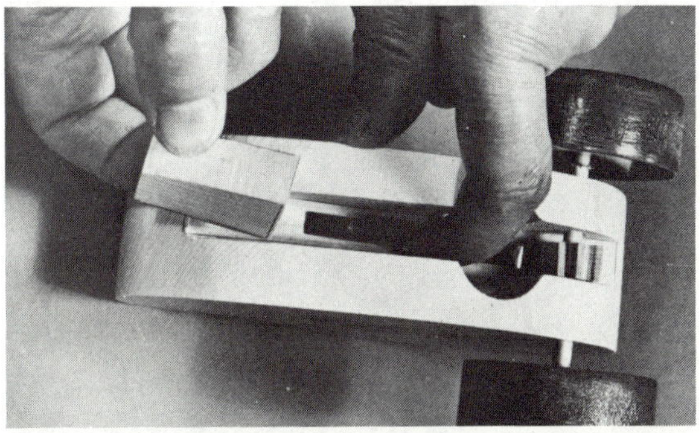

APPLY GLUE to wedge block, then insert block in slot to hold the spring against the cardboard and ratchet.

continued

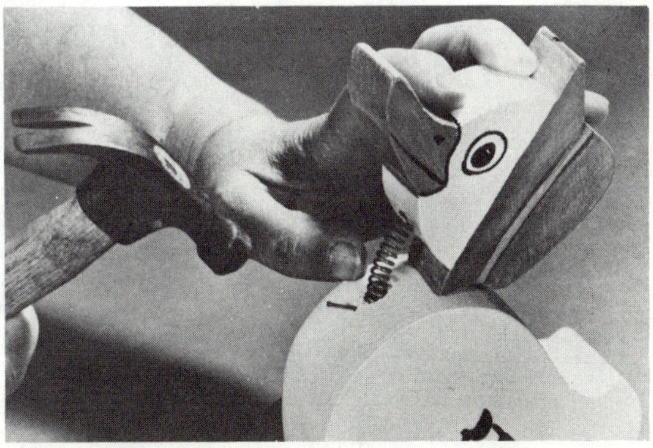

SMALL FINISHING nails, plus glue, are used to anchor neck springs in holes. Drive nails crosswise.

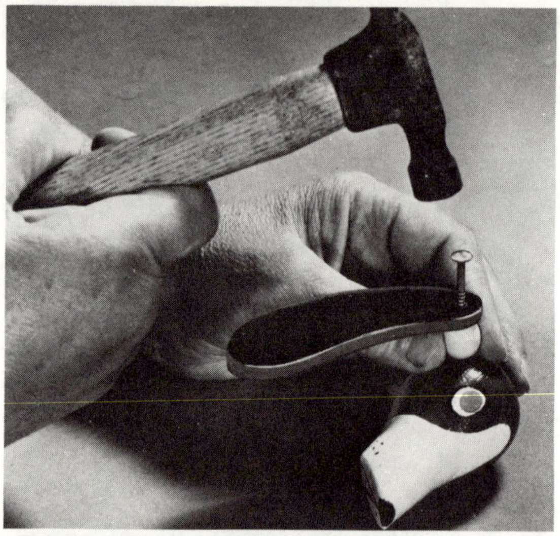

ATTACH EARS to head by driving nails through oversize holes in the ears, then through wooden beads.

in the center of the slot. A wedge block is inserted in the slot to hold the spring against the cardboard. Finally small finishing nails and glue are used to anchor the neck springs.

Basically, Danny is made the same way, the exception being that only his rear wheels are placed off-center. Waddle is produced by attaching his hind quarters with a nail in an oversize hole. His head is lathe-turned and then cut off at an angle to form nose and mouth.

The wheels can be cut easily from ½-inch stock with a hole cutter for either of the toys. Finally, sand all parts smooth and then paint with a nontoxic enamel.

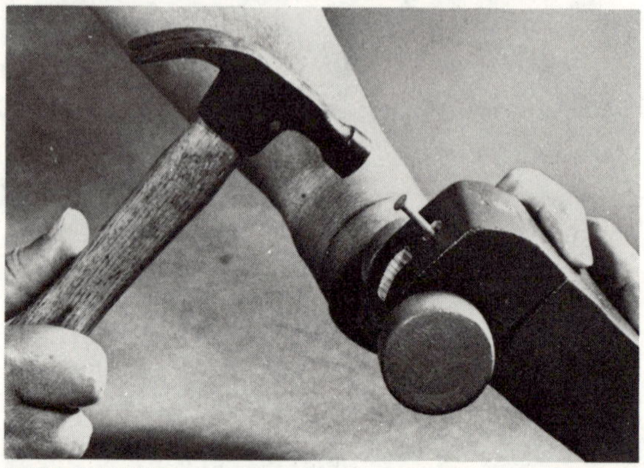

ATTACH HIND quarters to front section with washer between by driving nail through oversize hole.

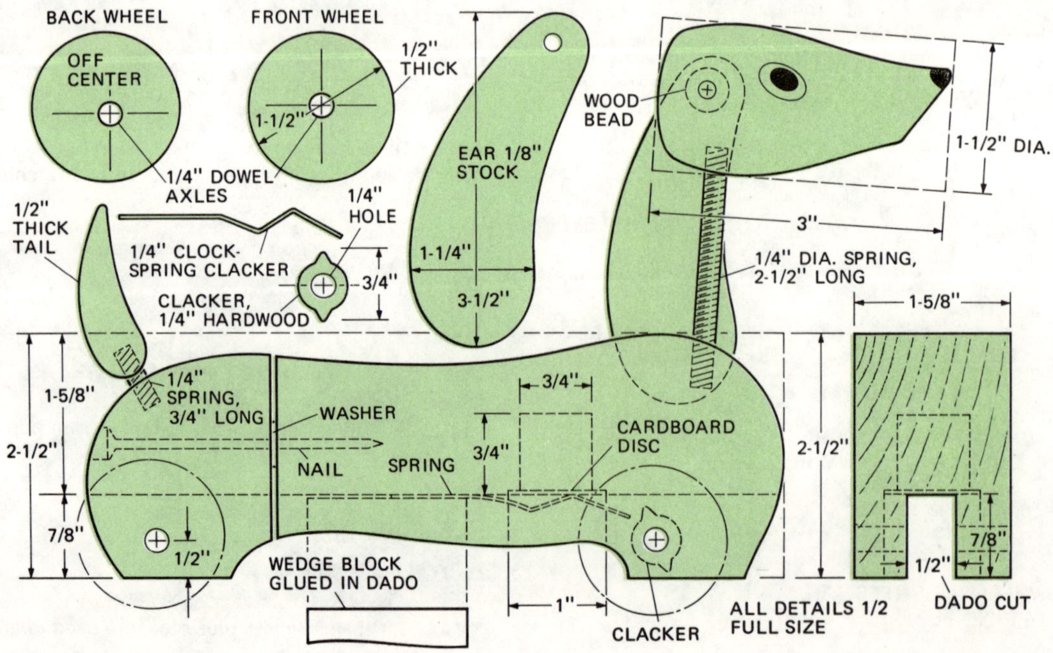

Buzzing bumblebee

By MERTON H. SLUTZ

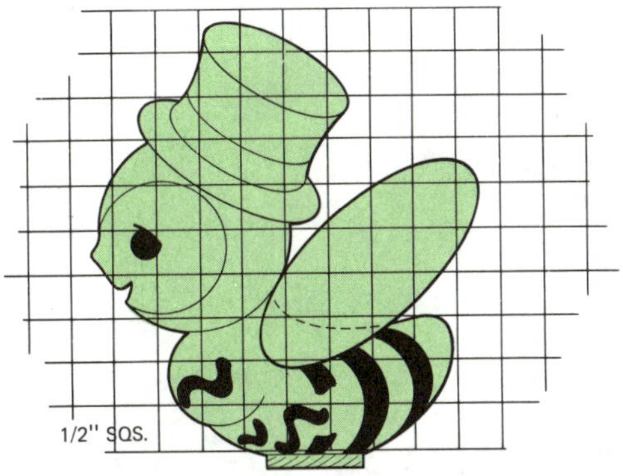

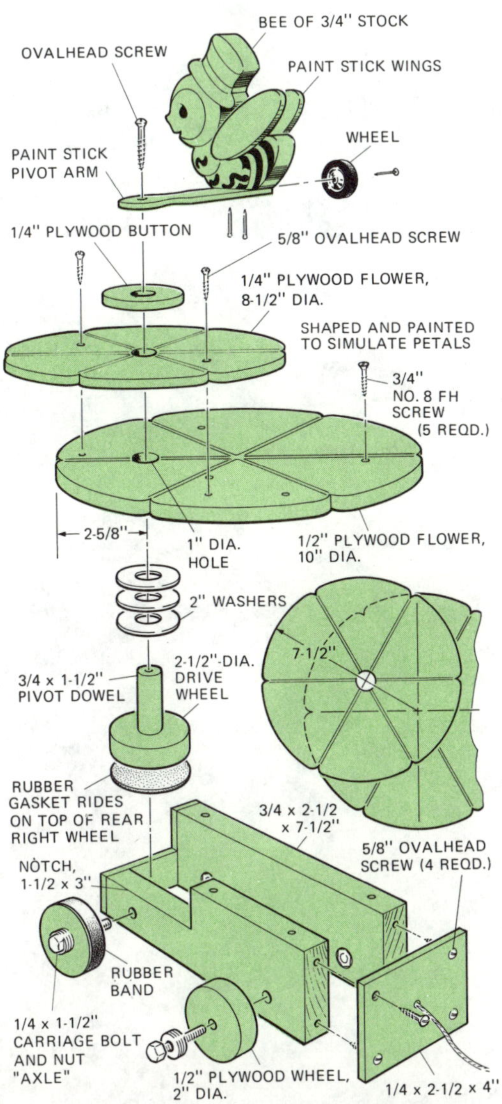

■ AS THIS TOY is pulled along by a youngster, the smiling bee "buzzes" around the petal continuously, "alighting" only when the pulling stops. While sure to delight toddlers, this pull toy will make parents happy as well because the "buzzing" is silent.

As can be seen in the drawing at left, the toy is far easier to make than one would suppose when watching the finished toy in action. Parts are easy to make and assemble; no sophisticated tools, techniques or knowledge are called for in the making. In fact, the project can be completed entirely with handtools using a coping saw for shaping petals and bee, brace and bit for all necessary boring. The rest of the job calls for gluing, sawing, nailing and finish-painting with nontoxic paint.

The wheels on the toy shown were cut from ½-in.-thick plywood. If you lack a jigsaw or holesaw—either of which must be used to cut perfect circles—buy a length of 2-in.-dia. hardwood dowel, and cut off ½-in.-thick pieces like slices of bologna.

It is best to tack-assemble the toy before finishing to assure that moving parts work as they should. When satisfied, disassemble the piece, do the finish painting and permanently assemble.

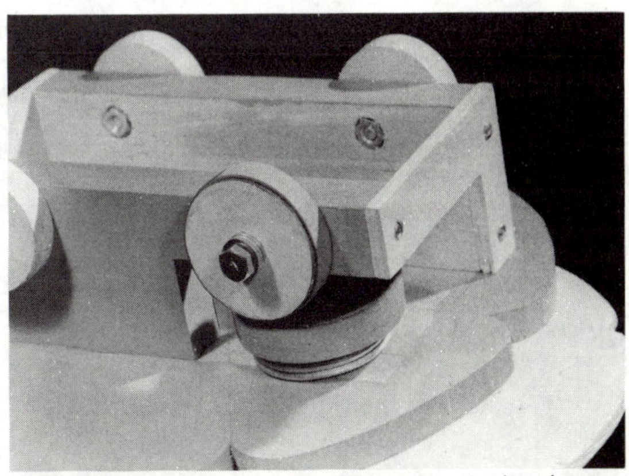

UPSIDE-DOWN view shows what makes the bee buzz—rubber gasket on drive wheel rides atop the rear wheel.

SEE ALSO
Dump trucks, toy . . . Gifts, Christmas . . . Playgrounds . . . Toys . . . Weekend projects

18

Build a putting green from artificial turf

This synthetic turf is easy to install and durable. It's perfect for laying your own greens

IF YOU'D RATHER spend Saturdays swinging a putter than a grass whip, Lawnscape Landscaping is the material that can make your dreams come true. The decorative "carpet" has a fiber facing that closely resembles living grass both in appearance and feel. The beauty of it is that once it is installed, there's no maintenance.

Made of second-generation polypropylene that is polymerized to withstand aging and the weathering of extreme outdoor conditions, Lawnscape is a product of the Ozite Corp., 1755 Butterfield Rd., Libertyville, IL 60048. The synthetic turf is sold nationally through carpet dealers and building-supply centers that also stock installation materials. Ask their advice regarding installation in your area.

The material can be installed professionally or by a do-it-yourselfer. Since the carpet comes in 6 and 12-ft. widths, the putting greens shown here are designed to utilize those modules.

The dirt or soil subsurface of the area to be covered should be shaped and well tamped. The manufacturer recommends either 1½ in. of asphalt or concrete over the compacted base for the Lawnscape to adhere to. (This minimum thickness will vary with load requirements.) Installation directly over earth is not recommended.

The surface finish should be as smooth and nonporous as possible. Because of the latter requirement, the covered area should be pitched slightly to direct water runoff where you want it to go.

The perimeter boards (headers) can be installed as shown in the drawings (page 10) or as in the photos below. The latter method creates shiplap joints by doubling up two-bys. Start by installing the headers because these can also be used for screeding the concrete. Once they are in and secured by stakes, the earth inside can be excavated and tamped. Then the concrete is laid

SEE ALSO

Carpeting, outdoor . . . Landscaping . . . Lawns . . . Paths, garden . . . Patios . . . Playgrounds . . . Swings . . . Tennis . . . Trees . . . Yard lighting

USE A NOTCHED TROWEL to spread adhesive on the base. When it's almost dry, put down the turf.

FOR INVISIBLE seams, press Seaming Pin-Tape into the adhesive. Its barbs will hold the turf.

up to the solid header and maintained approximately ⅜ to ½ in. below the header's top edge. This measurement should be as consistent as possible to maintain a uniform grass height. You can achieve it by using a notched screed on the header boards to level the concrete. If you use asphalt instead of concrete, seal the surface and allow it to dry overnight before installing Lawnscape.

Sweep the surface clean and patch any irregularities. Spread the synthetic turf in the sun to warm it and trim the edges to be butted. Then, using a $\frac{3}{32}$-in. notched trowel, spread Ozite AP 770 adhesive over the area of exposed width. When the adhesive barely transfers to your finger (10 to 20 minutes), the turf can be rolled onto the surface. You can assure invisible seams with Pin Tapes (see photos, page 2357). These are positioned astraddle the edge. The grass is simply tapped into place with a hammer.

Lawnscape and related material—flags, cups and instructions—come as a kit. Simply select the layout you want and order the amount of carpeting in the kit.

In addition to a putting green, you might want to consider the synthetic turf for swimming-pool aprons, patios, roof decks and the like. It's comfortable to walk on and durable.

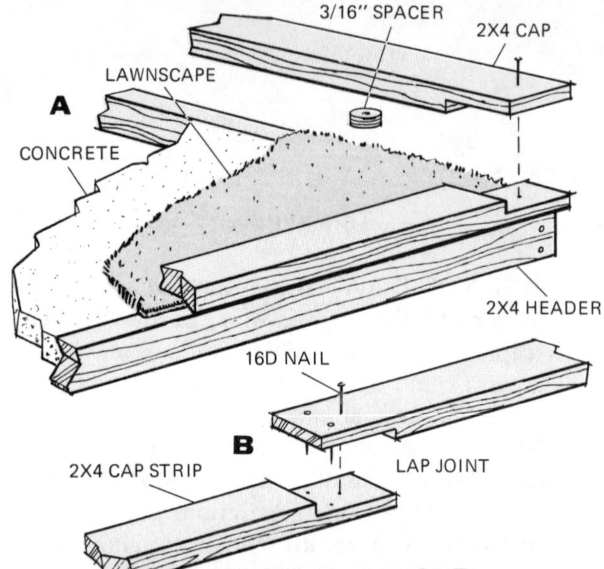

TYPICAL LAYOUT

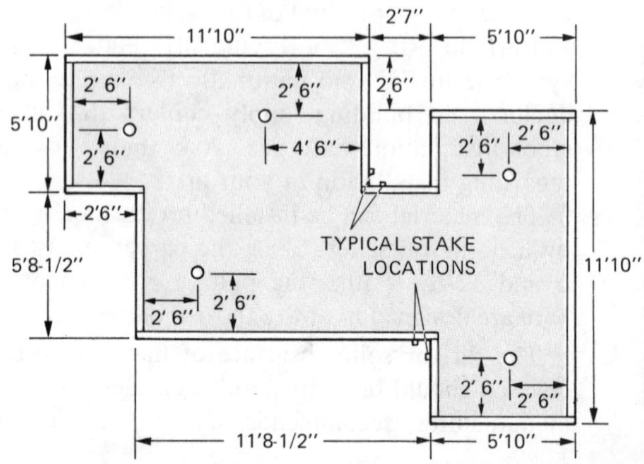

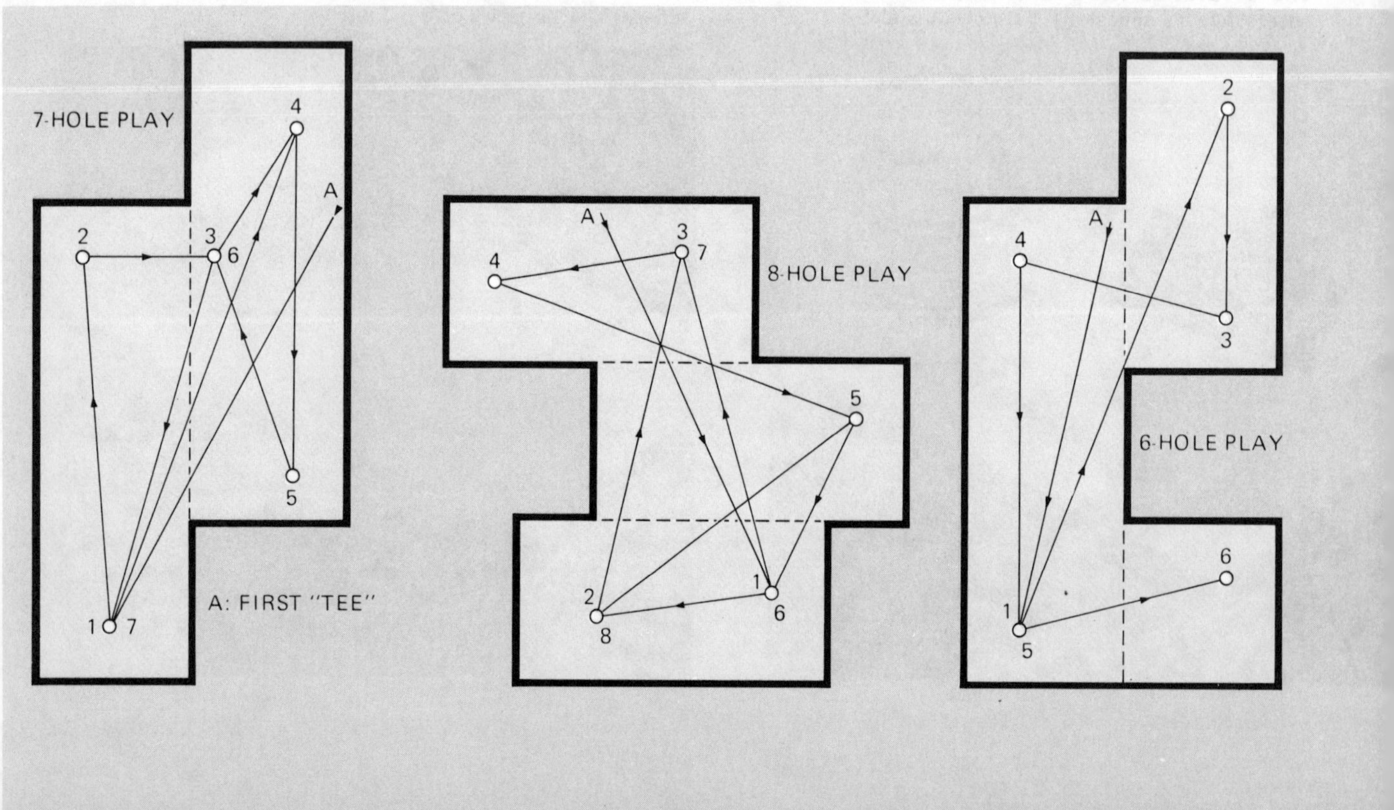

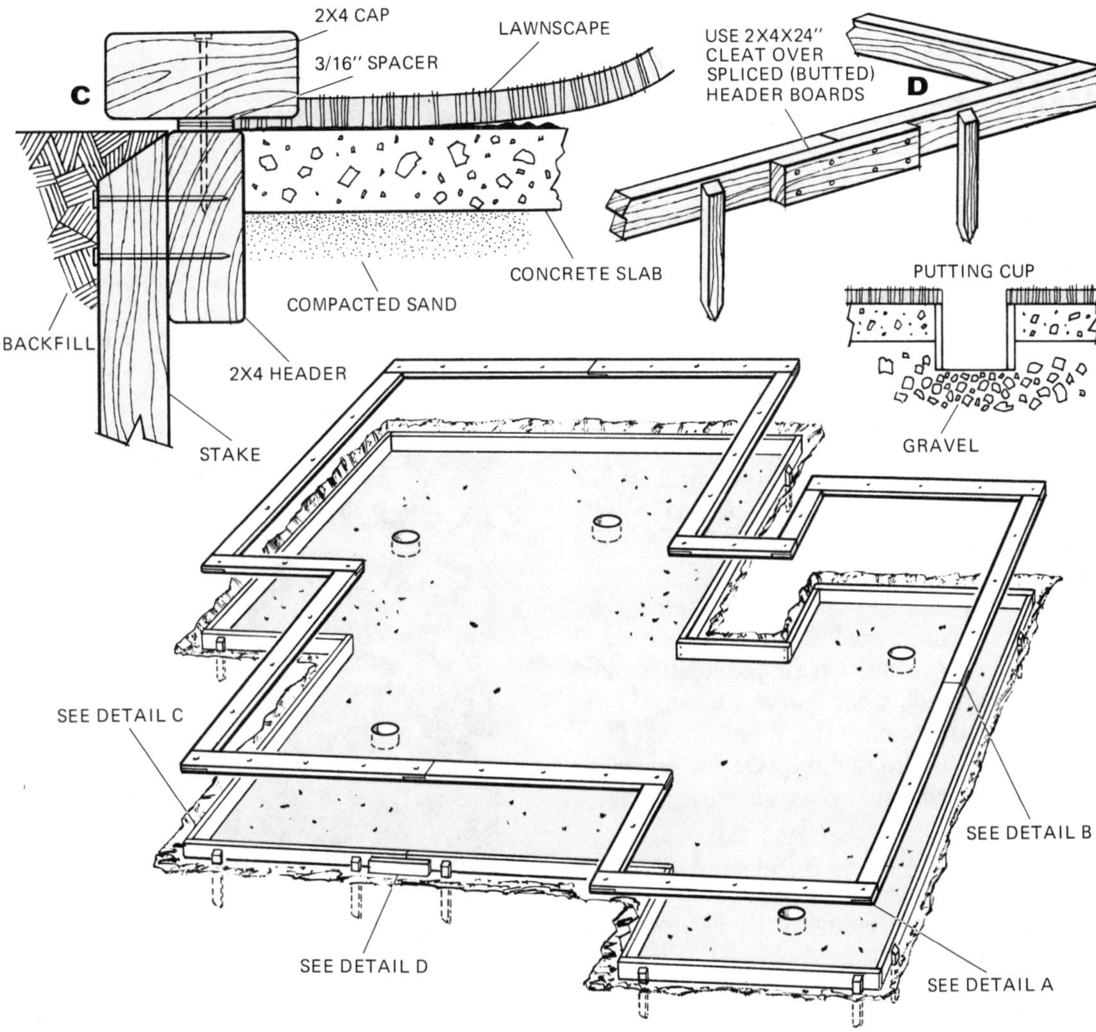
C
2X4 CAP
3/16" SPACER
LAWNSCAPE
CONCRETE SLAB
COMPACTED SAND
BACKFILL
2X4 HEADER
STAKE
D
USE 2X4X24" CLEAT OVER SPLICED (BUTTED) HEADER BOARDS
PUTTING CUP
GRAVEL
SEE DETAIL C
SEE DETAIL B
SEE DETAIL D
SEE DETAIL A

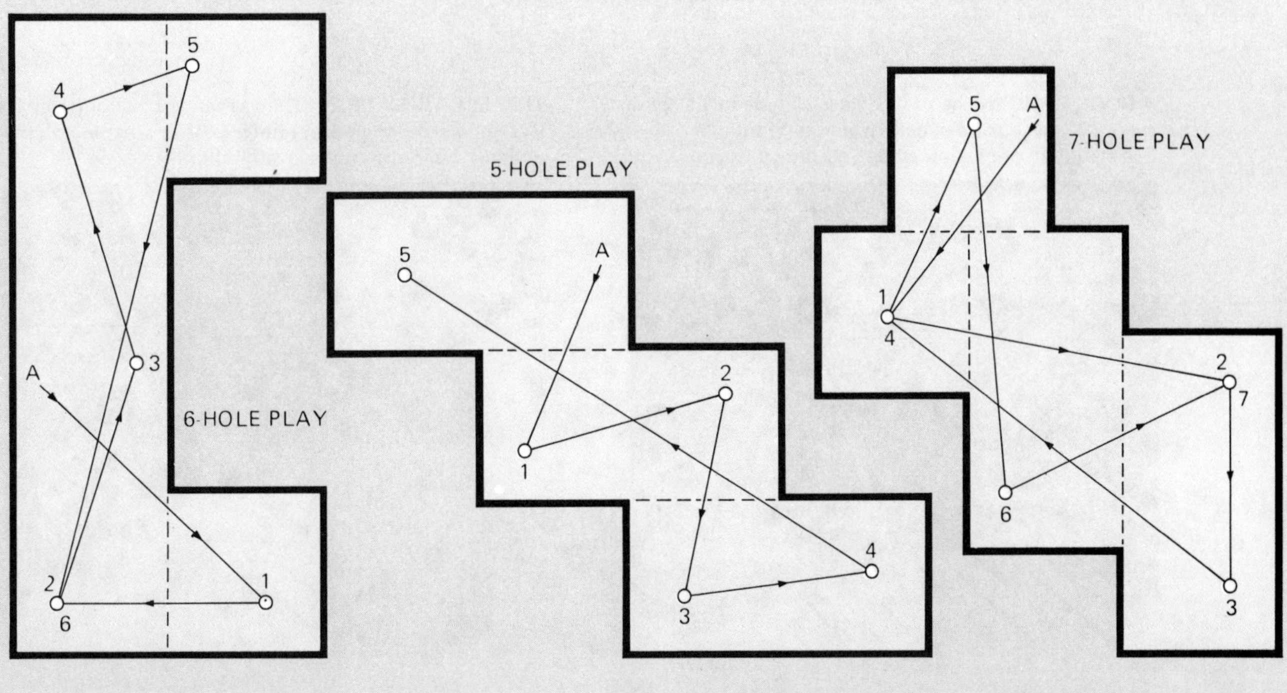
6-HOLE PLAY
5-HOLE PLAY
7-HOLE PLAY

At sea—with PVC

Versatile PVC pipe can take the water and weather exposure that comes with a large variety of boating jobs

By ROD RADFORD

WITH A NAME like polyvinyl chloride, it's no wonder they call it PVC. And with its no-sanding, no-scraping, no-varnishing qualities for easy maintenance, no wonder it's ideal for use afloat.

Many people have used PVC for lawn-sprinkler systems, saved $300, and discovered the inexpensive material is simple to shape and assemble with heat, a hacksaw and a can of PVC cement. In many other uses, it has proved itself almost impervious to salt, rot, rust and corrosion—so marine applications, as shown here, are a natural.

White is often used to reflect the heat of the sun. Either Schedule 40 or Schedule 80 pipe is ideal. Plumbing and hardware stores stock it in ½ to 16-in. diameters.

SEE ALSO
Accident prevention, water . . . Boating, safety . . . Knots . . . Life preservers . . . Outboard motors

PVC FLAGSTAFFS with upper 5-ft. sections of ¾-in. pipe reinforced with ½-in. pipe support flags.

A DOCK HANGER line of flexible PVC pipe in a strong, rigid PVC base is an excellent way to reduce line-handling confusion when you return to your slip.

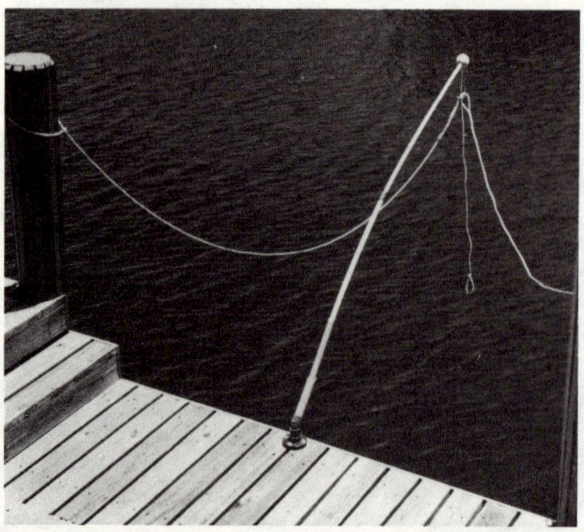

THIS MULTIUSE BRACKET was made by submerging PVC pipe in boiling water until soft, then stepping on the end and bending up the overall fitting.

A RIGID BASE made with a 45° PVC angle fitting and a smaller pipe insertion becomes a flag or rod holder.

A CHART STORAGE tube that floats can be made by sealing one end of a PVC pipe and capping the other.

THIS DOCK safety ladder fashioned from PVC piping and four flanges is impervious to rot and corrosion.

A PORTABLE LADDER uses 1½-in. PVC pipe joined by polyurethane cord with knots supporting rungs.

A FLOATING BOATHOOK is made with ¾-in. pipe, a vinyl-covered hardware hook and a rubber hand grip.

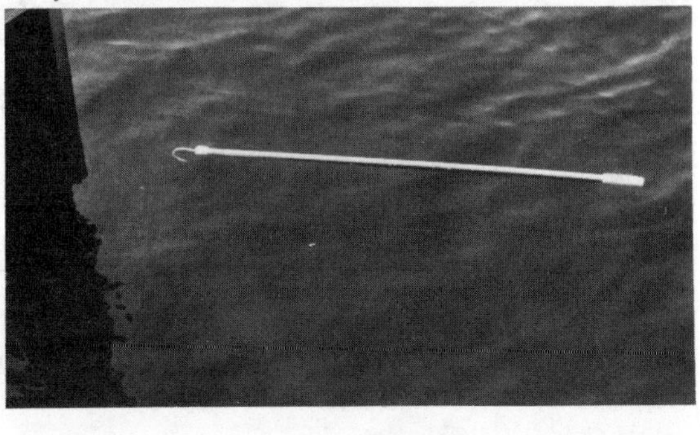

THIS CLUB for unruly fish is made by weighting one end of ½-in. pipe with cement and adding a handle.

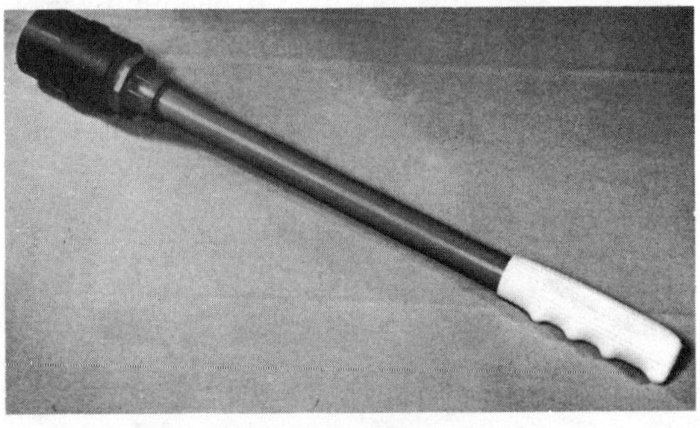

An entry floor that won't wear out

IF YOU HAVE wood floors, there are probably a few spots that are dull and worn. This is most likely to happen just inside your front or back door where traffic is heaviest. These areas take the worst beating in bad weather because they're the principal targets of muddy shoes, snow-covered boots and dripping raincoats. Quarry tile can provide a long-term solution. It's available in good-looking colors and a varied selection of sizes and patterns.

No matter which setting system you use, prepare the job by thoroughly cleaning the subfloor and squaring up your layout to minimize any cutting. Most tile suppliers have cutters and chippers that you can rent to avoid buying the tools for a one-shot job. Here's a rundown of the different applications that will give you a solid, long-lasting job.

application over concrete

■ **Organic adhesive** is a prepared material that comes in tubes or cans and is usually applied with a notched trowel. This method is clean, fast, and gives you flexibility in correcting tile placement. *Read the label cautions.* Most recommend thorough ventilation during use; some are flammable and their solvents may cause skin irritation. The recommended grout is a 1:2 ratio of

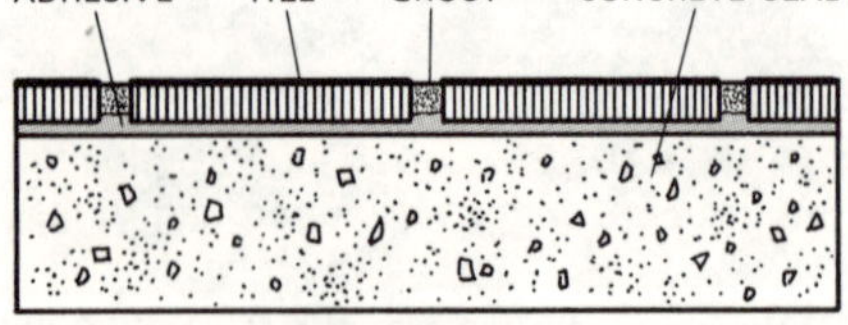

ORGANIC ADHESIVE

portland cement and sand. It should be wet-cured by covering the entire floor with polyethylene sheeting for three days. Water is spread on the surface the second day and the sheet replaced.

SEE ALSO

Entryways . . . Floors . . . Home improvement . . . Pier sets . . . Tile, floor

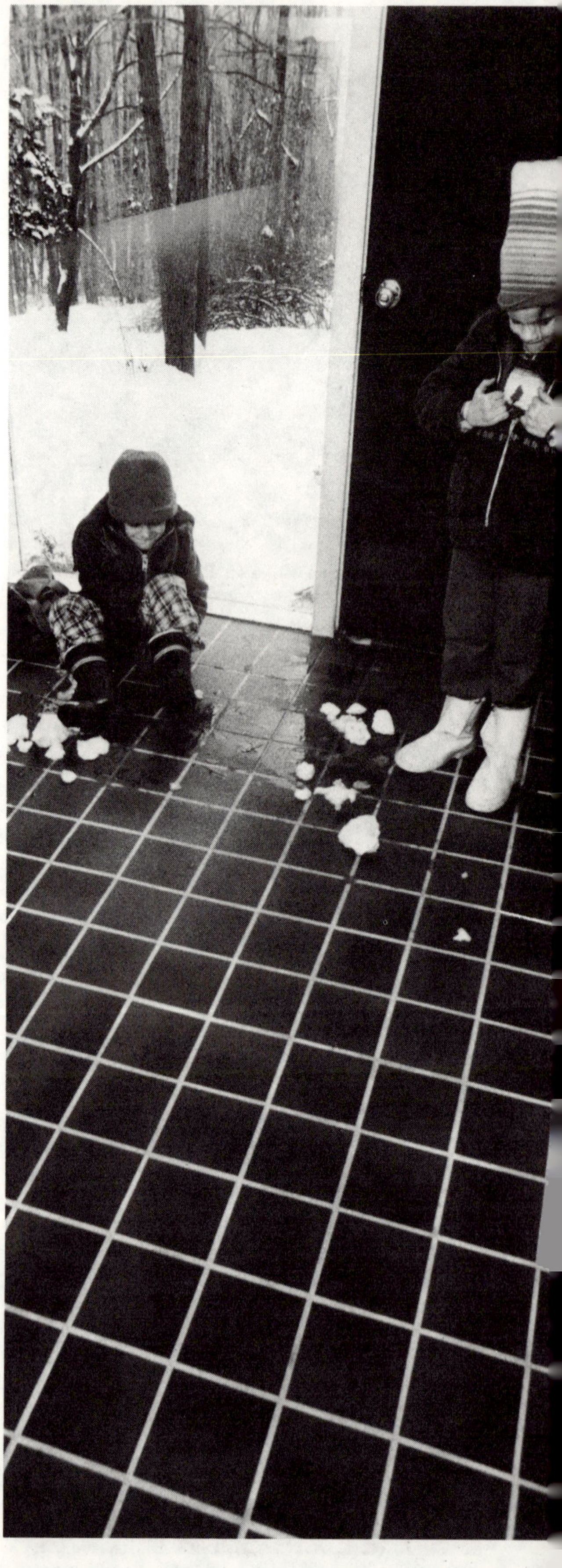

■ **Cement mortar** is a mixture of portland cement and sand in the proportion of 1:6. The mortar can be reinforced with metal lath or mesh.

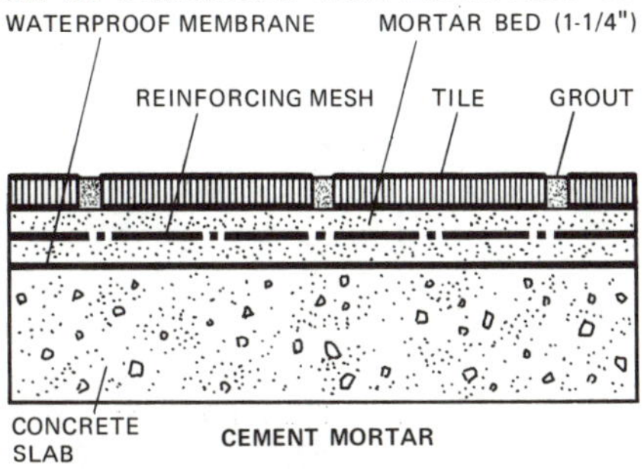

CEMENT MORTAR

This installation can withstand prolonged contact with water. The thickness of the bed (¾ to 1¼ inches) gives you enough room to compensate for depressed or irregular areas. Use the same 1:2 cement-to-sand ratio for grout.

application over wood

■ **Organic adhesive** is ideal here, too. Many homeowners are already familiar with this process because it is similar to installing vinyl tile. The recommended grout over a wood subfloor is latex-portland cement. The latex additive makes it less rigid than regular cement grout. The Tile Council of America sets standards calling for a ⅝-inch plywood subfloor and a ⅜-inch exterior-grade plywood underlayment.

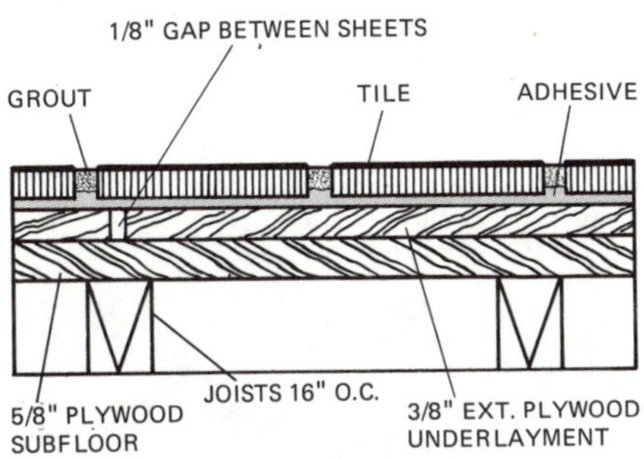

ORGANIC ADHESIVE

■ **Epoxy adhesive** combines resins and hardeners to provide high bond strength. It is recommended for renovations where ceramic tile is to be installed over existing resilient tile. This eliminates the need for a new layer of plywood. A latex-portland cement grout should be used.

The installation methods detailed above are rated for residential and light industrial use. There are even more elaborate procedures (although you won't need them) that use chemically resistant mortar on an acid-proof membrane that can withstand 300-pound loads on steel wheels as well as severe chemical exposure. Durability and low maintenance are the qualities that make ceramic tile more desirable than resilient tile. For these reasons, all of the platforms built for the new rapid transit system in Washington, D.C., will use ceramic tile. So don't worry when the kids come home covered with mud or snow—your quarry-tile floor can take it.

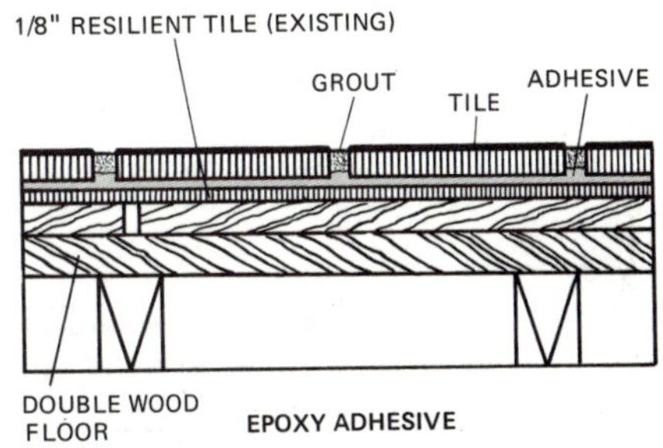

EPOXY ADHESIVE

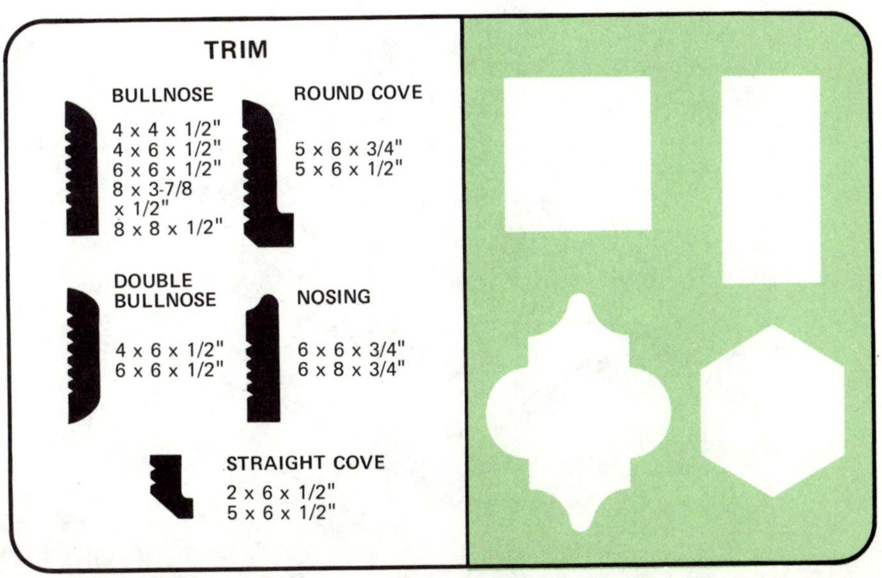

AS SHOWN at right, quarry tile comes in several sizes and patterns. Matching trim is available for edges and corners.

Tabletop bookrack

By KENNETH WELLS

■ DESIGNED FOR PAPERBACKS, this smart-looking metal rack will hold 36 or more books. It's a bend-and-solder project and the photo below shows how the bending jig is used in a vise for making neat bends at each end of the brass-rod backrest. It's later attached to the ends of the steel base by peening the tenoned ends. Notice that the holes for the 3/16-in. rods in the end pieces are drilled clear through except for the middle ones.

The various parts are soldered by first applying flux to the feed holes provided, heating the metal with a torch and touching solder to the holes. Capillary action causes the solder to flow around the joint. The legs are bent after soldering by slipping a piece of pipe over the protruding rod, and then fitted with ball feet of wood or plastic. Paint the steel parts flat black, polish the brass and coat with clear lacquer.

SEE ALSO
Book shelves . . . Bookcases . . . Bookends . . . Bookracks . . . Bookstands . . . Metalworking . . . Storage ideas . . . Tubing, metal

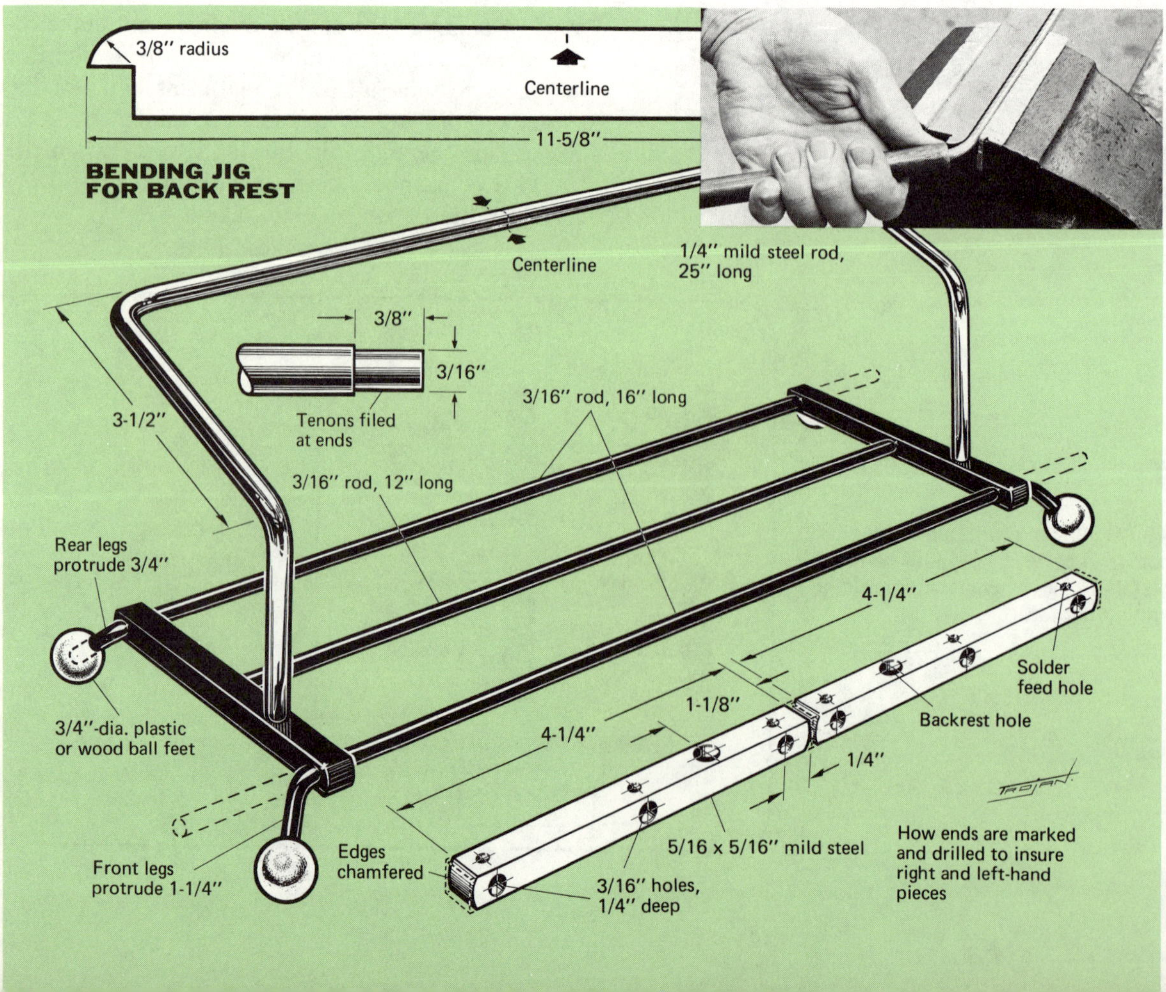

How to use a radial-arm saw

By W. CLYDE LAMMEY

From a simple power tool for crosscutting, mitering and ripping lumber, the radial-arm saw has evolved into a nearly complete power workshop in one unit. Using accessories and a variety of setups, you can do shaping, routing, grooving, sanding, dadoing and rabbeting

A RADIAL SAW is comparable to a table saw turned upside down. The motor, arbor, controls and mountings are all *above* the table rather than *below* it.

In crosscutting and mitering operations, and also in dadoing, you move the blade or cutter to the work, rather than the work to the blade or cutter as with the table saw. The exceptions are ripping, and some operations with accessories where the work is moved to the cutter, as in grooving, rabbeting, routing and shaping.

This "upside down" saw calls for a somewhat different operating technique and an extra measure of caution in all operations. This applies even when the blade housing and guard are in position. You will notice when making that first crosscut with your new saw that the blade tends to move, or "pull," toward you as the cut progresses. You are making what experienced operators of radial saws call a "climb" cut, where the blade tends to pull itself into the work. Here you make sure of that extra measure of caution and have a firm hold on the handle with which you draw the blade forward into the workpiece; you actually offer a slight resistance to the travel of the blade into the workpiece. Otherwise the cut may be too fast for smoothness, and the blade may exit from the cut unexpectedly, possibly endangering you. This is especially true when crosscutting or mitering wide pieces of stock 2 in. or more in thickness.

The rules for safe operation of the radial saw are quite simple and should quickly become habit: (a) Before you plug in the tool, make sure the motor switch is in the "off" position. (b) Make sure before starting the motor that all control handles are tightened properly. (c) Never—repeat, *never*—permit loose pieces of stock, other objects such as end cuttings, wrenches, clamps, etc., on the table when operating the unit. (d) Never—repeat, *never*—allow your attention to wander even for a moment while the unit is in operation. (e) Always operate the unit with both the blade housing and the blade guard in position.

All the precautions can be summed up in two words—*be careful!*

The manual that comes with the saw will tell: how to set it up and operate it when making the basic cuts; how to align the blade should this be necessary; and how to arrange the table spacer boards for in and out ripping.

Some radials may come with the table already grooved and recessed. If not you can easily cut these yourself. To make the crosscut groove, raise the blade to clear, slide the carriage back as far as it will go, start the motor, and lower the blade until it cuts into the table about 3/16 in. Then pull the blade forward as far as it will go. Cut the right and left miter grooves in the same manner, moving the arm 45 degrees to the right and left. Then raise the blade to clear, swing the arm to the 90 degree position, swing the yoke 90 degrees to the out-rip position, pull it forward as far as it will go, start the motor and lower the blade until it cuts into the table about 3/16 in. Push it back as far as it will go, very slowly, so that it cuts a concave recess in the tabletop. The purpose of the grooves and recess, of course, is to permit the lowering of the blade below the table surface so that it will cut all the way through the stock.

SEE ALSO

Bandsaws . . . Bench saws . . . Drill press techniques . . . Motors, shop . . . Power-tool stands . . . Saws, radial-arm . . . Shapers . . . Table saws . . . Workbenches . . . Workshops

CROSSCUTTING is a basic operation on radial saw. Blade is drawn only far enough to cut through material, then returned to starting position.

WHEN SETTING up for ripping, tilt blade housing to just clear the stock, then adjust kickback arm with a block the thickness of stock to be ripped.

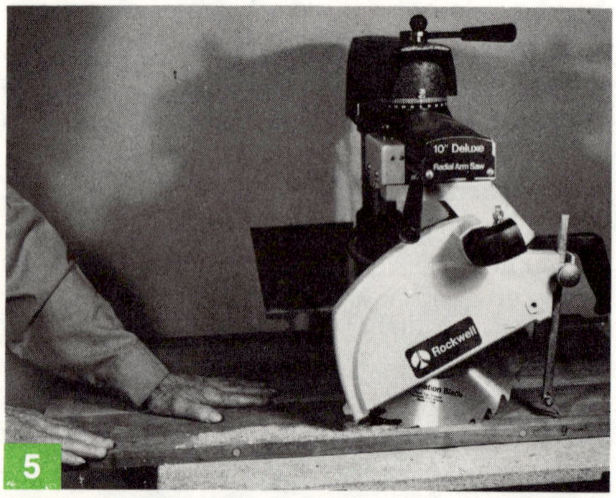

RIP CUT in relatively wide stock is common radial-saw operation. In rip cuts make sure carriage, yoke and blade housing are securely locked in place.

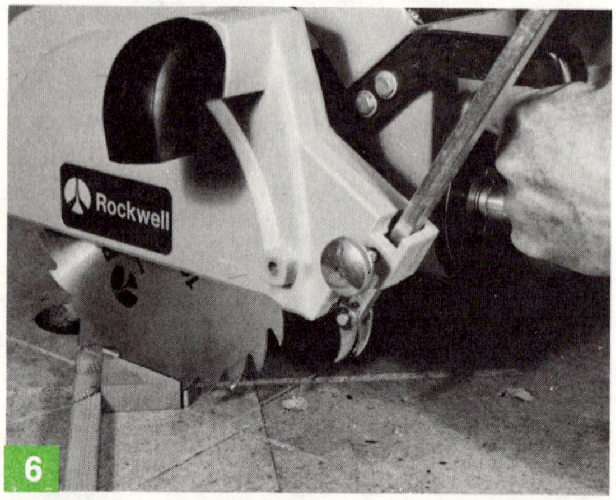

LEFT-HAND miter cut is perhaps less common of the two. As in all crosscutting, draw blade only far enough to cut through stock.

In making the crosscut, Fig. 1, you have a choice of left or right-hand pull. In the illustration, the left-hand pull is shown, as the longer stock is more conveniently held in the position by the right hand. If the workpiece were short, and only a small waste piece was to be removed, you could use the right-hand pull with left-hand hold. Either position is permissible, but you should know where that right or left holding hand is at all times!

When making the crosscut or the miter (either right or lefthand) don't pull the blade all the way past the stock. Stop when the waste is completely severed. This assures that when you move the blade back through the cut there is no chance that the portion of the blade coming up will catch the waste. The same is true when making the miter cuts.

Before you make a rip cut, always set the anti-kickback arm as in Fig. 2. First tilt the blade guard so that its rear edge will be about ⅛ to ¼ in. above the surface of the stock. Then, if ¾-in. stock is to be ripped, set the kickback arm with the swiveling points, or fingers, in the position shown, using a ¾-in. block. Next, if you have not already done so, set the pointers on the rip scale to the correct positions to assure ripping to the precise width desired, Fig. 3. (See your instruction manual.) In any ripping operation make sure *both yoke and carriage* are locked in position before starting the motor.

When ripping short, narrow stock as in Fig. 4, use a push stick and place the stick so that it contacts the material near the outer edge as shown. This will prevent any tendency of the workpiece to edge away from the fence. Fig. 5 shows the common procedure of ripping a long, wide workpiece. *Here the blade guard has been removed, as it has in other following illustrations, only for the sake of clarity.*

Figs. 6 and 7 show positions in cutting left and right-hand miters. The left-hand miter is the least

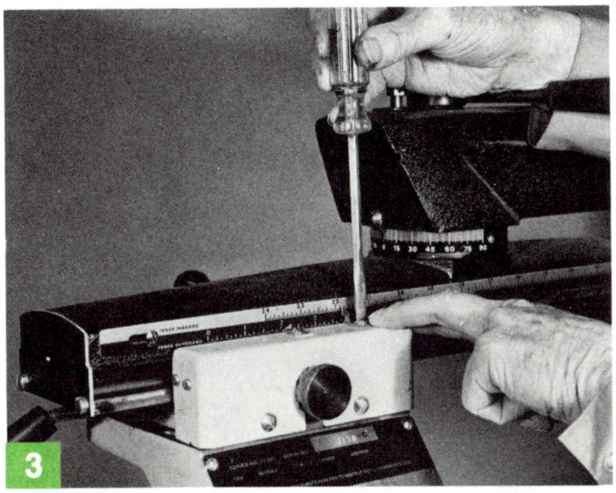

IF YOU HAVE NOT already done so, set rip-scale pointers for in and out-rip positions to assure accuracy. See instructions that come with your saw.

USE PUSH STICK when ripping short, narrow stock. Place stick near outer corner of stock to prevent it drifting away from the fence.

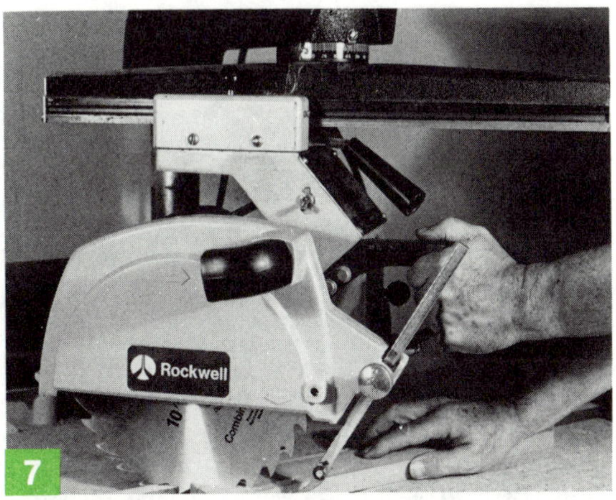

RIGHT-HAND MITER is made just opposite. After first cut, turn stock over and move to left to miter opposite end. Exception is mitering molded stock.

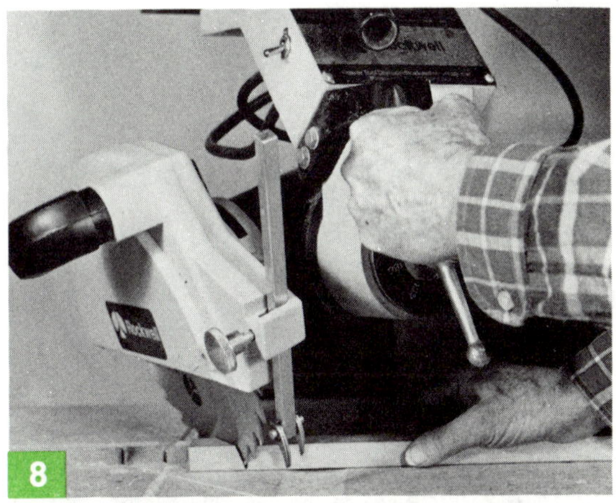

COMPOUND MITER is made by swinging the arm and tilting the blade the required number of degrees. Consult a table for proper degree setting.

used as it generally is possible to shift the stock from right to left positions after turning it over when necessary to miter both ends. The exception, of course, is mitering picture molding. The compound miter, Fig. 8, requires setting both the arm and the tilt to the required number of degrees to form the "hopper" joint. There are tables available which give the degree settings for this type of joinery on the radial-arm saw.

When you want to trim a number of small workpieces to exact length, you can clamp a stop to the fence as in Fig. 9. Make sure that the clamp is properly positioned and that it is *tight*. Remove each waste piece as it is cut only after the saw is moved back to its extreme rear position.

Your radial saw is a first-rate disc sander. You first remove the fence and substitute two ¾-in. square strips, placing these on each side of the disc as in Fig. 10. Then lower the disc through the slot thus formed as in Fig. 11. Be sure that the disc clears before starting the motor; also be sure that it just clears the fixed edge of the saw table. Use a medium to coarse grade abrasive disc for fast cutting and to avoid burning the end grain of hardwoods. Use the finer grades for finishing, and apply only light pressure to the work.

To use a drum sander, swivel the motor to the vertical position with the spindle, or arbor, down. Cut a half-round opening in the edge of each of the spacer boards, as in Fig. 12. The diameter of the opening should be about 1½ times the diameter of the drum. Leave the square spacers in position as shown in Fig. 11, but be sure that the table clamps are drawn tight so nothing can shift while sanding is being done. Be especially careful to avoid a finger or hand contacting the rotating drum; a rather painful burn can be the penalty. The same caution is necessary when using the disc. Also, in any of these operations, make sure that the yoke is

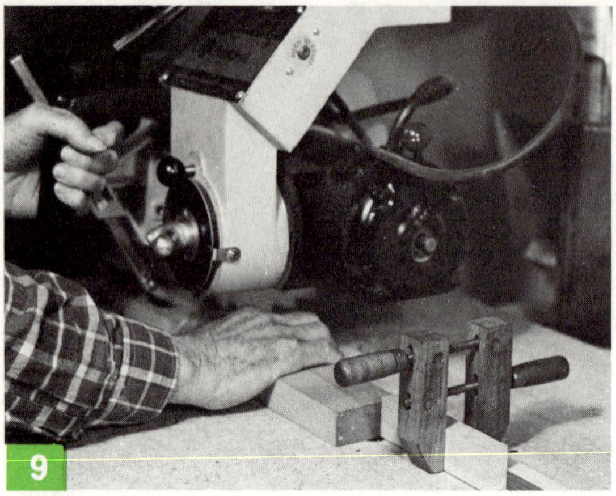

TO CUT DUPLICATE short lengths, clamp a stop to the fence and measure distance from blade to stop. Make sure that the clamp is drawn tight!

FOR DISC SANDING substitute ¾-in. strips for fence, one on each side of disc. Lower disc into opening and be sure carriage and yoke are locked.

WITH THE MOTOR still in the vertical position it's a straight router. If the groove is more than ⅛ in. in depth, cut in two or more passes.

REPLACE ROUTER CHUCK with three-knife shaper cutter and accessory spindle and you have a vertical-spindle shaper. Make the finish cut in two passes.

locked securely in position with the yoke clamp provided.

The radial is not only a useful drum and disc sander, it's a handy router, as you can see in Fig. 13. It takes only a minute to make the conversion. Leave the motor in its vertical position and replace the drum with an accessory router-bit chuck. Set the motor to the desired position to rout the groove, lock it in position, and feed the work slowly. If the groove is more than ⅛ in. deep you'll get a smoother job by cutting to the desired depth in several passes, each not more than about ⅛ in. deep.

In Fig. 14 the radial is set up as a spindle shaper, using an accessory spindle and a three-knife cutterhead of the type used on vertical-spindle shapers. The guard does not come with the accessory spindle; it's improvised from a sheet-metal disc and is not really necessary if one is cautious. In this operation it's best to make the cut in two or more passes for the smoothest work. Feed slowly in either hard or softwood; again, make sure the yoke is securely locked before starting the cut.

A quick conversion makes your radial saw a rotary planer, as in Fig. 15. Use the same two-piece fence as in shaping, change to the router-bit chuck, and fit a rotary planing head. As you can see, it does a smooth, clean job. If you must reduce the thickness of stock more than ⅛ in., make the cuts in two or more passes.

If you don't have the three-knife molding cutter pictured in Fig. 14, you can set up with the three-knife head such as that commonly used for cutting moldings on a table saw. Figs. 16 and 17 show how the setup is made, using the special guard furnished as an accessory. Notice in Fig. 17 that the motor is tilted about 5 degrees from the vertical. For this work you'll need to make the special fence, as shown in the inset detail, to obtain the necessary clearance. The molding shape is similar to that being cut in

WHEN SANDING end grain, use coarse abrasive and a light pressure to avoid "burning" stock. Don't permit hand or fingers to touch the rotating disc!

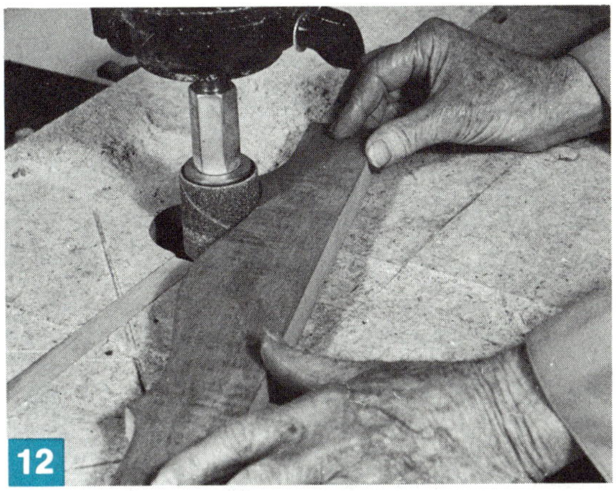

YOUR RADIAL SAW is also a drum sander. Swing motor to vertical position and cut half-round opening in spacer boards. Use ¾-in. spacers as shown.

REPLACE shaping spindle with that for router bit, insert planing head and you have a surfacer. Cuts should not exceed ⅛ in.

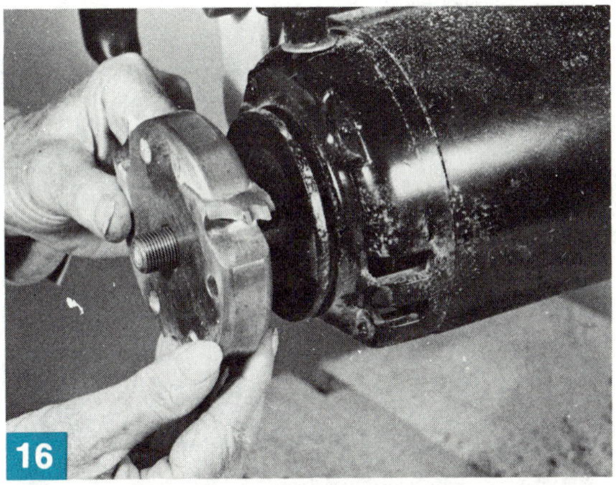

A MOLDING HEAD of the type used on the table saw will also work well on most radials. Here the three-knife head is being placed on the motor spindle.

Fig. 14, but of course other molding shapes can be cut with the same setup. In Fig. 18 a panel-raising cut is being made with the same setup, but using a straight knife on the cutterhead rather than the molding knife shown on the head in Fig. 16. You can also do rabbeting with this setup, tilting the motor back to the vertical position. Again the reminder: Don't forget when making any of these setups to lock the yoke firmly in place so that it cannot slide forward or back. And be just as certain that all controls are tight before starting the motor.

Figs. 19 and 20 show dadoing and grooving with a carbide-tipped cutter of the "wobble" type; the width of cut is adjusted by movable "washers" that form the hub. It's a simple gadget easily adjusted for various groove widths, and cuts extremely smoothly on both hard and soft woods. Notice in Fig. 20 that the blade housing has been tilted back so that the rear edge just clears the surface of the stock, as in the ripping cut with the saw blade; also that the kickback arm has been adjusted for ¾-in. stock.

In Fig. 21 the same type of head pictured in Fig. 20 is being used to make spaced dado cuts in a dentil molding. Here the cuts are spaced by means of a heavy pencil line on the table; if you need greater accuracy, make the special fence in the detail having a fixed stop, the stop entering each successive cut as you move the stock after making the first dado cut.

In ordinary shop work you'll not often be called upon to make a uniform bend in stock. In case you need to make such a bend, Fig. 22 and the insert detail show how it can be done. Once you get the spacing of the successive cuts, as in the detail, mark the location of the cuts on one face of the workpiece and then set the saw blade to cut within about ⅛ in. less than the thickness of the stock. Should it be necessary to hold the workpiece in the curved position until application, Fig. 21, place a few drops of glue in each

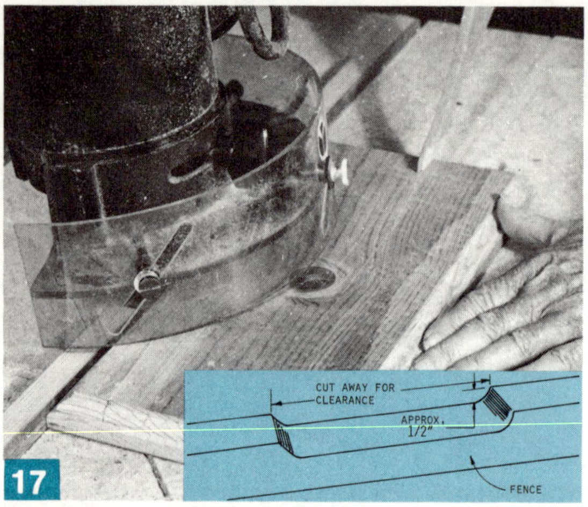

USING HEAD pictured in Fig. 16 and accessory guard permits doing a range of shaping work. When workpieces are small use push stick.

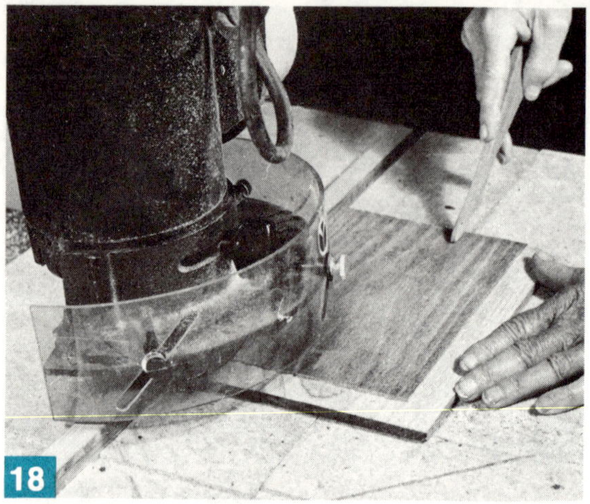

HERE'S A panel-raising job being done with the same head shown in Fig. 16, using a straight cutter. The motor is tilted and the same guard is used.

GROOVES are cut with the same head, the setup made as in ripping cuts. It's well to test for depth on waste stock to assure accuracy. Use the push stick.

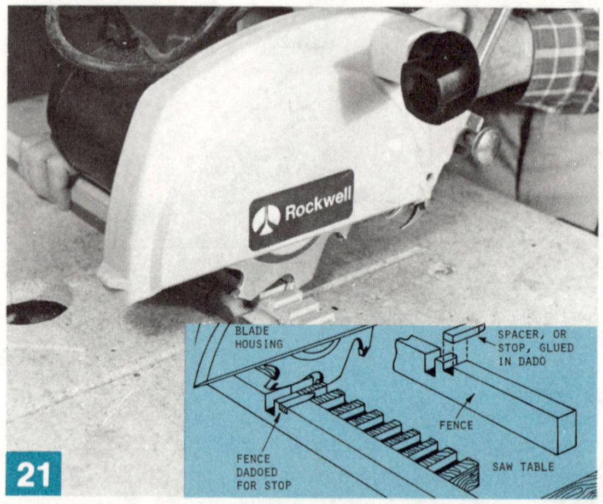

IN MAKING a dentil molding the cuts are simply spaced dadoes. For precise accuracy you can make the special fence shown in the insert detail.

JOINING NARROW pieces to build up to a given width is usually done by doweling but the pros generally prefer to cut a glue joint on the meeting edges.

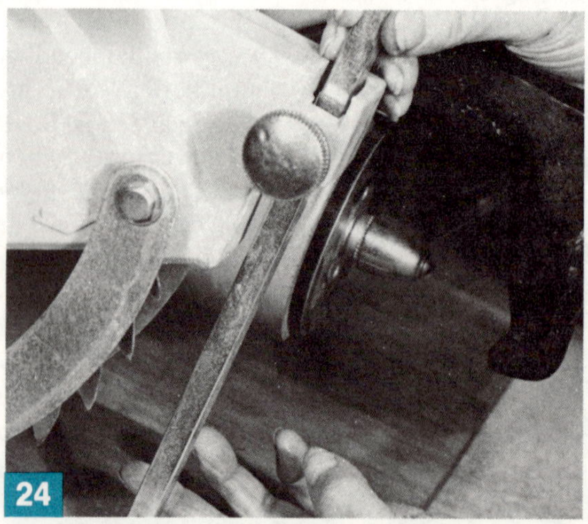

BY INVERTING the kickback arm in its opening in the housing it can form an additional blade guard for added safety when making repetitive cuts.

CUT DADOES from ¼ to ¾ in. with grooving head of the "wobble" type. Adjustments for width are made by rotating washers that form hub.

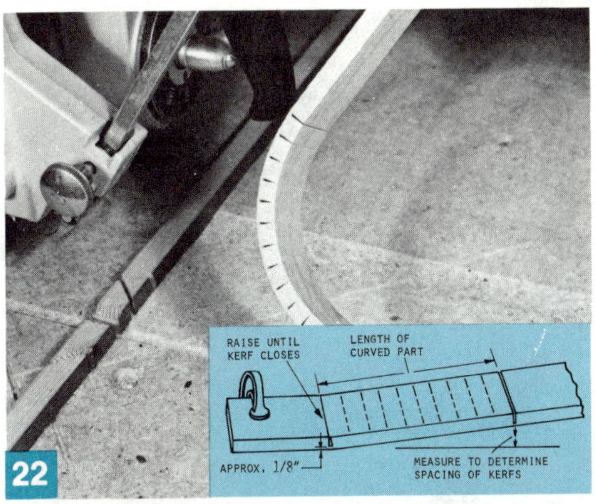

IT'S NOT OFTEN you'll need to bend material by kerfing but the photo and inset detail show how it can be done. Space the kerfs accurately.

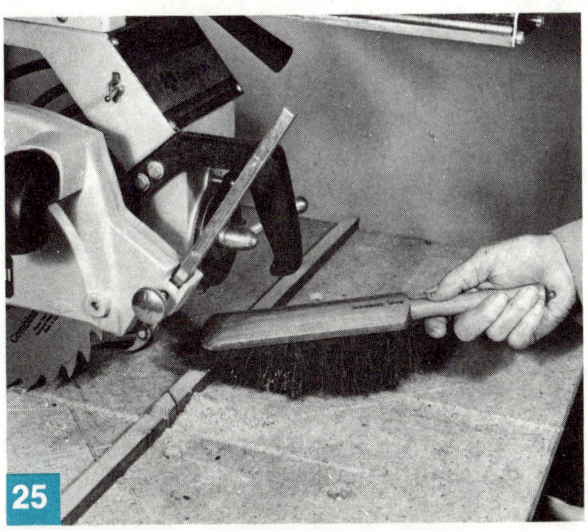

KEEP A BRUSH handy to clear away sawdust that tends to collect in front of the fence. It can cause inaccuracies and may be an operating hazard.

kerf, bend to the full curve and hold in place with clamps until the glue has set.

Home woodworkers generally join pieces edge-to-edge with dowels where it is necessary to build up to a given width with narrow pieces. Many pros prefer to cut glue joints on both edges of the joining pieces. This is easily done on the radial saw by using a three-knife glue-joint cutter and the same molding cutter accessory arbor as that pictured in Fig. 14; also the same two-piece fence. In this job you have to be especially careful to set the cutter to the precise height to cut accurately so that the joining pieces will fit together without any offset at the joining edges. It's best to check the setting by making test cuts on waste stock.

The kickback arm can provide additional guarding of the blade in some operations, such as making a series of repetitive crosscuts. Invert it in its opening and then slide it down so that the end just clears the surface of the stock being cut, as in Fig. 24. In this position it could, conceivably, prevent fingers of even a hand contacting the spinning blade. Make sure that the holding screw is tight and also be sure to replace the arm correctly when changing it back to its original position. On most radials you will have to remove the blade housing to make this change either way.

It's well to check the blade guard occasionally to make sure that all parts, such as the bolts holding the curved parts and the spacer at the back, are properly tightened. Any such metal parts that chance to come loose while the saw is in operation might be caught by the blade and thrown with dangerous force.

a necessary precaution

A final and very necessary precaution is pictured in Fig. 25. Keep a brush handy to clear away sawdust that tends to collect in front of the fence. It not only can cause inaccurate work, but can also be a hazard. It may be a cause of the blade binding suddenly due to the stock being inadvertantly tilted. This may stall the motor, damage the material or even cause an injury. And cautious operators who don't wear glasses always wear industrial goggles or a face shield to protect their eyes.

There are, of course, other operations than those shown which can be done on a radial saw, such as novelty cuts, crosshatching with dado cuts and the like.

In any case, a radial saw is one of the most versatile of all shop tools.

A fine cabinet for your radial-arm saw

By HARRY WICKS

This unique cabinet, which you can build in your shop, makes use of that wasted space beneath your radial saw— no matter what brand or size of saw you own

SEE ALSO

Drawers . . . Motors, shop . . . Power-tool stands . . . Storage ideas . . . Workbenches . . . Workshops

■ THIS CABINET for a radial saw was designed to provide a convenient, attractive and easy-to-keep-clean storage unit that will hold the accessories you need for your saw. This particular cabinet fits beneath Sears' 12-in. radial saw. However, the overall size can be easily altered to fit any make of radial saw.

To make cleanup a simple chore, we covered all exposed parts of the cabinet with Johns-Manville Melamite (plastic laminate). For appearance and eye-relief, we used avocado and white. Admittedly, the laminate is a luxury, but the thought of never having to repaint a dirt-smeared cabinet more than justified the cash outlay. However, if you prefer, the cabinet can simply be painted with an enamel.

How it's built. Constructed of ¾-in. A-D plywood, the box is actually symmetrical—with one exception: The top, bottom and sides are edge rabbeted to receive the ¼-in. hardboard back. Similarly, drawer slides at the back are set in for the back. All edges are flush.

When laying out your cabinet, take all dimensions directly from your radial saw. Then, if any dimensions vary from those shown in the drawing, simply mark the changes right on the drawing and custom-build your cabinet to suit your saw. Also, the dimensions shown do not allow for the laminate, so make certain that you make such allowance if you plan to cover your cabinet.

Also, when laying out your cabinet—and before doing any cutting, rabbeting, or dadoing—double check exact location of the four drawers at the front. If you've altered the cabinet dimensions, drawer depths must be adjusted accordingly.

The drawers. The amount of drawer space that the cabinet provides surprised me when we finished the project. In fact, there was more storage space than I needed for my radial-saw accessories, so I used the bottom drawer for table-saw items. And for the first time in 20 years I have all those items in one convenient spot.

For future flexibility, I decided simply to butt-join all divider/partitions. I used ½-in. pine, gluing and nailing them in place after positioning the various accessories in each drawer. Should my requirements ever change, it will be easy to knock out the old dividers and install new ones

BASIC CONSTRUCTION is symmetrical. The unit can be sectioned into identical quarters with one exception: Back edges of the sides are edge-rabbeted and drawer slides are let in ¼ in. to receive hardboard back. The ends are fitted with perforated board.

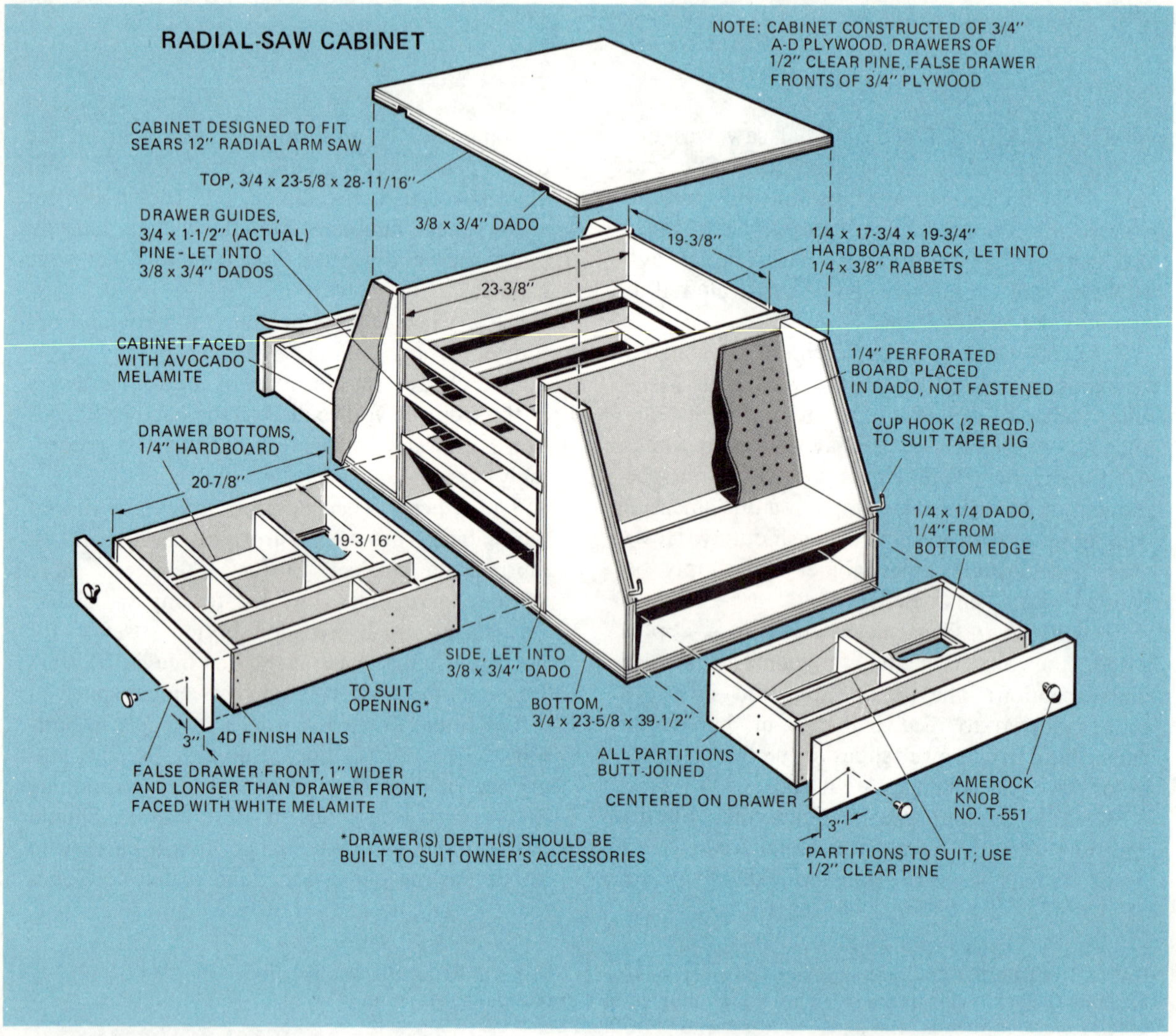

saw accessory cabinet, continued

where I want them. Location of accessories in the drawers is a matter of personal taste and working habits. I laid them all on the workbench and then, based upon frequency of use, placed them in the drawers.

The cabinet ends. Since there was space at both ends I installed a pair of shallow drawers. They are extremely handy for small items such as pencils, tape measures, dividers and the like—which seem to have a way of getting lost in the shuffle when left on the workbench. The perforated board was left brown (as it comes) and given two coats of McCloskey Heirloom varnish.

THE ACCESSORY cabinet sits on the base (below) and the whole assembly rides on casters.

Flexible drawer layouts

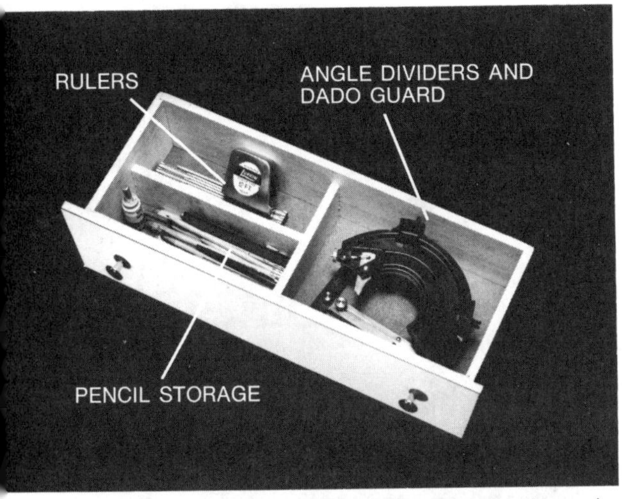

THE END drawer is shallow, ideal for frequently used items such as a tape measure and pencils.

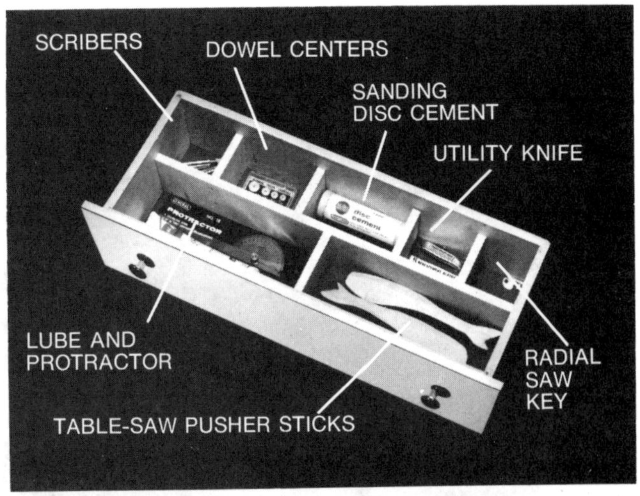

DRAWER at the other end holds more miscellaneous equipment, including the table-saw push sticks.

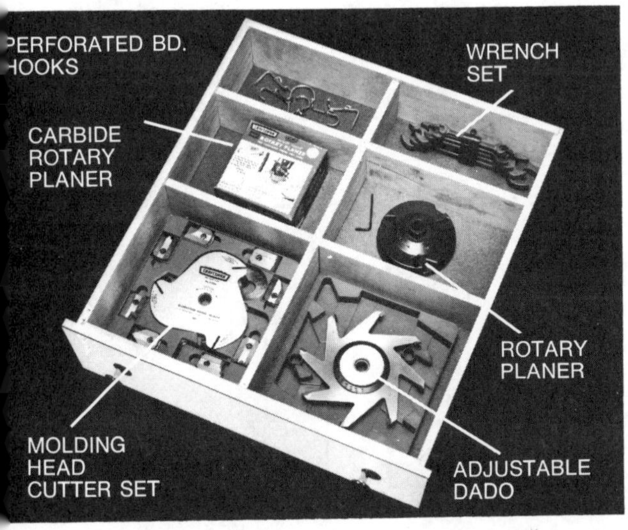

TOP FRONT drawer gets the most-used accessories plus such small items as the wrench set and hooks.

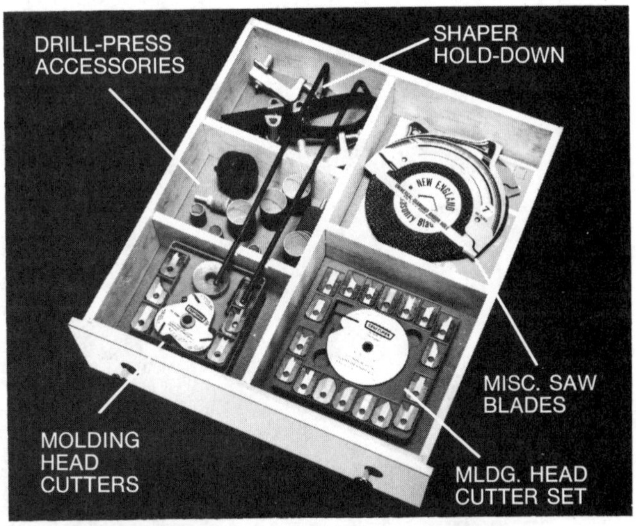

SECOND-DRAWER items are those used less often—for masonry- and metal-cutting blades, for example.

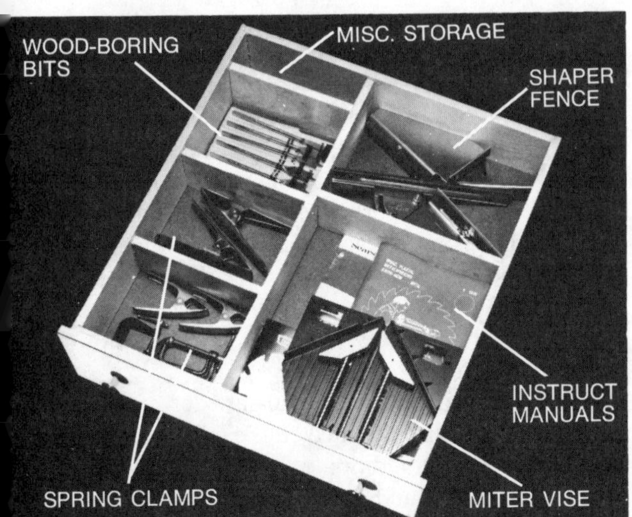

THE THIRD drawer concentrates the accessories for the saw's conversion to use as a drill press.

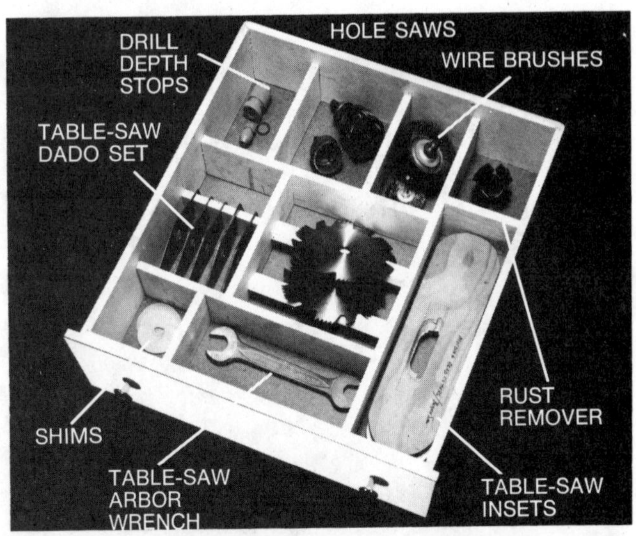

BOTTOM DRAWER keeps the bulk of the table-saw items together in one organized collection.

Removable perforated panels

SAW BLADES hang on a removable ½-in. dowel in the left end of the cabinet with separators.

PERFORATED boards aren't fastened permanently in place, but rest in dadoes as in the top sketch.

THE DOWEL'S block must be located with care; your blades' size will dictate its proper position.

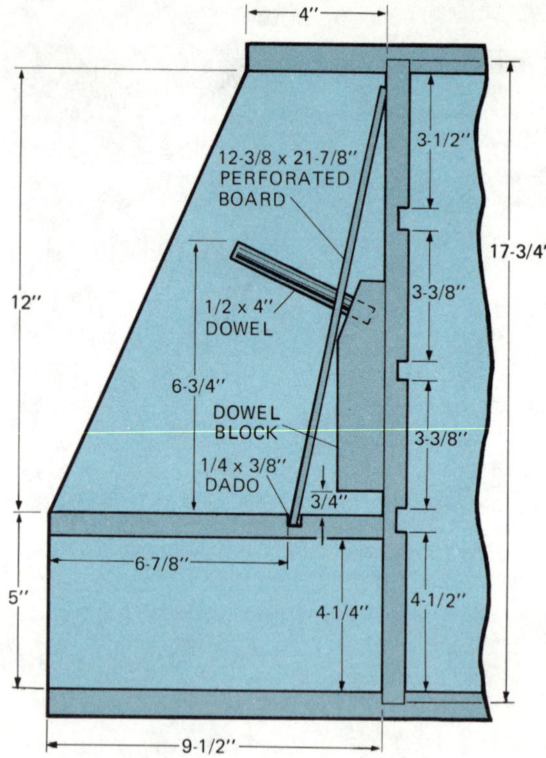

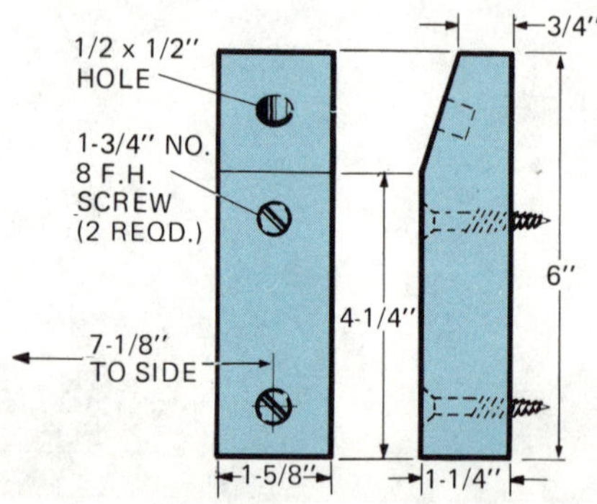

My feeling here was that if I painted them, dirt and smudge marks would inevitably appear and I would be constantly repainting.

The radial-saw blades are hung on a removable ½-in. dowel (see the sketch above). It's good shop practice to use spacers between the blades to keep them from dulling one another. (I used 6-in.-dia. circles cut from hardboard.)

The reason both perforated ends are removable is simply one of cleanliness. From time to time, the boards can be lifted out and the dust removed with a vacuum cleaner. To keep sawdust out of the drawers, the back is fitted with ¼-in. hardboard.

Even if the number of radial-saw accessories you currently own is limited, the cabinet shown will be a welcome addition to your shop. While in the process of building your accessory collection, you can use that valuable drawer space for almost any kind of storage.

Table extensions for a radial saw

By R. S. HEDIN

■ WHEN YOU'RE CUTTING long boards, the weight of the outboard section often makes the sawing operation a dangerous one. To avoid an accident under those conditions, a radial-saw table may be rigged with a pair of fold-down extensions. With proper support under those extra-long workpieces, cutting is a snap.

The extensions shown were made of plywood built up to match table thickness. Hinged to the saw table, they drop down when not needed, yet automatically engage when raised into position.

To fasten them to the saw table, lay a long board across and clamp the extensions to it. Use wood screws to attach them, and, if necessary, shim under the hinges to make the extensions flush with the tabletop. Notice in the drawing that the supports are offset 2 inches so that they pass each other when in the folded position.

SEE ALSO

Bench saws . . . Power-tool stands . . . Table saws . . . Workbenches . . . Workshops

DOUBLED-UP ½-in. plywood was used in these fold-down extensions to match the original table's thickness. You can shim the hinges if necessary.

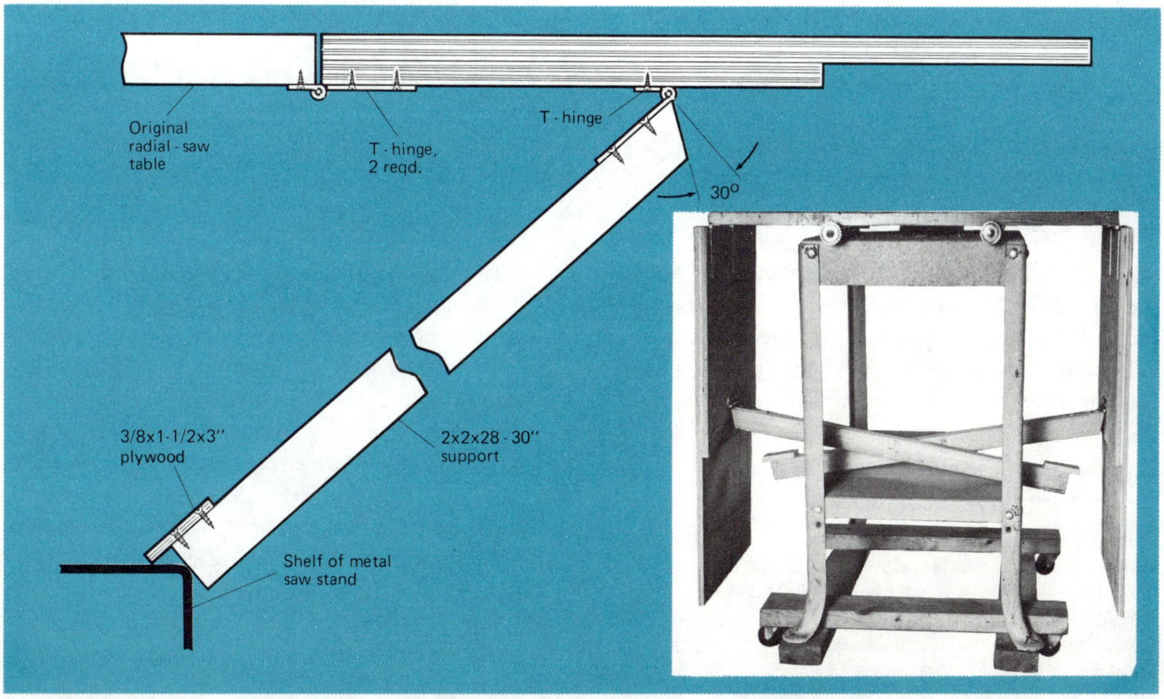

NO-NONSENSE, 16-ft. radial-arm saw bench has flip-away fence for oversize ripping. Generous-size drawers and storage tray offer space for accessories and in-progress work. Hefty casters make bench mobile and easy to align.

A radial saw bench with lots of storage

By LARRY KELLAM

■ A RADIAL-ARM saw bench that's close to being perfection can be yours by building this version for half the price of commercial models. The cost is about $200, using construction-grade, 2-inch stock for legs and rails. Drawers, cabinet front, cross members and tray edges are of 1-in. spruce stock. Drawer bottoms and cabinet sides are AC (good-one-side) plywood. The top surface is cut from a 4x10-ft. sheet of 1⅛-in. particleboard. Hardwood ties stabilize legs.

To begin, build the base, which has a front and rear rail, and eight connecting cross members glued into the dadoed rails. Clamp overnight. Notch the back rail and set ledgers at the correct height for your saw. Attach the eight legs, after checking that each measures exactly 32 in. from the top of its respective rail to the floor. In other words, the lap joint at the top of each leg must be set 2 in. below the rail's top edge. Next, glue and

SEE ALSO
Bench saws . . . Blades, carbide . . .
Circular saw blades . . . Power-tool stands . . .
Safety, workshop . . . Saws, bench . . .
Saws, radial-arm . . . Table saws . . .
Workbenches . . . Workshops

clamp the cabinet front, sides and back (½-in. AC plywood) into previously routed grooves in legs and bottom edges of rails.

Dress the fronts, sides and backs of the drawers to ½ in. and lay out as in drawing. The fronts may be rabbeted flush to their openings and dovetailed to sides, or built with butt joints and a screwed-on false front. (Use 2d nails and white glue at butt joints and ¾-in. No. 6 fh screws with white glue to attach the false front.) Pulls and slides used are the single-channel, three-roller type—standard hardware items.

Construct the storage tray separately. Slip the bottom into ¼-in.-deep grooves in the 1x4 sides and join at corners. Simple butt joints will do, but I opted to use dovetails for extra strength. Fit the

CONSTRUCTION DRAWING

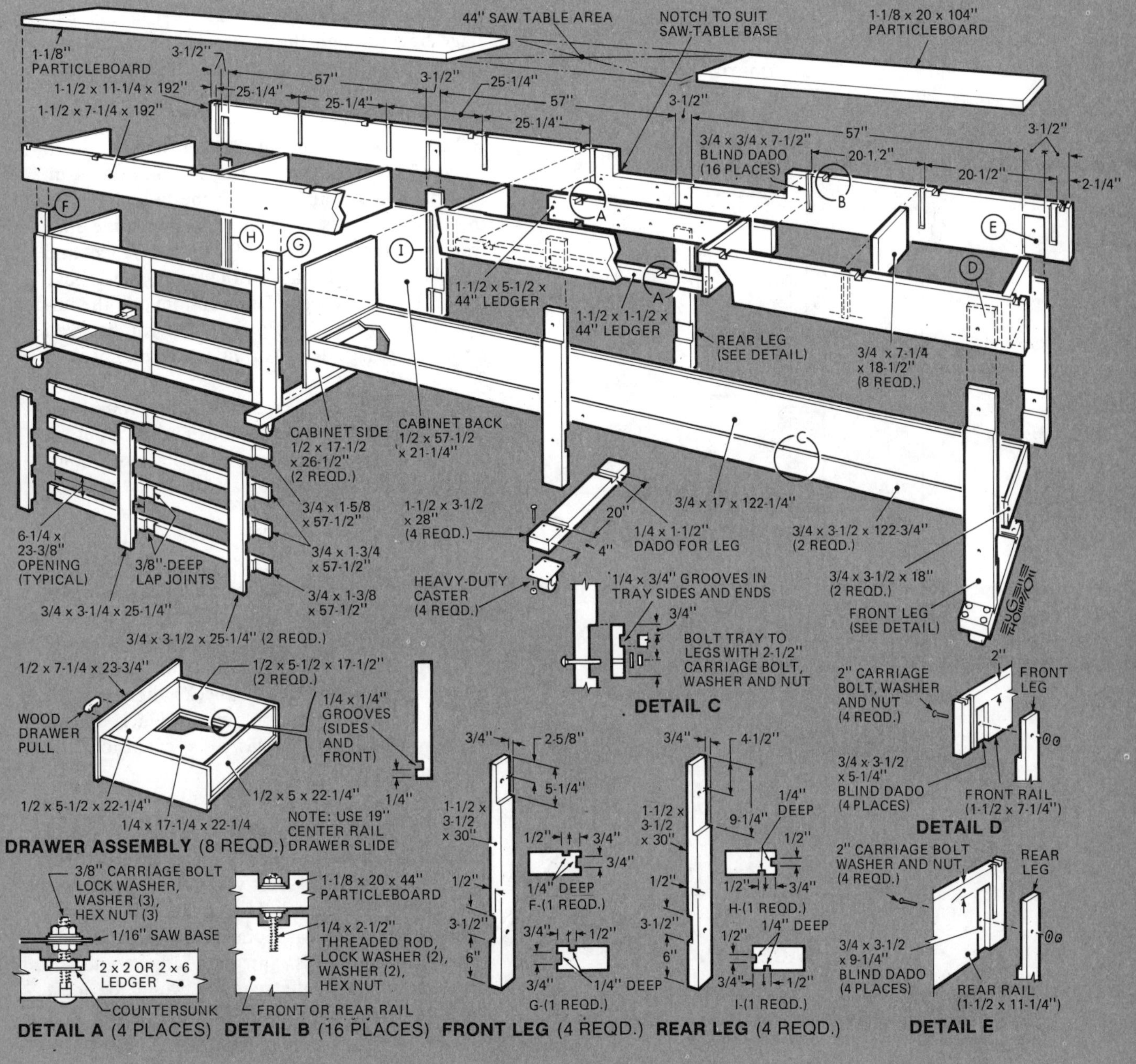

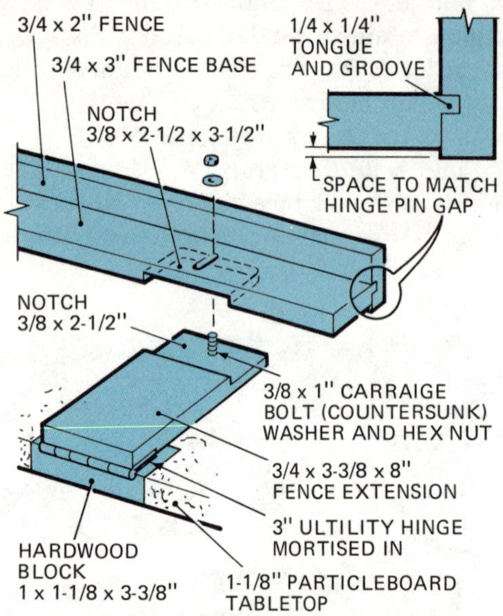

FENCE EXTENSION DETAIL

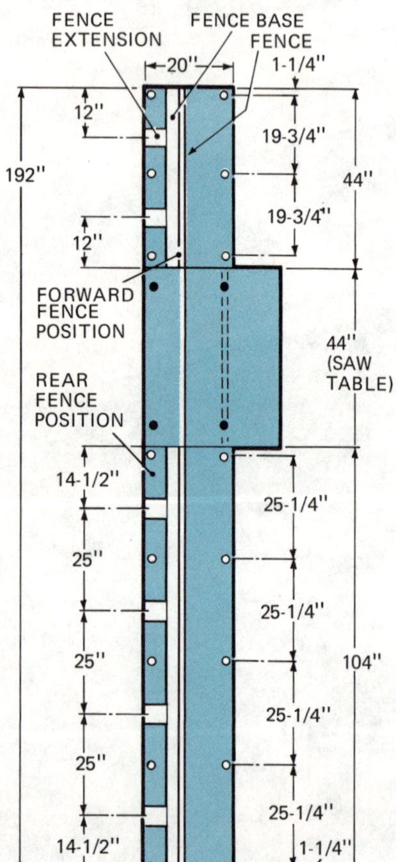

o EXTENSION LIFTS MOUNTED IN RAILS
• SAW LIFTS MOUNTED THROUGH LEDGERS

SURFACE PLAN

ARRANGE saw lifts at the corners of your saw base to suit, and extension lifts according to the plan above. Saw 16 2½-in. lengths of ¼-in. threaded rod for latter—it costs less than sawing off bolt heads.

completed tray component into previously cut leg notches.

Now add hardwood ties to the leg bottoms, with ample projection for heavy-duty casters. Secure casters with ¼x3½-in. lagbolts threaded into previously embedded ⅜-in.-dia. dowels.

When you need a wide rip or extra-wide crosscut, you can lift the hinged fence extensions, adjust your saw (including moving its central fence to the rear position) and begin ripping. To construct, mortise for and glue six hardwood mounting blocks into the particleboard table extensions to obtain solid hinge mounts. Position as on surface plan. Cut the six hardwood fence extensions and carefully countersink for a 1x⅜-in.-dia. carriage bolt through the center of the routed lap. Hinge fence extensions to the mounting blocks.

making the fences

The fences are made from a straight 14-ft. piece of 1x6 clear pine cut in 104-in. and 44-in. lengths. Rip a 3-in. width off the two pieces for the two fence bases. Then rip a 2-in.-wide strip from each remaining piece for the two fences and join these pieces to bases with tongue-and-groove joints. The lip between fence bottom and the underside of its base should equal the gap between hinge leaves (see detail) or the fence will not sit at 90° to the table.

Center and cut six slits into the completed fence sections. Flip the sections and rout out six recesses for corresponding hardwood extensions. Secure fences to extensions with bolts, washers and nuts.

To align, start by leveling the bench, using the storage tray as a base. Set up your saw according to manufacturer's instructions; then level the saw table by raising or lowering the nuts on the saw lifts. Carefully level each table extension to the tabletop. Gently move the saw and the two extensions into alignment. Check alignment of fence sections with a long piece of black thread. Tighten nuts firmly on saw lifts, extension lifts and fence adjustments.

adapting bench for your saw

This bench is designed around a Craftsman 12-in. radial-arm saw, but you can adapt it to almost any other model. The critical changes depend on the saw-base dimensions and adjustment-crank positions. Saw-base ledgers and the saw-base notch in the rear rail would be most likely to need modification. Carefully study your particular saw and your needs before you begin construction.

Spot-finishing metal cabinets

Edges of doors and drawers in my metal kitchen cabinets have small checks, or breaks, in the original white-enamel finish. Since I don't want to replace these, I'd like to know the best way to conceal the defects.—W.B., D.C.

Of several methods, I've found the best way is to cut a small opening, slightly larger than the break in the finish, in a piece of thin cardboard and use this as a mask. Buy a pressurized can of appliance enamel, place the mask with the opening directly over the break, hold it firmly and spray through the opening. Usually one full squirt will be sufficient. Remove the mask immediately, being careful not to slide it off. On corners, bend the mask around the corner and hold it firmly while spraying. You may have to make several masks with holes of varying size.

Patio chair stains

I have an aluminum patio chair that leaves a black stain on clothing. A grayish coating covers the metal. What is this, and how can I prevent it?—W.W., Tex.

An oxide coating forms on many metals exposed to the air, especially aluminum. The only thing you can do about it—and it's only a stopgap cure—is clean the metal and coat the "wear" surfaces with a metal lacquer. Any clear finishing material will do, but genuine metal lacquer will do the best possible job.

When and how to seed a lawn

It's about time to think about what to do with my lawn. I don't know how long it's been in existence, but it's thinning and I'm told it needs to be renewed. How do I seed an existing lawn?—D.L., Mo.

Your lawn also needs, no doubt, to be renewed by a scheduled fertilization program, starting this coming spring. I've had good success by mixing grass seed with the fertilizer in the spreader: a layer of fertilizer, a layer of seed successively in the hopper, then hand mixing until both seed and fertilizer are uniformly distributed. Don't expect immediate results. You may see little improvement the first season other than that brought about by feeding existing plants. But if you follow through you will notice a thickening of the sod the second season.

Small areas with few or no plants should be spot-seeded by first working the top soil, spreading the seed and covering lightly. Keep these areas well watered.

Condensate on aluminum storm sash

Why do my aluminum storm windows steam up when the temperature goes below freezing? The steam forms on the inside of the window frames and glass, runs to the sill and freezes. How can I stop this?—John Redmond, Birmingham, Ala.

The storms are at a lower temperature than the air leaking through inner sashes. That air contains moisture, which condenses on the colder metal and glass. Weatherstripping the inner sashes usually eliminates this or minimizes it so it is no longer troublesome. If your furnace is of the unvented, gas-fired type, it is a major source of excess moisture in your room air. It should be vented outside.

Cleaning acoustical-tile ceiling

How can I clean acoustical tile in a basement room? Will it withstand wetting?—Roy Adams, Lexington, Ky.

I've used a wallpaper cleaner—the kind you form into a ball or pallet and rub over the dry surface. It seems to serve very well, but you must work in good light and be careful to remove all streaks by overlapping each stroke of the cleaner. If the ceiling is dusty, cobwebby or otherwise soiled, it's wise to go over it first with a vacuum-cleaner floor brush to loosen dirt and other debris and draw dust from the partial perforations. Then use the cleaner. I've also used an artificial sponge dampened in soapy water and squeezed out nearly dry. After the first sponging, rinse with a nearly dry sponge.

Preventing paint 'skin'

How can I prevent a film from forming over paint after the can has been opened and a part of its contents used?—William Carpenter, Puente, Calif.

Clean paint from the rim of the can thoroughly, using a solvent that mates with the paint. Clean the groove into which the top fits tightly and press the lid firmly down as far as it will go. Then store the can upside down. In cans at least half full this usually prevents formation of film.

Another way is to cut a disc of wax paper to a true fit inside the can and lay this on top of the paint. There's also a liquid—available from your paint dealer—that can be poured in a thin film over the paint. I clean small paint cans in which paint leftovers can be easily stored. I fill these three quarters full, press lids tightly in place and then invert the cans.

Molding head fence for a radial saw

By. C.E. BANISTER

FENCE FITS flush in table in place of saw's own fence and rear table board which you remove. Hold-down fixtures shown can be bought separately from Sears.

■ USED WITH a molding head, this adjustable fence assembly makes your radial-arm saw perform like a real wood shaper. It drops in place flush with the table surface and occupies the area behind the saw's fence. You remove both fence and rear table board when you want to use it. Total thickness of the base must equal thickness of the saw's wood table. The ⅛-in. hardboard covering on the bottom of the fence provides for free movement over the table.

The square opening in the base provides clearance for the motor arbor and vertical cutter adjustment. Two ⅜x1½-in. capscrews, washers and Tee-nuts are used to lock the movable fence in place. I used oak for the two fences and rabbeted the edges. The rest I made of fir plywood. I glued and clamped the tempered hardboard to the surfaces indicated.

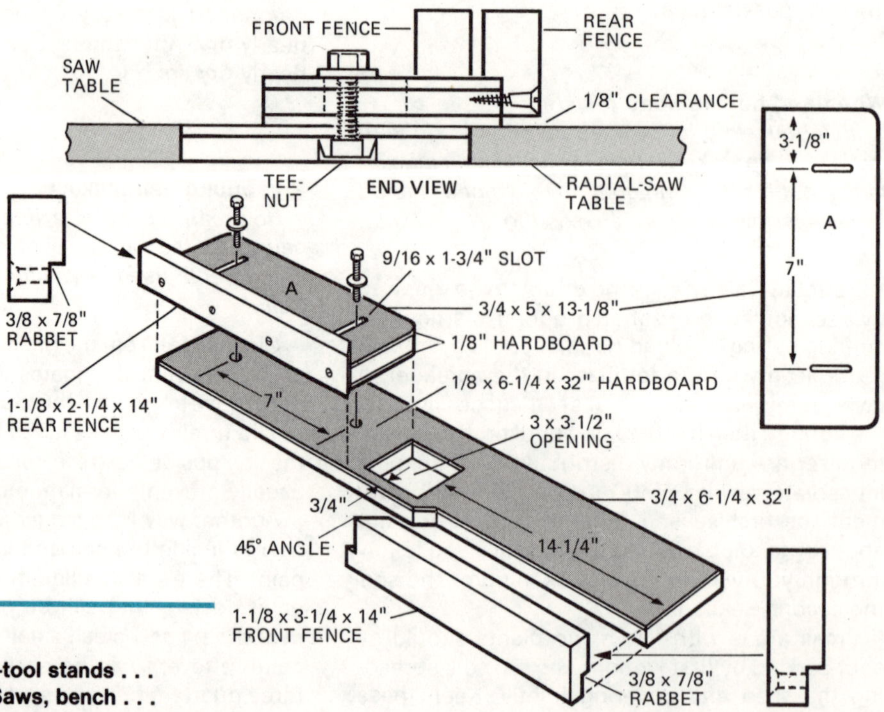

SEE ALSO

Bench saws . . . Power-tool stands . . . Safety, workshop . . . Saws, bench . . . Saws, radial-arm . . . Stands, bench saw . . . Workbenches . . . Workshops

Never try to work on a radial-arm saw that doesn't have a level table. To make simple leveling jacks you can use carriage bolts and nuts

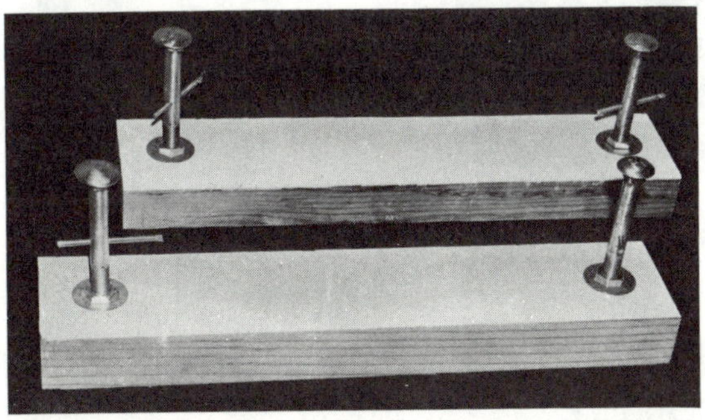

TWO PIECES of 2x4 (18 in. long) have ½ x 5-in. carriage bolts turned into holes at the ends and locked in place with nuts and washers. The cross handles in the bolts are simply nails—optional but handy.

Jacks quickly level a radial-saw table

By WILLIAM WAGGONER

■ THE IMPORTANCE of a perfectly level table is obvious in the case of a radial-arm saw. If the fixed table runs "down-hill," rabbets and dadoes will run downhill and vary in thickness from one end to the other. Only when the table surface is level with the saw's overarm will the saw cut rabbets and dadoes right on the button.

I find the best way to check the table on my DeWalt saw is with these leveling jacks. To use them you loosen the four bolts that hold the slotted rails, set the jacks in place as in the drawing, lock the motor in a vertical position and then move the motor and arm over the entire surface. When the motor shaft lightly touches the surface at all points, the table will be level. A slight turn of the jacks will correct any variance.

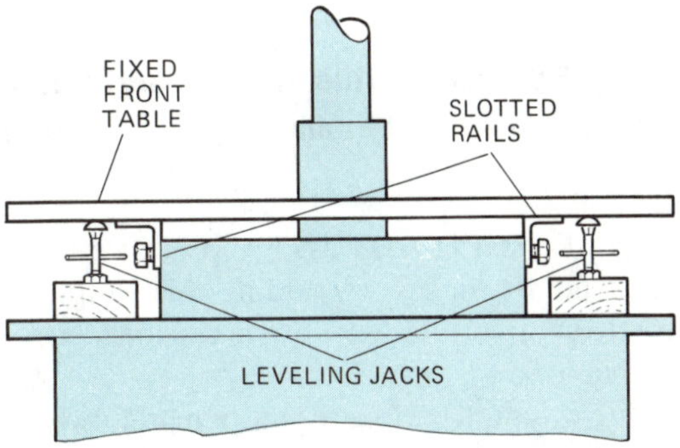

SEE ALSO
Power-tool stands . . . Workbenches . . . Workshops

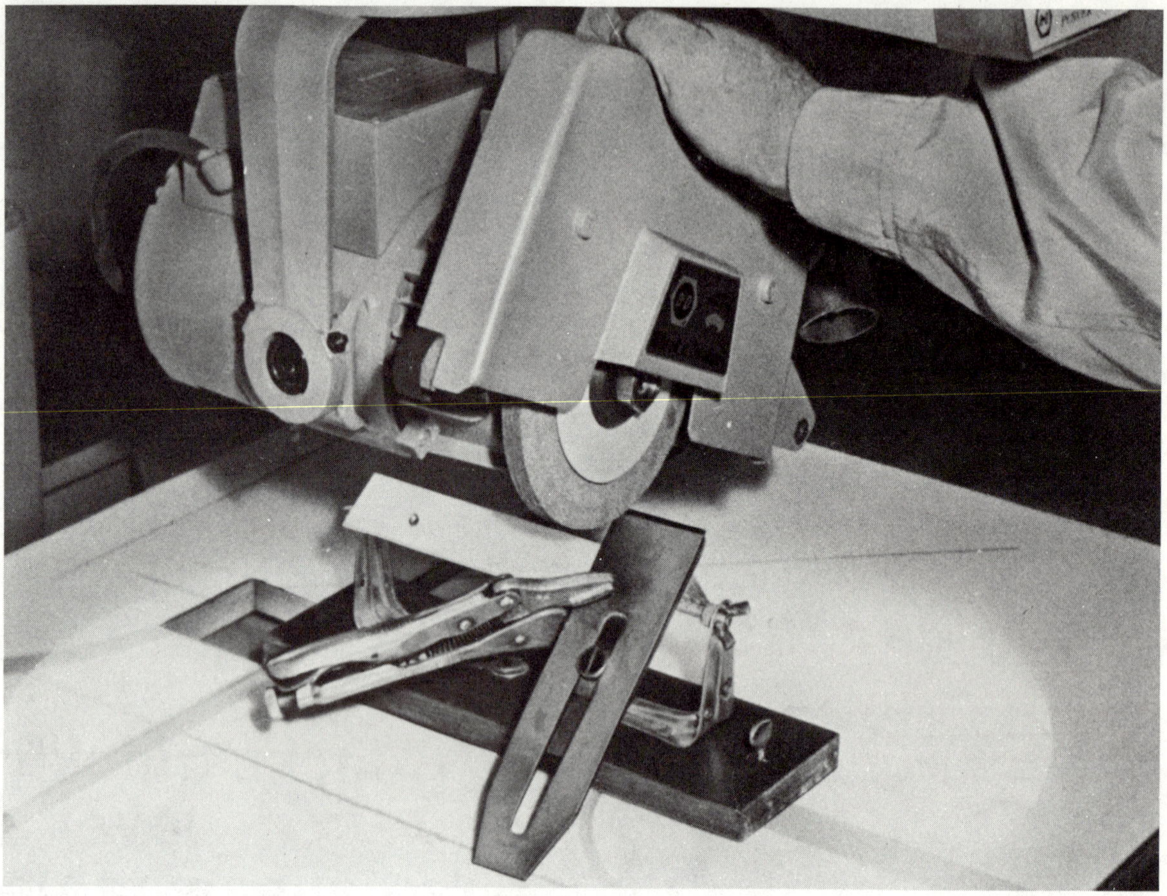

How to sharpen tools on your radial-arm saw

By WILLIAM G. WAGGONER

By building this little jig and putting an emery wheel on your radial-arm saw you can sharpen practically any tool around the house with a high degree of precision

■ TAKE FULL ADVANTAGE of your versatile radial-arm saw by adding this simple fixture that converts the saw to a precision sharpening machine.

With it, you'll be able to sharpen precisely just about any tool around your home, shop or garden, including hollow-ground chisels, plane irons, jointer and planer knives, wood bits, hedge trimmers, tin snips and other cutting tools.

SEE ALSO
Abrasives . . . Power-tool stands . . .
Saws, radial-arm . . . Sharpening, tool . . .
Workbenches . . . Workshops

As shown on the opposite page, the threaded studs welded to the angle iron are headless ¼-20 bolts 2 in. long, with about ½ in. of the threaded portions protruding at each end of the angle iron.

To insure alignment of the bolts with each other and with the holes in the shelf brackets, lay a section of ¾-in. angle on the inside of the 1¼-in. angle and position the bolts on the step formed by the smaller angle. Clamp the two pieces in place and tack-weld the bolts to the 1¼-in. angle. Remove the length of ¾-in. angle and complete the welding.

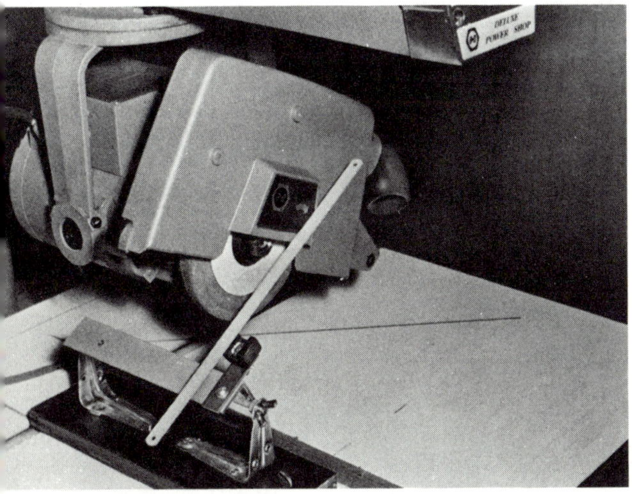

CORRECT POSITION of the angle iron is indicated when hacksaw blade falls slightly below the wheel arbor.

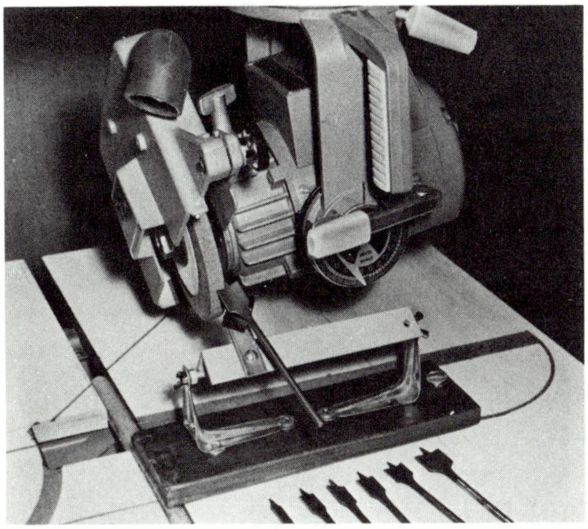

WING-TYPE wood bits are among many precision-ground tools you can resharpen quickly and accurately.

If necessary, enlarge the holes in the shelf brackets by reaming or drilling, then mount them on the bed of ¾-in. plywood. Note that two ¼-in. washers are placed under the bracket at the end of the bed fitted with the length of ¾-in. dowel. At the other end of the bed, a ¼-20 thumb-screw and Teenut are used to permit adjustment of the bed for slight angles or bevels.

The magnetic toolrest assembly consists of a 1-in. horseshoe magnet fitted to a 2½-in. length of ⅛ x ¾-in. flat iron. For light sharpening operations, the work can be held by the magnet alone, but for heavier sharpening chores, be sure to clamp the work firmly to the angle iron.

A 100-grit, 6-in.-dia. emery wheel is used on the radial saw. Because the sharpening is always done under the wheel, you can see exactly what you're doing, especially since there is no toolrest, wheel guard or motor housing in the way.

To get the proper plane for sharpening, lay a straightedge, such as a hacksaw blade, on the magnet and adjust the angle iron so the straightedge is slightly below the wheel arbor. Lock in this position. This procedure also provides the correct relief clearance.

Occasionally you'll find it necessary to dress the emery wheel precisely, using a diamond-tipped wheel dresser. Lock the dresser to the angle iron and position it so that it is at a "drag" position in relation to the wheel's rotation. This will also prevent the dresser from gouging pieces out of the wheel.

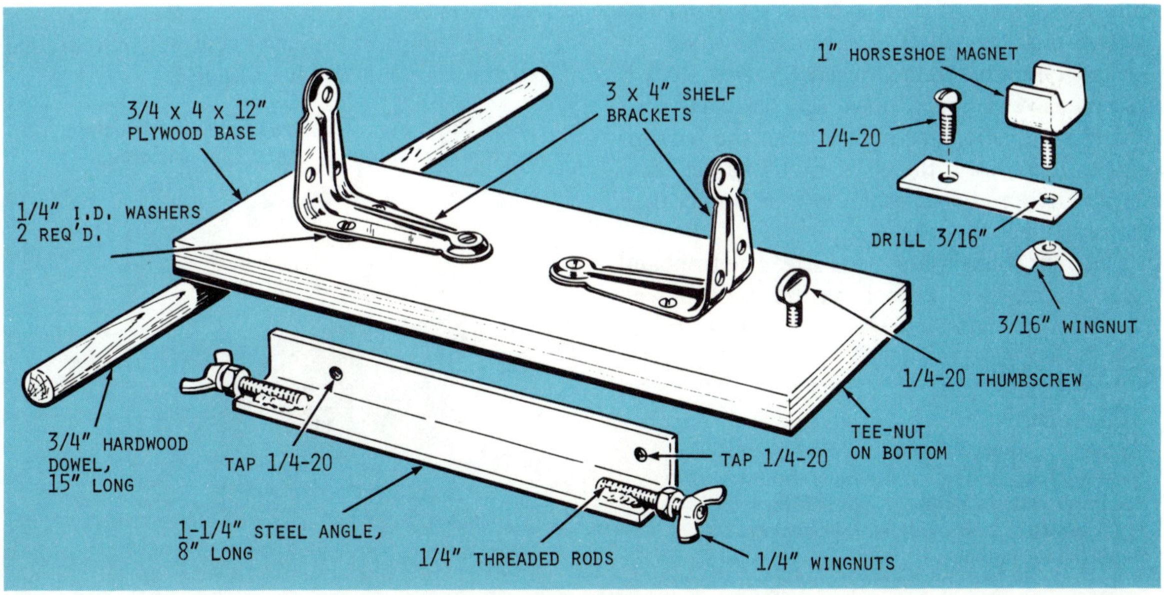

FILIGREE HARDBOARD cover hides a monstrous 82-in. radiator. Only two 2x6-ft. hardboard pieces are needed. Plywood filler pieces are attached at ends of cover. It is painted to blend with walls.

Easy-to-make radiator cover

By ROBERT LASSON

ONE HAPPILY SOLVED problem in my household was how to cover a 7-ft. radiator that doubled as an eyesore. Since it wasn't possible to buy a readymade cover for this monster, I shopped around for an inexpensive but attractive material to make one. The answer was ¼-in. filigree hardboard, available in a number of panel sizes and patterns.

The panels I installed measure 2x6 ft. By using plywood filler at the ends, I built the unit with only two panels. If your eyesore is 6 ft. or less pipe-to-pipe, you don't have to use plywood.

First I built the frame. Because 1x1-in. stock is so expensive, I ripped down several 2x4s. Your frame must be long enough to clear the radiator pipe at the ends. If there's a shutoff valve, allow for it. The top should be 1½ to 2 in. higher than the radiator.

Cut your frame members to size. The front and back are identical, except that the back has no bottom horizontal piece. Butt the boards at each joint and secure them with a dab of white glue and 2-in. finishing nails. Connect front and back with crosspieces.

When the glue is dry, cut the hardboard and attach it to the top with casing nails. The top material—hardboard or plywood if you need the filler—should extend ¼ in. beyond the frame to join with the front and side panels. Add the front and side panels, making sure not to damage the joints as you hammer. If you need access to a valve, make an appropriate cutout on the side.

You can paint the cover with a short-nap roller to make a good-looking disguise.

BACK VIEW of cover shows frame construction. Top extends over frame to form a joint with sides.

SEE ALSO

Boilers . . . Energy, saving . . . Furnaces . . . Heat pumps . . . Heating systems, home . . . Heating systems, solar . . . Humidifiers . . . Solar energy . . . Stoves, wood-burning . . . Winterizing, homes

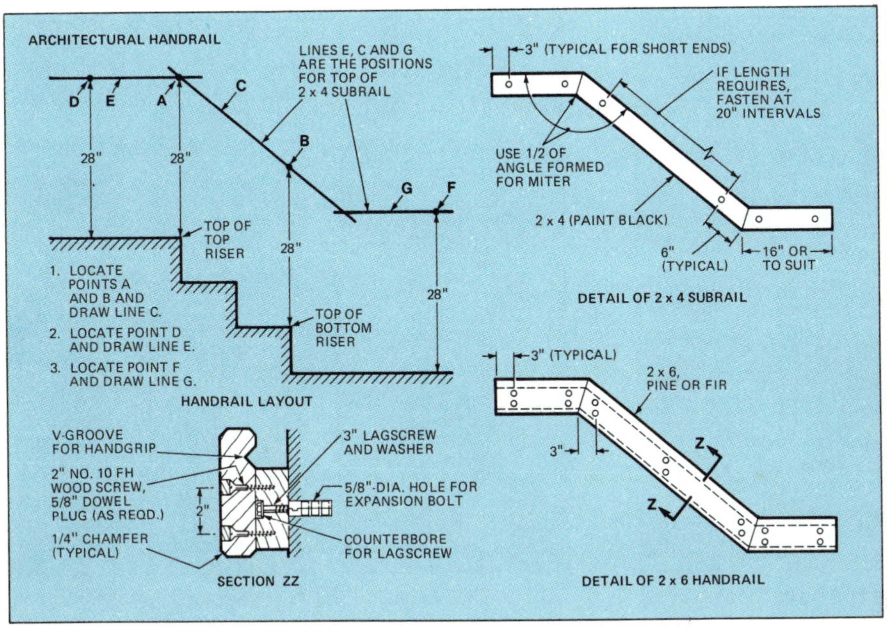

A handsome handrail

By JOHN E. GAYNOR

■ MANY TWO- and three-step entry stairs don't have handrails. Using stairs in icy weather can be dangerous, especially for oldsters.

If your steps run parallel to a wall, you can get the jump on safety by building the handsome handrail pictured. It's a good alternative to installing a standard wrought-iron rail. Painted or given a clear, polyurethane finish, the handrail lends a pleasing, substantial finishing touch to your entry.

Begin work on the handrail by drawing a line to indicate the top of the 2x4 subrail on the wall. Use the 28-in. standard banister height shown. Cut the pieces to length to suit your needs. Once you determine the joining angle, the remainder of the job is easy. Measure lengths off line drawn and cut the three 2x4 segments with desired angles.

HANDRAIL adds safety and an attractive touch to a home. Note the finger grip in detail.

In a masonry wall, use masonry bits to bore ⅝-in.-dia. holes for expansion bolts by first boring $\frac{3}{16}$-in., then ⅜-in. and finally the ⅝-in.-dia. holes. Countersink lagscrews in the subrail. In walls made of other material drive countersunk hefty wood screws into studs if you have vinyl or aluminum siding.

Use a bevel square to transfer the angle already determined onto the 2x6-in. handrail pieces and cut. Since this rail is set ¼ in. below the 2x4 bottom, the ends of the pieces will project slightly past the subrail.

Chamfer (bevel) 2x6 edges for hand comfort; rout, shape or saw the backs, above the 2x4, to make a finger grip. Space the fastening screws so they don't hit subrail fasteners. Add dowel plugs and apply finish.

SEE ALSO

Basement remodeling . . . Basement stairwells . . . Decks . . . Measurements . . . Stairs . . . Steps

NEWEL POSTS are used for the end posts, corner posts and intermediate posts. The number required is determined by the overall size of the stoop. A stoop that is the same width as the steps generally requires four posts. A stoop wider than the steps can require as many as six or more posts. Posts are anchored to the masonry stoop and steps by flanges that are attached with expansion bolts inserted in predrilled holes. A concrete bit is used to drill the holes for the bolts.

AFTER THE NEWEL POSTS are in place, preassembled, adjustable rail sections are marked for length. Here in order to maintain uniform spacing of spindles, excess length is cut from each end of the upper and lower rails. To cut the rails, you'll need a hacksaw. A vise is handy for holding the rails while they are being cut. Any burred edges should be smoothed with a file so connectors insert easily. Railings are usually installed 31 in. high and even with the tops of the new posts.

How to install wrought-iron railings

MAKE A ROUGH SKETCH of your stoop with measurements as shown at the right. To find the number of 4 or 6-ft. rail sections you'll need, measure from the house to the edge of the platform. To determine whether a 4 or 6-ft. rail section is needed for the steps, measure the length of the stairs, top to bottom as shown. To find the number of newel posts required, figure one for each corner of the platform and one each for the top and bottom of the stairs. If railings consist of more than one section, add one post for each added section.

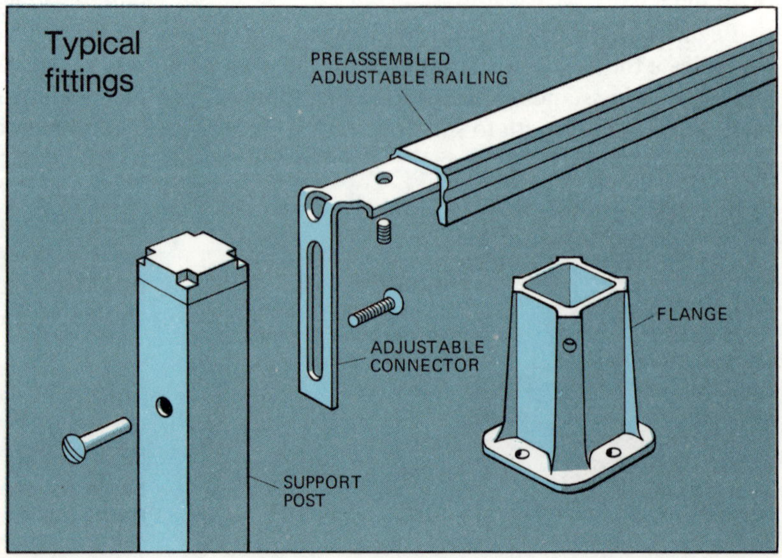

RAIL SECTIONS are attached to newel posts with adjustable connectors that require no drilling. Each connector slides inside the upper and lower rails and is tightened by a setscrew. Rail sections come in 4 and 6-ft. lengths and require support posts between sections. The same connectors attach the sections to the house. Before drilling holes, be sure to level the railing. If it's to be attached to wood, use regular screws; if to masonry, bolts in expansion anchors.

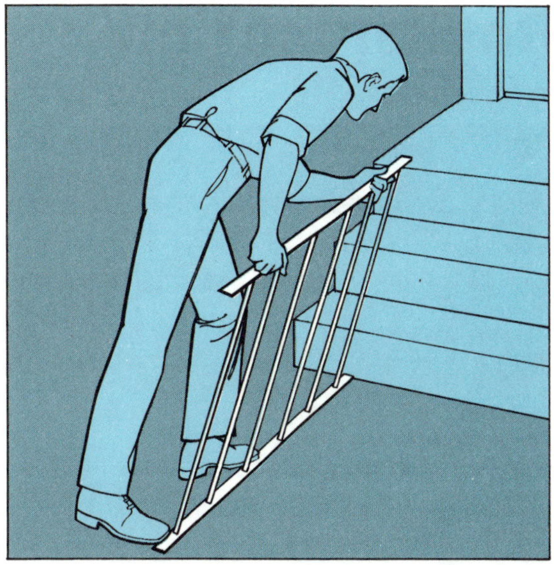

PREASSEMBLED RAIL SECTIONS adjust to any stair slope. To bend, put foot on the lower rail and push forward on the top rail to suit the stair pitch. Spindles are generally electrically fused to top and bottom rails to make the railing stronger than welded ironwork. Connectors are bent to the same angles as the rail section to join the section to the top and bottom newel posts. Extra wrought-iron scrolls, called lamb's tongue and finial, are available for the bottom newel post.

SEE ALSO

Basement stairwell . . . Concrete . . . Decks . . . Measurements . . . Patios . . . Spiral stairs . . . Stairs . . . Steps

ONLY FOUR basic parts are required to add a wrought-iron railing to any porch or stoop—rail section, support post, adjustable connector and flange. Support (newel) posts are 1¼ in. square, 35 and 48 in. high. Posts fit into flanges, which are attached with setscrews; flanges are anchored to wood or masonry with screws or expansion bolts. Adjustable connectors join rail sections to posts like an Erector set. Complete railings are made up of 4 and 6-ft. sections, joined end to end with a post between.

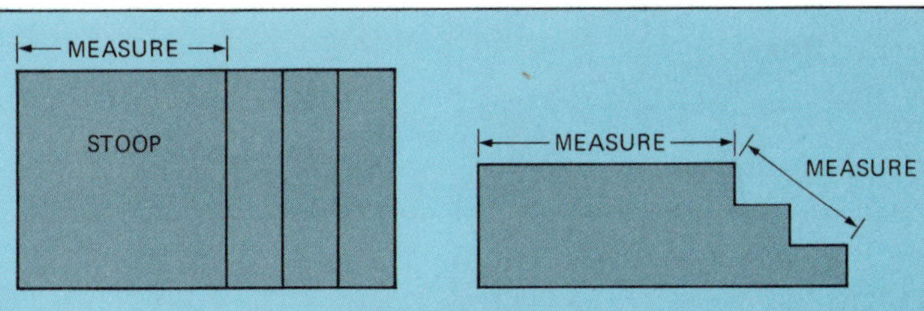

IF PLATFORM IS	ORDER
3 FT OR LESS	ONE 4-FT SECTION (CUT DOWN)
3 FT ON BOTH SIDES	ONE 6-FT SECTION (CUT IN HALF)
4 FT OR LESS	ONE 4-FT SECTION
6 FT OR LESS	ONE 6-FT SECTION
8 FT OR LESS	TWO 4-FT SECTIONS
10 FT OR LESS	TWO 6-FT SECTIONS (CUT DOWN)

Rocker 'car pit'

By GENE ROGERS

■ GETTING UNDER my car to work on it is no problem when I drive up this "car-pit" ramp. I made it to rock like a teeter-totter so it will raise the car front or back by simply tipping it. First you wedge struts in place at the front, insert the front-wheel chocks, drive up the ramp until the wheels hit the chocks and set the handbrake. Then you remove the struts, tilt the ramp downhill and insert a second set of chocks. Your car is now safely "locked" on the ramp.

To raise the car front or back for headroom, you merely lift up on the bumpers. To gain full access to the underside of the car, you insert struts at each end of the ramp to support it level. The ramp can be dismantled for storing by using bolts to attach the 2x4 tiepiece.

ROCKER RAMP will support the car uphill, downhill or on the level. Front-wheel chocks keep car from rolling, though for safety be sure to put it in gear and set the handbrake. The ramp will safely support up to 3000 lbs. and is made basically for compact cars.

SEE ALSO

Autos, body repair . . . Autos, ramps . . . Body care, auto . . . Brakes, auto . . . Lubrication, auto . . . Tune-up, auto

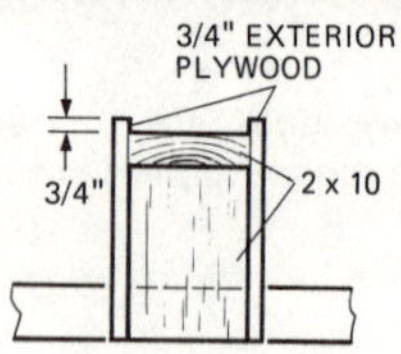

SECTION A-A

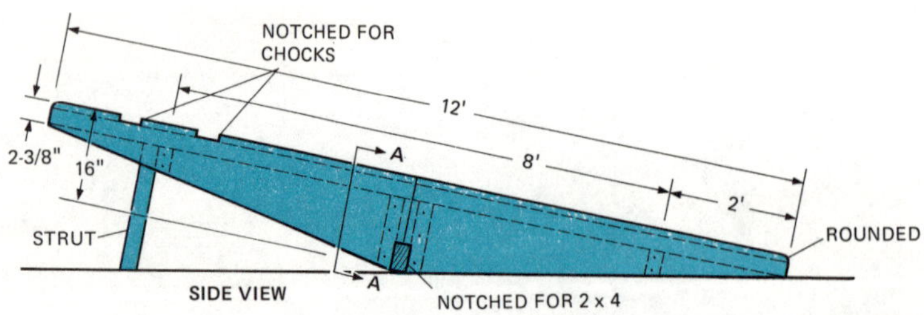

SIDE VIEW

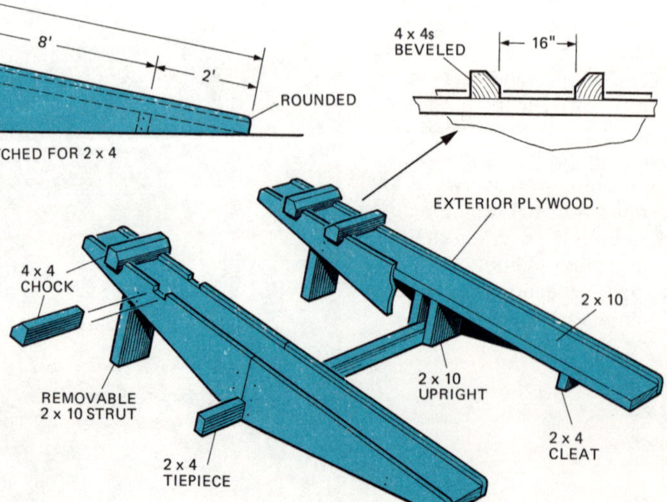

USE A 12-ft. 2x10 plank for treadway of each "pontoon" and, with spacers placed between, add sides of exterior ¾-in. plywood to produce girderlike beam. Use glue and screws. With economical cutting, you can get four sides from less than two 4x8 sheets. Each side is in two pieces, butted at the center to project ¾ in. above the plank, then notched at the front ends to receive 4x4 wheel chocks 16 in. apart.

How to troubleshoot your electric range

■ YOUR ELECTRIC RANGE is one of the simplest appliances in the house—it's really just heating elements and their controls. Although it uses 230-v. power, it's no more difficult to troubleshoot than a 115-v. appliance, so long as you show the respect you always should for the potential danger of electricity. And while the controls used on ranges have become increasingly sophisticated over the years, their basic principles have not changed.

Most electric ranges have four surface elements, two large ones and two smaller ones. The large elements can have a wattage of 2100 to 2600 w., while smaller ones range from 1150 to 1500 w. Older surface elements consisted of an open coil of wire fitted into a ceramic block. Elements of this type are rarely seen today, except on hotplates, as they burn out easily. They have been replaced by hermetically sealed elements. This element has a Nichrome resistance wire embedded in an insulating powder, usually magnesium oxide, housed in D-shaped stainless-steel tubing. The insulating powder keeps the resistance wire from touching the tubing sheath.

A surface element has either one or two resistance elements and two or four connections. For these connections, one of three types of terminal—banana, knuckle or screw-on—is used. These terminal types are shown below. A terminal block used with the surface element provides a positive connection point between element and switch wiring. Terminal blocks are usually attached to the underside of the cooktop with a screw. Screw-on terminals have, instead of a terminal block, a glass or ceramic covering over terminal ends to prevent shorting. Problems that can arise with surface elements are shorting, breaks in Nichrome wire and pitted or corroded terminals; terminal blocks are also subject to corrosion and pitting, and to damage from internal arcing.

Surface switches are used to regulate the amount of heat produced by surface elements.

SEE ALSO

Appliance repair . . . Appliances . . . Electrical wiring . . . Freezers . . . Garbage disposers . . . Kitchens . . . Mixers, food . . . Oven hoods . . . Toasters

SURFACE-ELEMENT ASSEMBLY

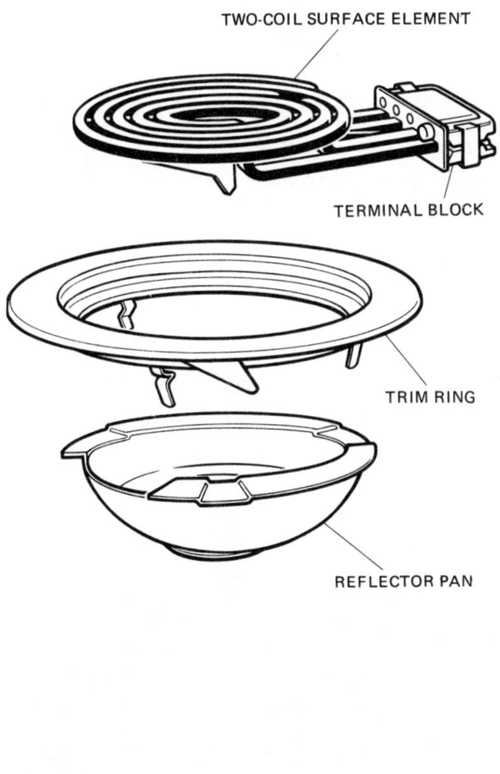

SURFACE-ELEMENT CONNECTIONS

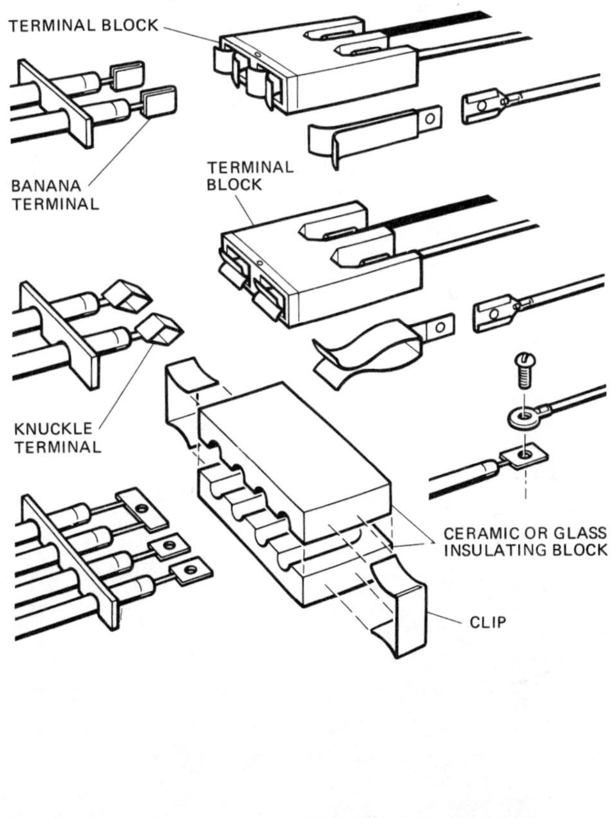

THERMOSTAT COMPONENTS

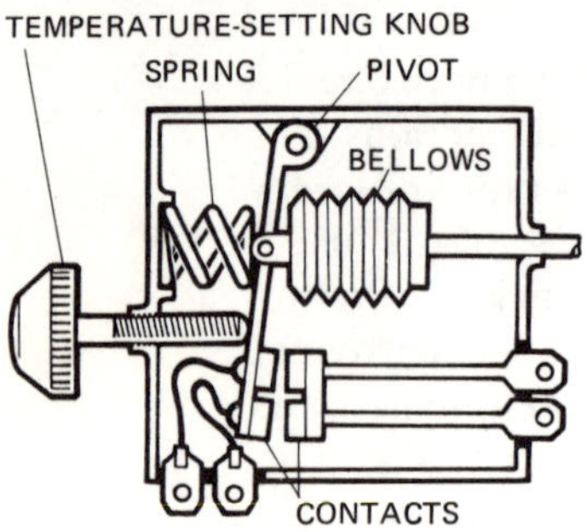

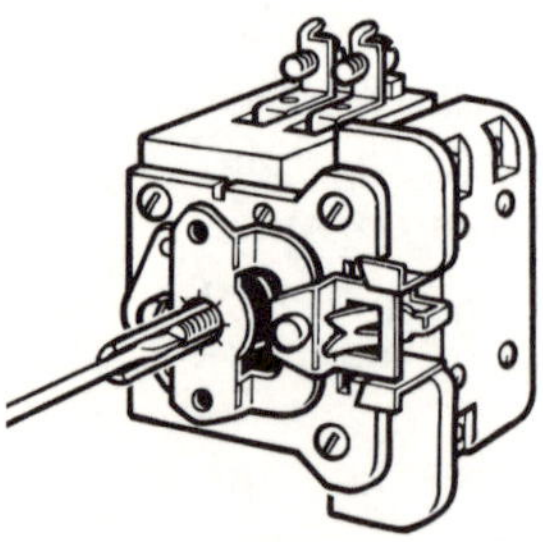

Oven does not heat

POSSIBLE CAUSES	WHAT TO TRY
1. Fuse blown or circuit breaker tripped.	Replace fuse or reset circuit breaker. If blowing or tripping is repeated, disconnect the power and check for shorts.
2. Automatic timer set improperly	Make sure timer is in "manual" position for everyday cooking. Refer to manufacturer's instructions.
3. Automatic timer defective.	Check timer for defective motor or contacts (see clock-timer discussion on page 2395). If gears are bound or broken, repair or replace timer.
4. Selector switch set improperly	Make sure that selector switch is set for type of cooking desired.
5. Thermostat defective.	Place voltmeter across thermostat input terminals; reading should be 230 v. Loosen bake element in oven and pull it forward a fraction of an inch to make terminals accessible; turn thermostat on and check voltage across bake-element terminals; reading should be 230 v. Otherwise, thermostat is defective and must be replaced. Check thermostat's broil operation the same way.
6. Element(s) defective.	Inspect bake and broil elements for breaks or cracks. Check elements one at a time as described above; if voltage is present but element does not heat, replace it.
7. Wires loose or shorted.	Disconnect power, check wiring for breaks or charring. Replace damaged wires. Be sure connections are tight.

THERMOSTAT CALIBRATION POINTS

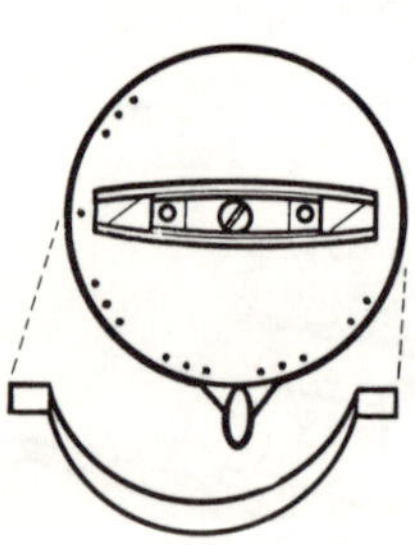

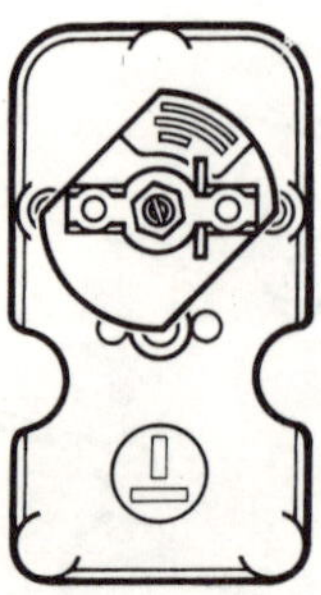

Oven temperatures are uneven

POSSIBLE CAUSES	WHAT TO TRY
1. Thermostat out of calibration.	Check oven temperature with an accurate mercury thermometer. Recalibrate thermostat according to the maker's instructions.
2. Door gaskets defective.	Open oven door and inspect sealing gaskets; replace any that are worn, cracked or flat.
3. Door fit uneven.	Check door alignment; if adjustment is needed, loosen door-hinge screws, realign door, then retighten the screws. Check door springs, too; adjust for equal tension if necessary.

SEVEN-HEAT SWITCH OPERATION

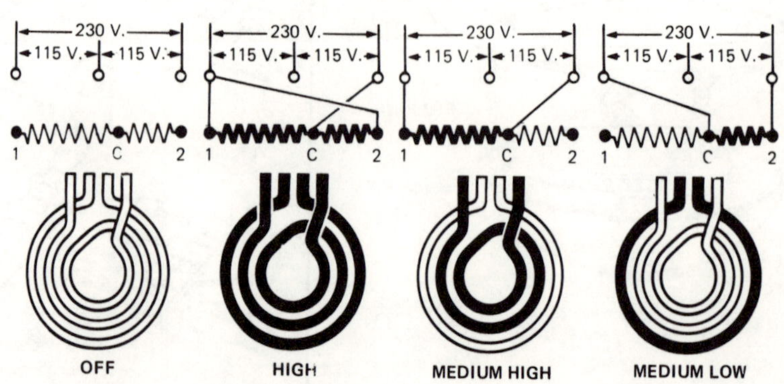

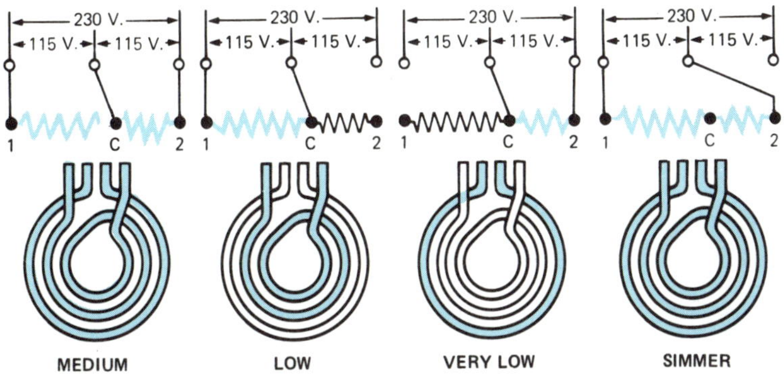

SELF-CLEANING OVEN COMPONENTS

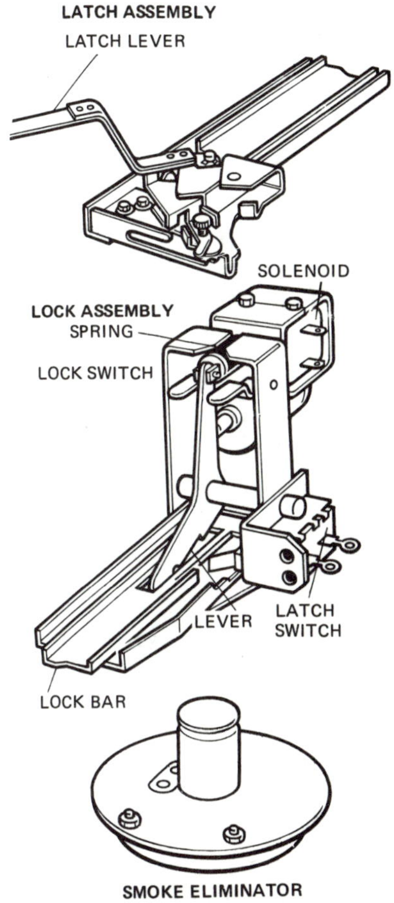

Oven does not shut off

POSSIBLE CAUSES	WHAT TO TRY
1. Thermostat defective.	Disconnect power, pull bake element (see first chart) and set thermostat in "off" position; reconnect power and check voltage across element terminals. If 230 v. is present, replace thermostat.
2. Automatic timer defective.	Set timer on "automatic," turn clock by hand until it clicks to the "off" position; there should now be no voltage to the thermostat. If there is voltage present, repair or replace the timer.

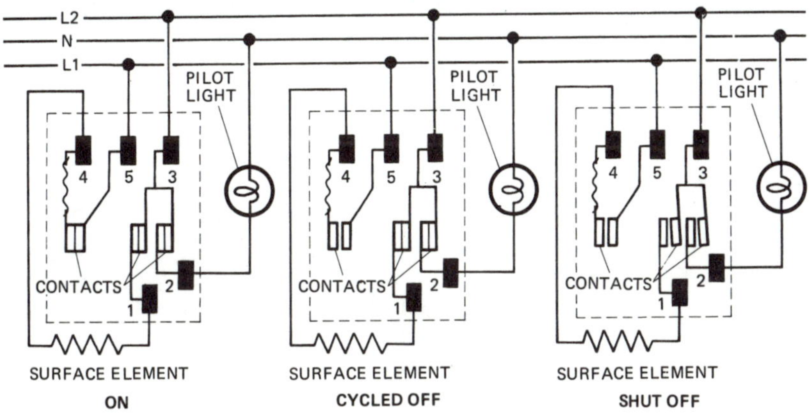

INFINITE-HEAT SWITCH

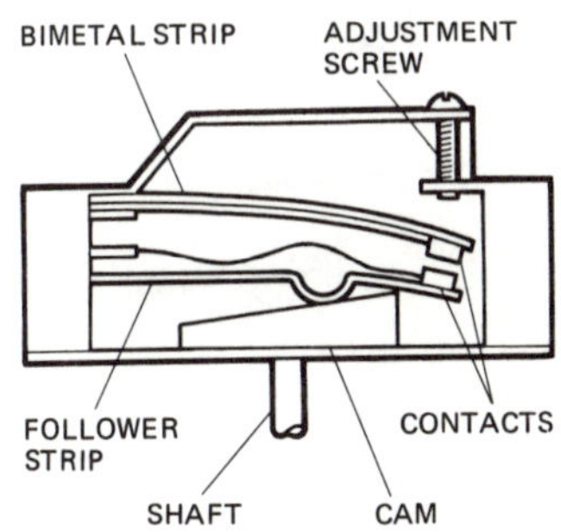

Timer does not operate properly

POSSIBLE CAUSES	WHAT TO TRY
1. Timer set incorrectly.	Refer to the manufacturer's instructions for correct settings.
2. Loose connection.	Disconnect power, tighten all loose connections, then reconnect power.
3. Motor defective.	Disconnect power, remove timer motor and test it directly with 115-v. power. If drive gear does not turn, replace the motor.
4. Blown fuse.	Inspect 15-amp. fuse behind control panel; replace if blown. If new fuse blows, disconnect power and check time for shorts (see clock-timer discussion, page 2395).
5. Gears worn, stripped or broken.	Inspect clock gears in timer; if any are visibly worn, broken or stripped, repair or replace timer. If gears are jammed, try to free them with silicone spray or a TV-tuner cleaner.
6. Contacts defective.	Make voltage checks on timer as explained on page 2395

OVEN ELEMENTS

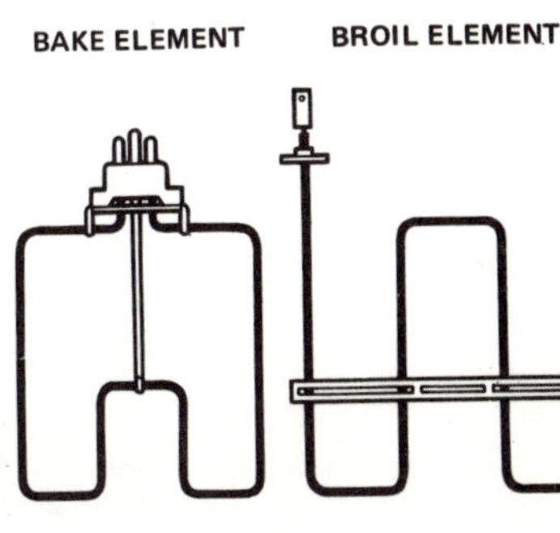

DOOR-HINGE ASSEMBLY

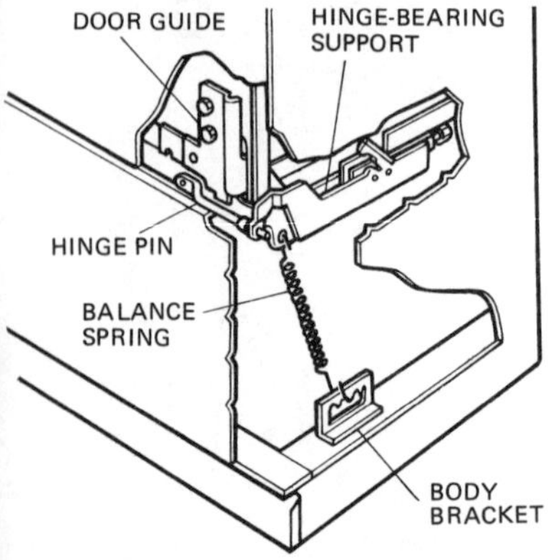

Surface unit does not heat

POSSIBLE CAUSES	WHAT TO TRY
1. Fuse blown or circuit breaker.	Replace fuse or reset circuit breaker. If blowing or tripping is repeated, disconnect the power and check for shorts.
2. Connection loose or shorted.	Disconnect power, tighten any loose connections and replace any charred wiring, reconnect power.
3. Switch defective.	Place voltmeter across switch's input terminals (usually labeled L1 and L2); reading should be 230 v. Turn switch on and place voltmeter across output terminals (to surface element); reading should be 230 v. Replace switch if you do not get these readings.
4. Terminal block defective.	Disconnect power. Inspect inside of terminal block. If it is charred or broken, replace it. If it is pitted or dirty, try to clean it with a contact file; replace it if this cannot be done.
5. Surface element defective.	If element is the plug-in type, unplug it and then plug it into one of the sockets into which the element is known to work; if it does not heat there, replace it. If element is the screw-on type, pull it forward, turn switch on and place voltmenter across surface-element terminals; reading should be 230 v. If voltage is present and element does not heat, replace it. Any replacement element must be of same size and wattage as the original and have the same type of terminals.

FLUID SENSING BULB

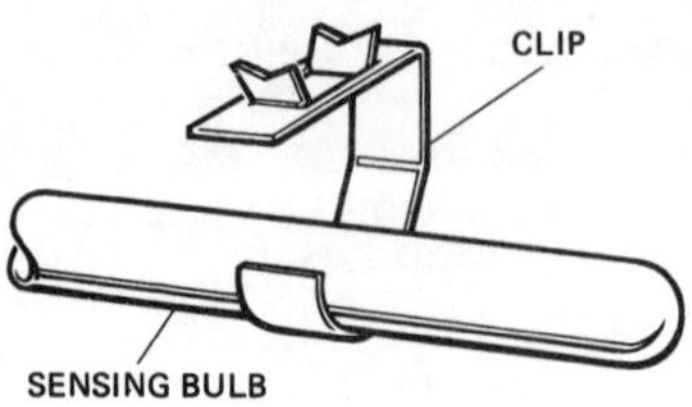

Oven door drops down or pops open

POSSIBLE CAUSES	WHAT TO TRY
1. Door out of alignment.	Loosen door-hinge screws, realign door and retighten screws. Check to make sure range is level.
2. Hinge pin worn or loose.	Disassemble door, inspect hinge pins, replace them if worn or broken—an 8d nail can sometimes be used.
3. Hinge worn.	Hinge worn: replace hinge if edges are worn.
4. Spring broken.	Open door slightly. If it fails to spring closed or drops easily, a broken spring is likely. Inspect springs; if one is broken, replace both.
5. Roller bearing broken.	If door is hard to open or close, a bearing is broken. Replace both.

Oven drips water or sweats

POSSIBLE CAUSES	WHAT TO TRY
1. Oven preheated improperly.	Preheat oven with door open at first stop.
2. Oven temperature too high.	Use an accurate mercury thermometer to check on calibration of oven thermostat.
3. Door not sealing.	Check door alignment and condition of the door gaskets; realign door if necessary (see chart, "Oven temperatures are uneven," page 2392). Replace any worn, cracked or flat gaskets.
4. Oven vent clogged.	Inspect oven vents for obstructions and clear them. If the oven uses a filter clean or replace it.

Oven lamp does not light

POSSIBLE CAUSES	WHAT TO TRY
1. Bulb loose or defective.	Tighten bulb in socket. If it still does not work, replace it with a new *appliance* bulb.
2. Switch defective.	Disconnect power, disconnect both leads to switch, place a continuity tester across both switch leads and turn on the switch. There should be a reading of continuity. Turn the switch off. There should be no reading. Replace the switch if you do not get correct readings.
3. Bad contact in socket.	Disconnect power and remove bulb from socket. With finger or blade of a small screwdriver, bend the center socket contact outward a fraction of an inch. Replace bulb and reconnect power.

AUTOMATIC TIMER

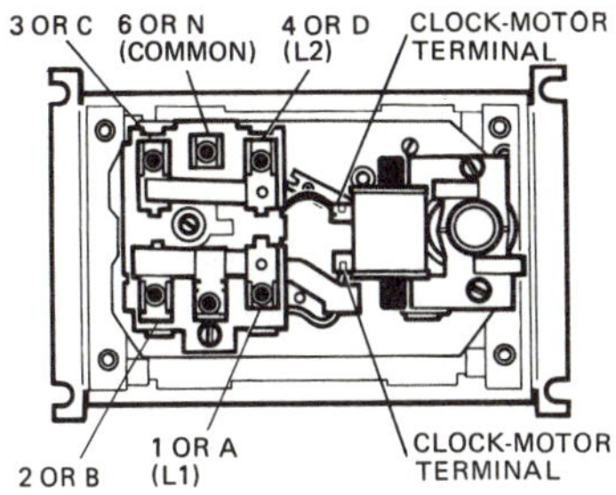

No heat for cleaning (self-cleaning ovens)

POSSIBLE CAUSES	WHAT TO TRY
1. Controls set improperly.	Refer to manufacturer's instructions for setting controls for cleaning cycle; after setting controls, wait a minute to determine whether they are working.
2. Fuse blown or circuit breaker tripped.	Replace fuse or reset circuit breaker; if blowing or tripping is repeated, disconnect the power, check for shorts.
3. Thermostat defective.	See chart "Oven does not heat" (page 2392).
4. Door unlocked.	Inspect door for firm seat against oven, make sure latch is all the way over in locked position; if not, check both door and locking mechanism for alignment.

TESTING AUTOMATIC TIMERS: Motor: voltage across terminals 1 and 6 should be 115; if not, check for blown 15-amp. fuse behind panel; if fuse is good, see whether motor drive wheel is turning; if not, replace motor. Switch: voltage across 1 and 4 should be 230, as across 2 and 3 with timer set on manual and when the timer has turned the oven on in automatic operation. If these voltage readings are not obtained, the timer must be repaired or replaced.

Cleaning is incomplete (self-cleaning ovens)

POSSIBLE CAUSES	WHAT TO TRY
1. Controls set improperly.	See chart "No heat for cleaning."
2. Cleaning time short.	See maker's instructions on length of cleaning time.
3. Oven elements defective.	See chart "Oven does not heat" (page 2392).
4. Line voltage low.	Check voltage at terminal block at rear of range; it should be within 10 percent of 230 v. If it is lower than 207 v., call local power company.
5. Smoke eliminator defective.	Disconnect power, locate smoke eliminator and disconnect its leads; then place continuity tester across eliminator terminals. Replace eliminator if there is no reading or if there are visible breaks in its mesh screen.

continued

The switches most commonly used are the step switch and the infinite-heat switch. The step type is a rotary or pushbutton switch that provides a choice of from five to seven different heats (wattages) by connecting the resistances in the surface element in parallel, in series, or singly to either 230-v. or 115-v. current. Typical wattages for a seven-heat switch could be 212, 287, 500, 850, 1150, 2000 and 3000. Operation of a seven-heat switch is shown schematically on page 2492.

The infinite-heat switch, which provides a continuous range of settings between "high" and "off," uses an internal bimetal strip, which is anchored at one end and has a switch contact at the other end. As current passes through the bimetal and heats it, it curls up and away from the cam-follower strip that carries the switch's other contact. The position of the cam determines how long the element will be on before the bending bimetal breaks contact and cycles the element off. In its extreme position—the "high" setting—the cam holds the contacts together without cycling.

Like surface switches, oven controls vary. Some ovens have only a thermostat, while others also have a selector switch and automatic clock. The selector switch is used where a range has more than one oven or there is more than one function for the thermostat to perform, or it can determine which oven elements are supplied with current and whether they are connected in series or in parallel.

The thermostat that regulates oven temperature has a fluid-filled sensing bulb, similar to the bulb at the end of a thermometer, suspended within the oven. Expansion of the fluid with increasing temperature activates a bellows in the thermostat that forces contacts apart, cutting off current to oven elements and cycling the oven off; reduced oven temperature and contraction of fluid bring the contacts together again, cycling the oven back on. The thermostat's control knob varies tension between contacts.

checking oven thermostat

Thermostat calibration can be checked by putting a mercury (not bimetal) thermometer in the oven and setting the thermostat at 400° F. Let the oven cycle three or four times, then check the temperature; if it is more than 15° F. above or below the thermostat setting, the thermostat requires recalibration. Calibration instructions are usually stamped on the thermostat, but if none can be found, assume that a quarter turn equals 25° F. Turn the calibration screw in either direction, then observe the result. Check calibration annually, more often if the oven gets unusually heavy use. (A source of calibration thermometers is Charles Connolly Distributing Co., 41 River Rd., North Arlington, NJ 07032.)

Construction of oven elements is similar to that of surface elements. The broil element usually has two resistances, with a maximum of 3000 w; the bake element is a single resistance rated at about 2500 w. Elements are fastened to the oven's rear wall, but can usually be lowered or lifted slightly.

A range clock may be fully automatic or nothing more than a clock with a buzzer timer. The fully automatic timer is connected to the oven controls.

self-cleaning ovens

Electric self-cleaning ovens use temperatures of 850° to 1000° F. to decompose oven soil. The process, called pyrolysis, leaves only a loose ash that is easily removed. The self-cleaning oven has more insulation, heavier body metal, larger and more durable controls and a number of safety features.

The cleaning cycle uses the oven thermostat, a bias circuit and door-locking circuit. The bias circuit lets the thermostat run in the higher temperature range required for pyrolysis. The door-locking circuit assures positive locking of the oven door at temperatures over 550° F. and keeps the cleaning cycle from starting if the door is not locked; this circuit is essential for safety, as a rush of air mixing with carbonized soil at high temperature could cause an explosion.

The self-cleaning cycle also involves a cooling fan that circulates air in and around the oven liner and, usually, a smoke eliminator, a device that promotes the decomposition of smoke.

Setup sequence for cleaning and duration of cleaning vary among manufacturers. The appearance of the soil remaining at the end of a cleaning cycle indicates cleaning effectiveness. If it is brown and soft, no cleaning has taken place; if it is dark brown, cleaning has been incomplete. Loose gray ash indicates complete cleaning.

Continuous-cleaning ovens require none of the extra circuits and safety devices self-cleaning ovens do. They differ from ordinary noncleaning ovens only in the porcelain with which they are lined. This is somewhat porous, and allows fat spatters to spread out and then decompose at normal cooking temperatures.

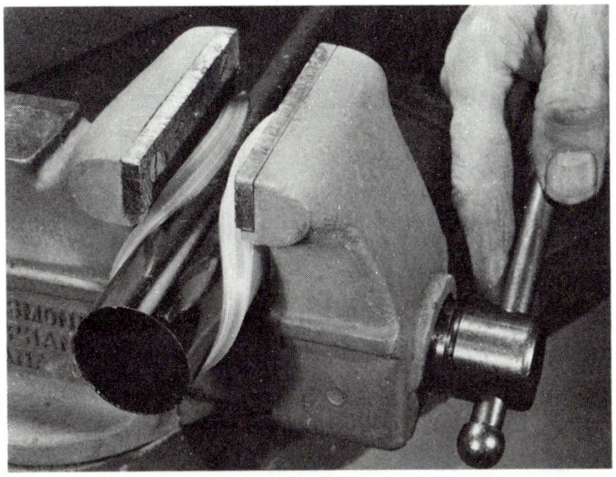

THE PLASTIC LID taken from a 2-lb. coffee can will securely grip thinwall tubing in a bench vise without damaging it in any way. Simply wrap the plastic lid around the tube or length of conduit, then bend the ends and pinch them in the jaws of a bench vise. This is especially handy when working with plated tubing that could be scratched or cracked.—*Albert Pippi.*

SAWDUST ACCUMULATION along the fence of your radial-arm saw can be avoided with this self-clearing device. Simply bore a row of ¾-in. holes along the edge of the front table insert. Thus when you slide the work along the fence to position it, the board automatically pushes the sawdust down through the holes to the floor. If you prefer, you can achieve the same results by making the holes in the edge of an auxiliary table and using it as shown in the photo.—*Victor Lamoy.*

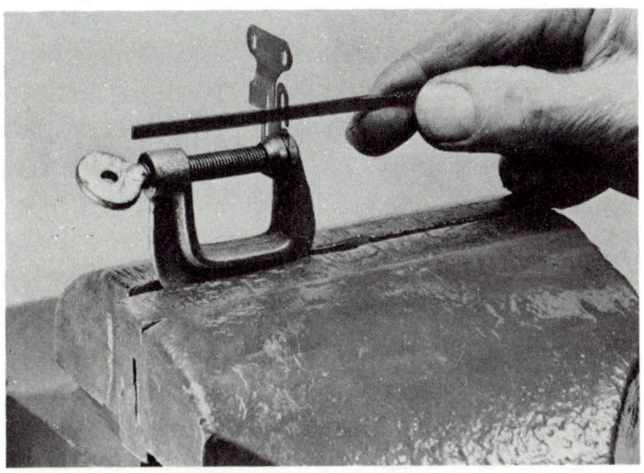

THIS MINIATURE VISE will hold tiny parts while you're working on them and avoid possible damage in the knurled jaws of a conventional bench vise. First clamp the work in the jaws of a small C-clamp, then secure the backbone of the clamp in the jaws of the vise. Now you can quickly insert or remove pieces of work without removing the clamp from the vise. If you use a regular clamp with a long adjusting handle, be sure the handle will clear the vise.—*Martin Steinagle.*

A MITERBOX will support your work while you cut small pieces of wood or metal with a sabre saw. This keeps the free end of a workpiece from vibrating when you're working on the other end, a problem which arises if the work is supported in a vise. Simply set the work over the miterbox, letting the saw blade cut between the two uprights. If you don't have a suitably deep miterbox, try improvising a simple sawing jig from a length of 2 x 4 and a few pieces of scrap pine.—*Harold Miglin.*

Record care: it pays to be tender

A little care can extend the life of your records. Here's a look at some of the products on the market for keeping your records and stylus clean

TRACK YOUR records clean with (from top): Audio-Technica AT-6002, \$10; original Watts Dust Bug, \$7; conductive Decca Record Cleaner, \$15, controversial Lencoclean which keeps grooves wet, \$13.

■ DON'T BLAME YOUR RECORDS if they're full of noise, warps and scratches—blame yourself. Long record life is up to you.

It doesn't cost a penny to store your records properly (on edge, packed firmly together but not tightly squeezed), or to be sure you put them back in their dust jackets as soon as you've played them. And take care never to touch the recorded grooves—your fingertip oils will glue down airborne dust.

A dust cover for your turntable will keep records from getting dirtier while you play them and will slow down the rate at which the turntable collects dust it can transfer to the records later.

What's left is getting the records clean to start with. Shown here are a variety of tools for record cleanliness: devices that clean records as you play them, tracking along the grooves just as the tone arm does (above); gadgets to clean the discs just before you play them; devices to get dust off your stylus and to remove static electricity that attracts falling dust; plus a new lubricant.

Some of the best, shown here, are the Zerostat, the Discwasher, the Decca Record Cleaner, the Manual Parastat and Sound Guard.

Polishing cloths don't clean down in the grooves where the dirt matters; and I suspect them of leaving dust-catching residues on the record surface. Record sprays are even more likely to catch dust.

One possible exception to this is Sound Guard, a new, dry lubricant which does actually seem to reduce record wear in lab tests.

Most of the cleaners shown on the next page

RECORD CLEANERS vary in design: 1. Schweizer Designs Hydro Cleaner ($10) has a built-in fluid atomizer. 2. Decca Record Brush has conductive bristles to avoid static, also a stand with a built-in bristle cleaner ($15). 3. Watts Parastat ($15) has bristles in the center to loosen dust and plush ends to pick up dust. 4. Discwasher ($15) has one-way slanted bristles and a pocket to hold the solution bottle. 5. Watts Preener ($4) is moistened by an internal wick. 6. Ball Brothers Sound Guard is a dry lubricant.

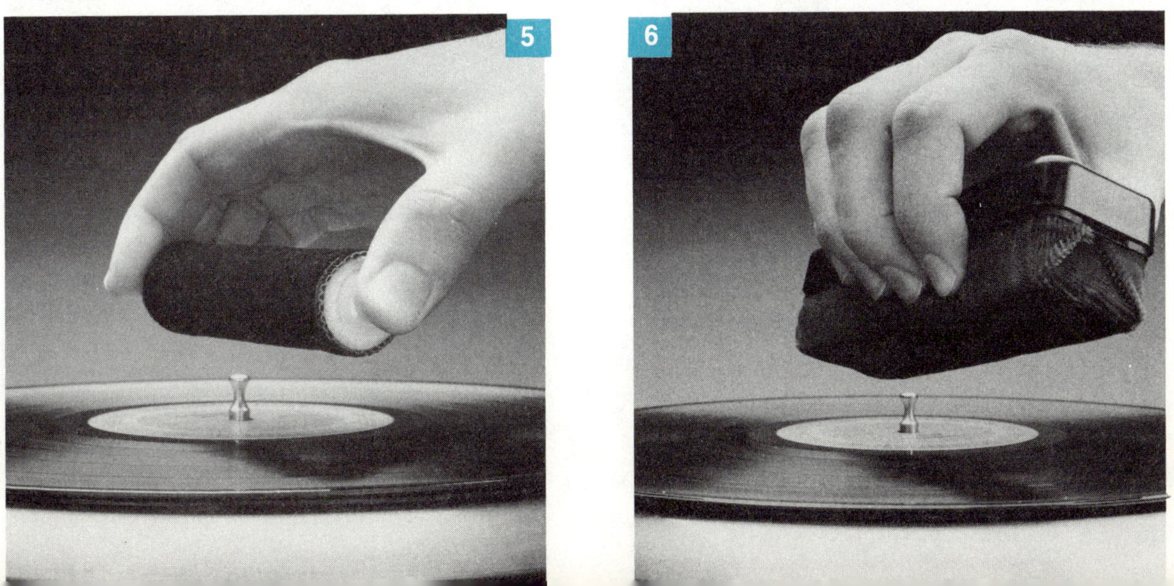

are used damp—but *not* wet—the better to pick up dust without building up static. Europeans, though, swear by devices like the Lencoclean, which soaks the grooves as the record plays; but some experts feel this makes the record noisier if you play it dry thereafter; so if you start wet, stay that way.

TO CLEAN dirty styli, try: Schweizer Designs No. 210 (rear, $3); Audio-Technica AT-607 (center, $3); Watts Stylus Cleaner (right rear, $1.25); Discwasher cleaner with inspection mirror ($6).

UNDER THE MICROSCOPE, you can see thin shavings worn by even a fresh stylus (above, left) accounting for some of the fuzz that gathers on the stylus. But lubricated with Sound Guard (above, right) the record appears fuzz-free. The grooves on the record shown average 0.003 inches in width.

TO KILL static attracting dust, try the Staticmaster 500 brush with a 1-year Polonium ionization strip ($15).

THE ZEROSTAT gun ($30) generates ions as you squeeze and release the trigger. These eliminate static.

METRIC CONVERSION

Conversion factors can be carried so far they become impractical. In cases below where an entry is exact it is followed by an asterisk (*). Where considerable rounding off has taken place, the entry is followed by a + or a - sign.

CUSTOMARY TO METRIC

Linear Measure

inches	millimeters
1/16	1.5875*
1/8	3.2
3/16	4.8
1/4	6.35*
5/16	7.9
3/8	9.5
7/16	11.1
1/2	12.7*
9/16	14.3
5/8	15.9
11/16	17.5
3/4	19.05*
13/16	20.6
7/8	22.2
15/16	23.8
1	25.4*

inches	centimeters
1	2.54*
2	5.1
3	7.6
4	10.2
5	12.7*
6	15.2
7	17.8
8	20.3
9	22.9
10	25.4*
11	27.9
12	30.5

feet	centimeters	meters
1	30.48*	.3048*
2	61	.61
3	91	.91
4	122	1.22
5	152	1.52
6	183	1.83
7	213	2.13
8	244	2.44
9	274	2.74
10	305	3.05
50	1524*	15.24*
100	3048*	30.48*

1 yard =
.9144* meters
1 rod =
5.0292* meters
1 mile =
1.6 kilometers
1 nautical mile =
1.852* kilometers

Fluid Measure

(Milliliters [ml] and cubic centimeters [cc or cu cm] are equivalent, but it is customary to use milliliters for liquids.)

1 cu in = 16.39 ml
1 fl oz = 29.6 ml
1 cup = 237 ml
1 pint = 473 ml
1 quart = 946 ml
= .946 liters
1 gallon = 3785 ml
= 3.785 liters
Formula (exact):
fluid ounces × 29.573 529 562 5*
= milliliters

Weights

ounces	grams
1	28.3
2	56.7
3	85
4	113
5	142
6	170
7	198
8	227
9	255
10	283
11	312
12	340
13	369
14	397
15	425
16	454

Formula (exact):
ounces × 28.349 523 125* =
grams

pounds	kilograms
1	.45
2	.9
3	1.4
4	1.8
5	2.3
6	2.7
7	3.2
8	3.6
9	4.1
10	4.5

1 short ton (2000 lbs) =
907 kilograms (kg)
Formula (exact):
pounds × .453 592 37* =
kilograms

Volume

1 cu in = 16.39 cubic centimeters (cc)
1 cu ft = 28 316.7 cc
1 bushel = 35 239.1 cc
1 peck = 8 809.8 cc

Area

1 sq in = 6.45 sq cm
1 sq ft = 929 sq cm
= .093 sq meters
1 sq yd = .84 sq meters
1 acre = 4 046.9 sq meters
= .404 7 hectares
1 sq mile = 2 589 988 sq meters
= 259 hectares
= 2.589 9 sq kilometers

Kitchen Measure

1 teaspoon = 4.93 milliliters (ml)
1 Tablespoon = 14.79 milliliters (ml)

Miscellaneous

1 British thermal unit (Btu) (mean)
= 1 055.9 joules
1 calorie (mean) = 4.19 joules
1 horsepower = 745.7 watts
= .75 kilowatts
caliber (diameter of a firearm's bore in hundredths of an inch)
= .254 millimeters (mm)
1 atmosphere pressure = 101 325* pascals (newtons per sq meter)
1 pound per square inch (psi) = 6 895 pascals
1 pound per square foot = 47.9 pascals
1 knot = 1.85 kilometers per hour
25 miles per hour = 40.2 kilometers per hour
50 miles per hour = 80.5 kilometers per hour
75 miles per hour = 120.7 kilometers per hour